Clay Lancaster specializes in the cultural interchange between Asia and the West. He has taught in New York City at Columbia University, the Metropolitan Museum of Art, Cooper Union and New York University, and at Vassar College. He is the author of eighteen published books and numerous articles, and he has contributed to many scholarly anthologies on three continents. His best known work is *The Japanese Influence in America*, which first appeared in 1963 and was reprinted in 1983.

THE INCREDIBLE WORLD'S PARLIAMENT OF RELIGIONS

He is less remote from the truth who believes nothing
than he who believes what is wrong.

Thomas Jefferson

for
EMAREL (M.R.L.) FRESHEL
who attended the
World's Parliament of Religions
as a Christian Scientist
and
because of what she heard there
became a Buddhist

and for the
ANAGARIKA DHARMAPALA
chief protagonist
of the foremost religion of
wisdom and compassion
at the Parliament

THE INCREDIBLE
WORLD'S PARLIAMENT
OF RELIGIONS

AT THE CHICAGO COLUMBIAN EXPOSITION OF 1893

A Comparative and Critical Study

CLAY LANCASTER

CENTAUR PRESS
FONTWELL SUSSEX
1987

First published 1987 by Centaur Press Limited
Fontwell, Sussex, BN18 0TA

British Library Cataloguing in Publication Data
Lancaster, Clay
    The incredible world's parliament of religions at the Chicago
    Columbian Exposition of 1893 : a comparative and critical study.
    1. World's Columbian Exposition *(1893 : Chicago)*—Religious
    aspects
    I. Title
    291.1'785   BL46.W6

    ISBN 0-900001-25-9

Printed in Great Britain by Villiers Publications Ltd.,
26a Shepherds Hill, London N6 5AH

CONTENTS

PREFACE: THE TWO CATEGORIES OF RELIGION

THE WORLD'S MAJOR RELIGIONS originated in Asia. Ancient religions were based on mythology. They centered upon the relationship of man to gods that he had created in his own image. These gods, he believed, made and conducted the world; and primitive religious practices had to do with keeping on good terms with the gods in order to receive the most benefits for man himself. This anthropomorphic and materialistic concept underwent serious modification in the intellectual ferment that crossed Eurasia beginning in the sixth century B.C. In that portion of Europe affected by it, Greece and its colonies from Italy to Ionia, it was embraced by isolated groups or schools of philosophy without altering religion, whereas in Asia, specifically in India and China, it resulted in philosophy religions. The native Indian religion, Hinduism, shifted emphasis from gods to an all-pervading principle; and the two chief manifestations generated by this movement, Buddhism and Taoism, were neither myth-centered nor materialistic from the start. It will be noted that this wave of intellectualism kindled only the great ancient civilizations whose people came from Central Asia — the Chinese, who had spread eastward, and the Aryans, who had migrated down into the Indian subcontinent and westward to lands on the Aegean and Adriatic seas. With the religious innovations occurring in India and China, we may speak of the philosophy religions as belonging to Farther Asia.

Modern Europe and America received religion from another source, from Western Asia or the Near East. Foremost is Christianity. As Buddhism grew out of Hinduism, Christianity began as a branch of a religion of equal antiquity, Judaism.

1

Its founder, Jesus, considered himself as a reformer of the parent faith. The third Near Eastern religion is Islam, inaugurated by Mohammed in the seventh century A.D. He drew upon both Jewish and Christian sources for many of his ideas, but these are acknowledged by his followers only insofar as Mohammed himself declared them, and thus Islam became autonomous. Similarly, Christians came to accept only those teachings of Judaism assigned to Jesus, and Christianity became a separate faith. Jesus and Mohammed are prophets who are held in equally high esteem by their devotees, but the former also is deified by Christians. Judaism responded to the great sixth-century movement of Farther Asia only insofar as the later prophets softened the severity of the tribal god; and although Christianity and Islam came into existence many hundreds of years later, all three religions remained essentially at the. archaic level, clinging to gods in human form, the creation myth, and an ingrained outlook.

There are, of course, numerous religions other than the six named, some of considerable importance. Confucianism, for example, exerted a stronger influence in China than Taoism, but Confucianism is primarily a social and political system and only secondarily religious. Jainism, a contemporary of and similar to Buddhism, remained in its native land to become virtually a denomination of Hinduism, whereas Buddhism, like Christianity, flourished elsewhere. Japanese Shinto has retained its ancient mythological form, and it and older Hinduism, which still persists, have more in common with the Semitic faiths than with later Hinduism, or with refined Buddhism and Taoism. It must not be overlooked that many of the elements of the older religions were retained or adopted into Buddhism and Taoism, and that these forms also are related to the Near Eastern group. Sects engaging in such overt aspects may be more numerous and more in evidence than those concentrating on the essentials, but the fact remains that higher Hinduism, Buddhism and Taoism constitute a body of advanced religion diametrically opposed to the earlier types; and representatives at the Parliament subscribed to and expounded the pure form. It was Dharmapala, general secretary of the Maha Bodhi Society, in his talk on "The World's Debt to Buddha," who characterized Buddhism as a "Philosophy Religion."

For a capsule understanding of the scope of present-day religions, the following chart depicts contents and attitudes common to the categories representing the two geographic divisions and the two generations of religion, contrasting the one with the other. As in the attempt to deduce principles pertaining to any evolved, protracted and complicated movement, there inevitably will be leftover minor exceptions, thus these comparisons are to be regarded only as basic distinctions. The noncommital subtlety of Taoism presents a justifiably arguable case in a number of instances. The three Near Eastern religions often are at bitter odds with each other on specifics, as in Islam's declaring the absurdity of a god being killed by human enemies. Within parentheses, following each of the ten numbered sets, will be found references to chapters in the present book wherein the subject is discussed.

PRINCIPAL NEAR EASTERN RELIGIONS *Judaism — Christianity — Islam*	PRINCIPAL FARTHER ASIAN RELIGIONS *Later Hinduism — Buddhism — Taoism*
1. THEISTIC gods are personified, and they control human destinies according to their dispositions; they may be appeased through sacrifice and devotion; Judaism is henotheistic, Christianity trinitarian, and Islam monotheistic	1. MONISTIC spiritual principle is inherent in nature and operates constantly according to uniform laws; in Hinduism the Ultimate is Brahman, the Universal Soul; in Buddhism It is Dharma, the Law of Cause and Effect; and in Taoism It is Tao, which is Reason or the Cosmic Essence

(Chapter Two)

2. UNIVERSE CREATED
   AND DOOMED
the phenomenal world was manufactured by God(s) as a spontaneous act; it will be destroyed by the same agent, returning to the nothingness whence it came

2. UNIVERSE EVOLVED
   AND INDESTRUCTIBLE
the material world was unfolded so gradually as virtually to have existed forever; as it has undergone recurring cycles in the past, so it will continue in the future

(Chapters Two and Three)

3. SELECT SALVATION
survival of death is physical and is reserved for the faithful and righteous (however, as qualifications differ in each of these three religions, in each case members of the other two are excluded automatically)

3. UNRESTRICTED
   IMMORTALITY
the spirits of all living beings pass from one state of existence to another; generally their status at any moment is determined by their past deeds; one must be united with the All to attain eternity

(Chapters Four)

4. SELF-CENTERED
concern focuses on the ego and the tribe or other limited social unit; the individual maintains personal contact with the deity and seeks eternal selfness

4. AWARENESS OF ONE'S
   PLACE IN NATURE
regard is for all beings in the universe; little attention is paid to organizational distinctions; escape from the round of births and deaths is achieved by rejection of ego for union with the Eternal (see Point 3)

(Chapters Five and Eight)

5. SUBMISSIVENESS TO
   AUTHORITY
these religions foster congre-

5. SELF-RELIANCE
devotions are individual, study or attendance at

gational worship, impose pre-determined dogmas, and require unqualified acceptance of their sacred texts; the principle of grace assumes members to be pawns whose fate is in the hands of deity; the word Islam means submission

lectures is voluntary, and no authority is imposed as to what members should think; there is, however, behavior discipline for those who assume orders; spiritual attainment is through one's own efforts alone

(Chapters Five and Six)

6. FAITH
accounts of God's laws, legends regarding the hierarchy (both in heaven and on earth), and fantasized afterlife must be accepted as revealed; they vary in each of these religions

6. REASON
through direct observation of the world and its workings, rationally considered, universal principles are arrived at; they are identical for all liberated, normal mentalities: in Taoism, Reason is the Cosmic Essence (see Point I)

(Chapter Seven)

7. RIGHTEOUSNESS
"good" behavior is largely worship practices directed toward deities; prohibitions against wrongdoing toward others are sectarian and only vaguely include outsiders

7. ETHICS
ethics is realistic and universal, based on Nature, with greatest consideration conferred upon the higher forms of life; it is humaneness and conservation, insofar as they are practical

(Chapter Eight)

8. MATERIALISTIC
preachers and missionaries are on fixed salaries; petitionary prayers are for mundane and career gains; sale of

8. NON-MATERIALISTIC
members of orders are forbidden to receive money for their services, only food or other necessities, freely given,

indulgences fill church coffers for promised benefits

being acceptable; modern departures among certain sects may be attributed to Western influence

(in adopting the system from Buddhism, Catholicism includes the non-materialistic principle in its monasticism)
(Chapter Six)

9. AGGRESSIVE
religious beliefs have prompted brutal atrocities against other nations (as in the usurpation of Canaan under Moses and Joshua, the Crusades, and the Jihad) and meted death to those opposing established doctrines (early scientists)

9. NON-AGGRESSIVE
respect for life prohibits participation in armed conflicts or violence of any kind; wars sponsored by these religions and punishment of men making new discoveries are unthinkable

(Chapters Nine and Ten)

10. COMPLEXITY
contradictions in dogma, diverse attributes of God, changing rules of conduct, stress of legend content stem from preoccupation with particulars in poor agreement: scriptures are badly organized, vague, and rambling

10. SIMPLICITY
adherence to constant premises, universal concept of ethical conduct, negation of religious narrative and texts in logical and precise language minimize extraneousness: as expressed in the Zen precept, one should eliminate the non-essential

(Chapters Two through Nine)

Relatively few people today belong to the philosophy religions. Their homeland is Farther Asia, and being non-congregational in character these religions do not tend to organize or to proselytize. But this is a scientific age — at least at the upper level — and millions are aware of the vast difference between the dubiousness of chance faith as against the greater reliability of critical observation. They are stifled by the myths, rites, dogmas, scriptures, and religious tyranny that fostered the Dark Ages, and they are aware it was secular man who established social, political, and educational reforms and threw off the yoke of church oppression. They are repelled by the long history of inhumane practices of Western religion and by its lack of an adequate ethical code. For these reasons thinking individuals will find the characteristics in the right-hand column of the preceding chart more acceptable than those in the left; and it is primarily to them that this book is addressed. Its writing, admittedly, is biased against the superstitions, injustices, cruelties, and unprincipled practices propagated by narrow sectarian religions, their intolerance or mere tolerance of others, and by their bigotry that calls adverse attention to their pettiness.

INTRODUCTION TO THE PARLIAMENT TALKS

THE WORLD'S COLUMBIAN EXPOSITION at Chicago celebrated the four-hundredth anniversary of the discovery of America. Christopher Columbus first landed on the island of San Salvador on 12 October 1492, and although he made three return trips he never set foot on the American continent. Nor did he suspect that he was anywhere other than in Asia. Some of the buildings at the Chicago fair were dedicated in 1892, but the fair itself was held the following year, and therefore it was on the four-hundredth-and-first anniversary of Columbus' first debarkation in the West Indies.

Although not known at the time, Europeans had preceded Columbus to America by three thousand years, and those first adventurers were not the least bit deluded by thinking that they were in Asia. They were primarily Norsemen and Celt-Iberians, the latter having taken to the sea through intermingling with the ancient world's master mariners, the Phoenicians. They engaged in copper and fur trade with the aborigines until their intercourse with America was interrupted by a change in climate, a drop in temperature around 800 B.C., which made voyages across the North Atlantic too hazardous to be continued.[1] Stragglers left behind in the New World were absorbed by the natives, giving rise, centuries later, to tales of the existence of "White Indians."

In the fifth century A.D., a Chinese monk named Hui Shan led a small party of confreres across the Pacific to the West Coast of America, which he called Fu-sang. He recorded the event. His account was deposited in the Chinese Imperial Archives, and it was translated into French during the eighteenth century. An eight-hundred-page tome by George

8

Leland, an American, was published at London in 1875, which was in ample time for it to have become known to the founders of the fair honoring Hui Shan's belated successor from Europe.[2] Archaeologists have had a field day comparing medieval art of Central America with that of Asia, which led to finding more ancient similarities, suggesting that the Japanese (perhaps fishermen blown off their course) had been here at least as early as the Celt-Iberians. Being racially akin to the American Indians, who had crossed the Bering Strait or the Aleutian Islands some thirty-thousand years earlier, later Asians would have left no distinguishing marks on their progeny.

Europeans again made voyages to North America from the late tenth century to the middle of the fourteenth century. They were the Norsemen, whose adventures were recounted in the Viking sagas. Whereas small dugout temples throughout New England are inscribed as being the work of the Celts, the round tower at Newport, R.I., resembles nothing better than a North European monk's turret of the Middle Ages and, whether constructed by Norsemen or the Irish (as has been suggested), retains its European origin. The "Vineland" of the sagas has to be somewhere in America, either in Canada or in New England.[3] It is not unlikely that Columbus heard about voyages to a continent across the Atlantic Ocean when he visited Iceland in 1476.

New York had emulated the 1851 London Exposition held in the Hyde Park Crystal Palace by building a huge conservatory on the site of present Bryant's Park and presenting its own world's fair in 1853-54. The official celebration of the one-hundredth birthyear of the nation was an international exhibition held in Fairmount Park, at the first capital, Philadelphia, in 1876. For memorializing the beginning of the buildup of America, Chicago was deemed the appropriate location because its youth and rapid growth symbolized the essence of the movement. The larger or western half of the United States had been settled and come under its jurisdiction within the preceding century; a railroad first had linked its two shores within the last quarter of a century. The machine had greatly accelerated the process, and the theme of the Columbian Exposition centered upon the industrial and mechanical accomplishments of recent times.

The great exhibition offered the proper atmosphere and accommodations for conferences on various phases of civilization. About fifty were held under the auspices of the World's Congress Auxiliary. Among them was a subject that no previous exposition had included, one purporting to round out the material theme of the fair by encompassing the spiritual aspirations of man: this is religion. It was propagated by members of local, national, and closely related international bodies, primarily Christian and secondarily Jewish, which, ironically, were among the more materialistic religions and had contributed to making the West into the materialistic hemisphere. However, presentations were to cover the whole range of ancient and modern, Eastern and Western manifestations. Talks or papers had to be submitted in or translated into English. In the spring of 1891 a sixteen-member General Committee was appointed, headed by the Rev. John Henry Barrows, pastor of Chicago's First Presbyterian Church. Meetings were scheduled for the fall of 1893, and they were to be held outside the fairgrounds, at the Art Institute of Chicago.

The event was called the World's Parliament of Religions. "Parliament" was an appropriate term insofar as it suggests an assembly which makes laws. The denominations behind the undertaking belonged to the revelation class of religions, whose founders had made pronouncements purporting to be God's laws, claiming divine inspiration. They proclaimed their dogmas too mysterious to be brought under the scientific scrutiny of perceptive observation. The one element in science that was most distasteful to them — and it surfaced a number of times during the lectures — was the relatively new Darwinian theory of evolution; it ran counter to the creation myth to which they subscribed. That other religions had progressed beyond the mythology stage and for two-and-a-half millennia had looked rationally and critically at the workings of the universe was to be a great awakening to them at the forthcoming Parliament. That is, it was to be an awakening to those capable of accepting ideas and ideals that better accorded with reality than those in which they had been trained.

Some who were invited to participate never got so far as giving their absorption powers that test. The Archbishop of Canterbury declined due to "the fact that the Christian religion is the one religion," and it could not become "a member of a Parliament of Religions without assuming the equality of the other intended members." Further, its "faith and devotion" were "too sacred" to be subjected "to public discussion." The churchman's reply was rather presumptuous for one whose domain was an island smaller than New Guinea, whose religious essentials were bogged down by an irrelevant institutionalism, whose beliefs centered on a legend most of whose documentation came no closer than almost a century to the events they supposedly recorded, and whose tenets were so irrational that they had to be accepted on what the archbishop himself called "sacred" faith or not at all. The attitude of the Archbishop of Canterbury is said to have "excited the wonder of some of the friends of that liberal-minded prelate in Great Britain." It made underlings hesitate to attend the Parliament, some of whom might have had the capacity for recognizing higher verities had they been exposed to them. Yet the British participants included the Hon. W.H. Fremantle, Canon of Canterbury; Prof. A.W. Momerie of King's College; the Rev. Drs. H.R. Haweis and George F. Pentecost of London; W.T. Stead, editor of *Review of Reviews*; and there was a paper submitted by the eminent scholar Prof. Max Müller.

Some replies to invitations were more insolent than the archbishop's. An obscure Christian missionary in Hong Kong blasted back that the project denied the sovereignty of the Lord. "If misled yourself," he wrote, "at least do not mislead others nor jeopardize, I pray you, the precious life of your soul by playing fast and loose with the truth and coquetting with false religions. I give you credit for the best intentions, but let me warn you that you are unconsciously planning treason against Christ."[4] The zealot was living in a heathen land, which (until Westerners came) had never known a religious war; had never beheaded, hanged, or burned heretics at the stake; had never engaged in prolonged acts of torture because of the victims' differences in belief from those held by their overlords or conducted an inquisition. Near the close of the nineteenth century, when such extreme (Western) religious acts had become archaic, the vicar of Christ at Hong Kong could only admonish iniquitous trespassers, who chanced to cross his path, of the dire consequences they risked from Higher Authority.

Chairman Barrows made it a policy not to acknowledge such unmannerly outbursts. He took the positive approach, setting forth the objects of the Parliament in statements that were widely circulated. These were (1) to bring together the leading representatives of the great religions, (2) and (4) to show how many important truths they held in common, (3) and (10) to deepen the spirit of human brotherhood with the hope of securing international peace, (6) and (9) to define what effects various religions have had on other aspects of culture, (7) to inquire into what religions have contributed to each other, and (8) to publish an account of all that would be said and otherwise transpire at the forthcoming meetings. Omitted here is one point (5), which was to "indicate the impregnable foundation of Theism, and the reasons for man's faith in Immortality, and thus to strengthen the forces which are adverse to a materialistic philosophy of the universe."[5] The "materialistic philosophy" ran counter to the moral and social stability for which the Parliament stood, being considered the root of evil and anarchy. History provided such an occurrence as the French Revolution; its reign of terror was directed against church as well as state, as the royal armies had been used to stamp out the Protestant heresies as being a threat to the nation's religion, Catholicism, and this was as offensive to the citizens as temporal oppression. The foundations of theism were found to be not "impregnable." Man's "faith in Immortality," or in anything, is the most irrelevant substitute for proof that was ever devised. Faith is an emotional and not an intellectual affirmation, and it, in itself, is unable to discern between reality and imagination. Theism, faith, and immortality will be discussed more fully in this book.

The subject to which the Parliament paid every deference was humanity. The twelfth-day session coincided with the thirty-first anniversary of President Lincoln's Emancipation Proclamation. It was duly observed at the evening meeting on September 22, featuring two members of the African Methodist Church, the venerable Bishop Daniel A. Payne, who presided, and Bishop Benjamin W. Arnett. The latter reviewed the progress made by Blacks over the last three decades in matters of education, religion, government, industry, music, stage, and the press, leading up to his presentation of a book to the Hon. J.M. Ashley of Ohio. The volume contained antislavery speeches made in 1865, when Ashley was a representative to Congress in Washington, printed by the Afro-American League of Tennessee. Mr. Ashley acknowledged the presentation graciously.

Another group receiving acclaim at the Parliament was the distaff side. The preface in the publication on the conference noted that "as Columbus discovered America, the Columbian Exposition discovered woman"; thus the Parliament was but a sharer in that greater tribute to the sex. It declared: "The Home, the Church and the State find their purity and light in her. The Parliament of Religions gratefully recognizes the supreme and splendid offices which woman has performed in the history of humanity's noblest development." The rather dubious statement is made, in the light of the outcome of the legend, that "Paradise was not perfect without woman." The two-volume recording of the Parliament proceedings was dedicated to "The Beloved Wife," whereby the editor, General Chairman John Henry Barrows, acknowledged his indebtedness to her "whose kindly and farseeing wisdom, unwearied helpfulness and unwavering faith in the high ends of the Parliament of Religions, were my constant solace and inspiration."

A number of the women who appeared at or contributed papers to the Parliament had acquired national fame. If their reports were not of great significance, as regards what they had to say about religion, at least their presence or efforts lent prestige to the occasion. Subjects of their talks generally veered into side issues. Elizabeth Cady Stanton, protagonist of abolition and women's rights, expounded on "The Worship of God in Man," which might better have been defined simply as human dignity. It was read by Susan B. Anthony, Elizabeth's friend and co-founder of the National Woman Suffrage Association. A speech framed along similar lines was called "A White Life for Two." It was the offering of Frances E. Willard, remembered for her role in organizing the Women's Christian Temperance Union.

The Rev. Olympia Brown, one of the first women to be ordained a minister, which was in the American Universalist Church, spoke on "Crime and Its Remedy." The solution, she said, was eliminating underprivileged conditions. The Rev. Anna Garlin Spencer, another minister and wife of a Unitarian clergyman (William H. Spencer), talked about "Religion and the Erring and Criminal Classes." These people needed democratic and humane treatment. Mrs. Julia Ward Howe also had married into her career, assisting her husband Dr. Samuel Gridley Howe in editing the *Commonwealth*, an abolitionist paper. She helped found a world peace organization, but she became more famous for writing the words to the stirring "Battle Hymn of the Republic." Her comments on "What Is Religion?" in Chicago dealt more with what it was not rather than what it was, the suppression of trickery by priests and the use of religion for human inequalities being cardinal flaws.

Not least known among women preachers was Mary Baker Eddy, founder of Christian Science, whose paper on this subject was read at the Parliament by Judge J.S. Hanna before a meeting held exclusively for the sect. One recalls Paul's mandate against women taking part in religion: "Let your women keep silent in the churches: for it is not permitted unto them to speak; but they are commanded to be under obedience, as also saith the law. And if they will learn any thing, let them ask their husbands at home; for it is a shame for women to speak in the church" (I Corinthians XIV, 34-35).

Henrietta Szold pursued a feminine theme in her essay on "What Has Judaism Done for Woman?" It was to give her the privileges due a lawful wife and nothing more. Miss Szold later was to launch the Zionist women's organization Hadassah. She long served in it and in the youth-rehabilitation facility, Aliyah, in Palestine.[6]

A young woman given an enthusiastic reception when she appeared on the platform at the congress was Jeanne Sorabji of Bombay, possessed of the large lustrous doe eyes and regular features of her race. Her father had been a Parsee convert to Christianity at eighteen, and in this faith Miss Sorabji was reared. She spoke on "Women of India," a subject of certain appeal, and she read an essay on Parseeism written by a countryman.

Equal to Miss Sorabji's reception was that given Mrs. Laura Ormiston Chant, a London social reformer, whose enthusiasm for religion suffered her to sit through talks containing "words that almost dislocate the jaw in trying to pronounce, words that almost daze the brain in trying to think out what their meaning is." Her own approach was simplicity itself, without burden of creed or nationality. She looked forward to that glorious day, she said, when vocabulary will be the worshipper's own speech, with "God, our Father, answering the prayer of the Japanese in the Jap's own language."

Thoughtless use of slang or indecorous words against groups was nowhere brought out more prevalently at the Parliament than in referring to Moslems as "Mohammedans," which is worse than calling Christians "Jesusites" (each derived from the founder's given name), because no Moslem ever worshipped Mohammed. The religion is called Islam, "to submit," referring to the will of God, and a member is called a Moslem, sometimes rendered Mussulman, "one who submits." The chief exponent of Islam at Chicago was an American proselyte, Mohammed Alexander Russell Webb. He was a handsome man with finely chiseled features who sported a full beard (as did more than half of the other male speakers) and a white turban. His address on the tenth day was entitled "The Spirit of Islam," in which he mentioned, near the beginning, that all Moslems believe that theirs will eventually become the universal religion. Probably most of the people there cherished the same hope for their belief, and at least a dozen speakers had'or were to express the same sentiment about Christianity. Such was accepted as a matter of course. But Webb's statement, followed by the mention of polygamy, called forth a volley of hisses and cries of "Shame!" As regards polygamy, it was as though the audience had never heard of King David and King Solomon, whose Psalms and Proverbs were recited with reverence, and whose wives exceeded by hundreds the Moslem limitation to four; besides which they had hundreds of concubines of slave status for their sexual gratification. On the eleventh day Webb attempted to ease the situation by claiming that polygamy had no official sanction in Islam, and his remarks were met with "some slight expression of applause." At the next meeting Webb was dressed down by the Rev. Dr. George E. Post, Christian missionary from Beirut, who laid aside his scheduled speech to read passages from the Koran showing that it not only condoned the practice of polygamy but that the Prophet himself had several wives.

One other session brought forth cries of "Shame!" The speaker was a young Japanese, Kinza Riuge M. Hirai, and the outbursts were in sympathy with his remarks about injustices perpetrated by Christian missionaries in his native land. He cited the incident in 1637 when foreigners (Jesuits) and their Christian converts "caused a tragic and bloody rebellion . . . intended to subjugate Japan to their own mother country." The insurrection prompted Japan to close her doors against the world for three centuries, until opened by Commodore Perry's visit in 1853 and the treaty with the United States made a year later. It was followed by similar treaties between Japan and Europe in 1858. Japan's feudal government in those days was inexperienced in international affairs, and the Western powers took unfair advantage by reserving matters of extraterritorial and tariff rights to their own jurisdiction. Hirai also referred to the ban against Japanese entering universities and public schools in San Francisco and else-where in the United States. The warm response from his listeners was gained by his neat appearance, his sincerity, his "eloquent command of the English language," and by his voicing a viewpoint that struck a premeditated chord of inconsistency among them — namely, the divergence between what Christianity preaches and what Christendom practices. It was this factor that provided the breakthrough for what-ever degree of enlightenment Westerners derived from the Parliament experience.

The policy of grouping previously prepared talks on the same subject led to vital disparagements and contradictions, especially among the religions based on faith rather than reason, which was practically all of them in Europe and America. Sometimes the differences lay in the minor remarks of one talk and the major of another. The sixth day of the Parliament was devoted to the world's scriptures, and the first speaker was Prof. Charles A. Briggs of New York.

Although he acknowledged other books of this category, Prof. Briggs limited his remarks to the Bible. His viewpoint was conservative, as regards the value of its contents, but he pointed out that the book was full of "historical mistakes, ... important discrepancies, ... bad grammar, of the incorrect use of words, of inelegant expressions, and of disorderly arrangement of material." He noted that it contained elements "which are hard to reconcile with an inerrant revelation," referring, in particular, to the numerous acts of human sacrifice and murder recorded in the Old Testament.

Prof. Briggs was followed immediately by Mgr. Robert Seton of Jersey City, whose topic was "The Catholic Church and the Bible." Mgr. Seton stated that Catholicism still supported "the emphatic declaration of the Council of Trent held in the year 1546," which was: "No one, relying on his own knowledge, shall presume to interpret Scripture ... contrary to that sense which Holy Mother Church ... both held and doth hold." In this he was specific: "The church teaches that the sacred Scriptures are the written Word of God and that he is their Author. ... This gives a distinct character to the Bible which no other book possesses, for of no mere human composition, however excellent, can it ever be said that it comes directly from God."

On the sixteenth day of the Parliament, Prof. William C. Wilkinson of the University of Chicago spoke on "The Attitude of Christianity toward Other Religions." Among its instances of intolerance he repeated several sayings of the founder himself: "The hostile attitude of Jesus toward any and every offer other than his own to save, is to be recognized in many supremely self-asserting, universally-exclusive sayings of his, such as these: 'No man cometh unto the Father (that is, no man is saved) but by me;' 'I am the bread of life;' 'If any man thirst, let him come unto me, and drink;' 'I am the light of the world;' 'I am the door of the sheep. All that came before me are thieves and robbers;' 'I am the door; by me, if any man enter in, he shall be saved.' " Wilkinson proceeded to talk about Paul's condemnation of other faiths, quoting him as saying: "The things which the Gentiles sacrifice they sacrifice to devils and not to God," and such will "provoke the Lord to jealousy." The professor concluded that, "The attitude, therefore, of Christianity towards religions other than itself is an attitude of universal, absolute, eternal, unappeasable hostility," though its attitude toward men is toleration.

Following Prof. Wilkinson on the sixteenth day, the Rev. James S. Dennis of New York, discussing "The Message of Christianity to Other Religions," took the saccharine view: "Its spirit is full of simple sincerity, exalted dignity and sweet unselfishness. It aims to impart a blessing, rather than to challenge a comparison. It is not so anxious to vindicate itself as to confer its benefits. It is not so solicitous to secure supreme honor for itself as to win its way to the heart. It does not seek to taunt, or disparage, or humiliate a rival, but rather to subdue by love, attract by its own excellence, and supplant by virtue of its own incomparable superiority." Had history vindicated Dennis' claim, Prof. Briggs would not have been prompted to say, "With few exceptions the Christian religion was not extended by force of arms."

Rabbi Emil Hirsch of Chicago presided at the evening session on the thirteenth day of the Parliament, and the first speaker was the Most Rev. Dionysios Latas, Archbishop of Zante, whose opening statement was, "I am not a Jew. I am a Christian, a profound believer of the truth of the gospel." This was met with applause. He announced that he wished to present a paper of an urgent matter and handed it to the assistant chairman to read. It began, "In the East the belief is current among the ignorant masses of the population that the Jews use for purposes of religious rites the blood of Christian children, and in order to procure such blood do not shrink from committing murder. In consequence of the belief, outbreaks against the Jews are frequent, . . . such erroneous ideas are also current among the ignorant of other countries, and . . . during the last decade both Germany and Austria were the scenes of trials of innocent Jews under the accusation of having committed such ritual murder. . . . The circulation of such slander against the adherents of a monotheistic faith is un-Christian. The origin of the calumny must be traced to the Roman conceit that early Christians used human blood in their religious observances. . . . it is in the interest of Christianity's good repute that I ask this Parliament to declare that Judaism and the Jews are innocent of the imputed crime as were the Christians of the first century."

Cardinal James Gibbons, Archbishop of Baltimore, in his speech on "The Needs of Humanity Supplied by the Catholic Religion," read by Bishop Keane, condemned the pre-Christian world: "Before the advent of Christ the whole world, with the exception of the secluded Roman Province of Palestine, was buried in idolatry. Every striking object in nature had its tutelary divinities. Men worshiped the sun and moon and stars of heaven. They worshiped their very passions. They worshiped everything except God only to whom alone divine homage is due. In the words of the Apostle of the Gentiles, 'They changed the glory of the incorruptible God into the likeness of the corruptible man, and of birds and beasts and creeping things.'"

The scholar Manilal M. D'vivedi in a paper on "Hinduism" at one point inserted several remarks about "idol worship" in his native land: "no Indian idolater, as such, believes the piece of stone, metal, or wood before his eyes is his god, in any sense of the word. He takes it only as a symbol of the all-pervading, and uses it as a convenient object for purposes of concentration, which, being accomplished, he does not grudge to throw it away." Another Indian, Swami Vivekananda, speaking also on "Hinduism," asked with regard to "idols" in the West, "Why does a Christian go to church, why is the cross holy, why is the face turned toward the sky in prayer? Why are there so many images in the Catholic Church, why are there so many images in the minds of Protestants, when

they pray? My brethren, we can no more think about anything without a material image than it is possible for us to
live without breathing. And by the law of association the
material image calls the mental idea up and *vice versa*."

To underscore Vivekananda's remark, one may ask, where
is the likeness of God more similar to that of "corruptible
man" than in the Sistine Chapel of the Vatican, the headquarters of the Western Church? In five major ceiling panels
having to do with the creation, Michelangelo depicted God
with flowing white hair and beard, and as belonging to the
same race as Adam and Eve — as well as the numerous slaves,
kings, and prophets in the various Old Testament scenes.
Nowhere in Farther Asia is God or the gods shown so photo-
graphically human as in Christian art.

Swami Vivekananda was one of the more colorful speakers
at the World's Parliament of Religions; his portly figure
resembled that of the successful Chicago industrialist, and he
appeared on the platform "clad in gorgeous red apparel, his
bronzed face surmounted with a huge turban of yellow." In
the brief introductory remarks allowed each participant at
the first meeting, Vivekananda addressed the assembly as
"sisters and brothers of America," which prompted "a peal
of applause that lasted for several minutes."

Another striking Oriental was the Buddhist Dharmapala,
founder and secretary of the Maha Bodhi Society from
neighboring Ceylon, who brought the only religious antique
art treasure displayed during the talks, a fifth-century Gupta
stone stele of the Buddha in meditation — *bhūmisparsa*. (The
separate Congress of Missions, which followed the Parliament,
superfluously concurred that there was not "any idolatry
in the fact that one of the speakers exhibited a statue of
Buddha.") Dharmapala spoke on the rational teaching of the
Buddha, its high ethical code and its self-reliant way to spiritual attainment and ultimate wisdom. Unlike Vivekananda,
Dharmapala was slender, and he dressed in a long, toga-like
garment of yellow; he wore a youth's beard and mustache,

and his wavy hair was pushed back shoulder-length from his handsome, swarthy face. To many in the audience — especially the women — he appeared to be the incarnate Christ, and he was pursued accordingly. To Dharmapala, as to any earnest seeker after perfection, nothing could be more distasteful than being mistaken for a personal savior, and he dispelled many flights of fancy with his declarations of simple common sense. Whatever distinction Dharmapala achieved at the Parliament was due to what he presented and how he treated it, and certainly not in drawing attention to himself as the possessor of mysterious powers or divine affinities.

An Easterner whose name later was to become more famous in America and the West than that of any of the others was Daisetz Teitaro Suzuki. He did not compose a paper for nor read one at the Parliament, but he translated "The Law of Cause and Effect" from Japanese into English for his master, Soyen Shaku. Suzuki continued as translator for Soyen's *Sermons of a Buddhist Abbot*, published by Paul Carus's Open Court in 1906. Suzuki also translated Carus's own work *The Gospel of Buddha* (1900) from English for a Japanese edition. D.T. Suzuki wrote many books on Zen Buddhism, published during the 1950s-60s, besides one on *Shin Buddhism* (1970), and another on *Mysticism, Christian and Buddhist* (1957).

For his prodigious output of books on Asian religions, attention should be called to Max Müller, a German philologist and orientalist, who had transferred to Oxford University. Here he compiled a six-volume work on the *Rig-Veda with Commentary* (1849-73), and he edited fifty-one volumes in the Sacred Books of the East series (1875-1900). His contribution to the congress was a paper on "Greek Philosophy and the Christian Religion," in which he advised Christians to return to an ante-Nicean faith.

Foremost among those of West Asian ancestry was Isaac Mayer Wise, a native of Bohemia, who came to the United

States in 1846. He served as rabbi to orthodox Jewish congregations in Albany and (after 1854) Cincinnati, both of which he transformed into Reform synagogues. The Congregation B'nai Yeshurun at the latter place later memoralized him by calling its building the Isaac M. Wise Temple. Dr. Wise founded the Hebrew Union College at Cincinnati. He wrote extensively on historical and religious subjects. He was called upon to speak on the theology of Judaism on the first day of the Parliament talks (Chapter Two).

Associated with Dr. Wise at the college in Cincinnati was Prussian-born Rabbi Gustav Gottheil, later a founder of the Federation of American Zionists. Gottheil's discourse on Moses is referred to in Chapter Nine.

A native American, mentioned earlier in this introduction, was Mgr. Robert Seton, who was well qualified to present the Catholic standpoint on the authorship of the Bible. He spent ten years of study in Rome, and for a while he served as private chamberlain to Pope Pius IX. At the time of the Chicago meetings he was rector of St. Joseph Church, Jersey City, and an active historian and archaeologist.

The World's Parliament of Religions attracted the participation of many leaders of liberal Christianity. Some had suffered expulsion from their posts by hide-bound authorities. Charles A. Briggs, who preceded Seton, had been suspended from the Presbyterian clergy by the General Assembly, only to take the professorial chair of Hebrew at New York's Theological Seminary. Subsequently he became an Episcopal minister. His book on *The Higher Criticism of the Hexateuch* was published during the year of his Chicago appearance. For heresies similar to Briggs', Crawford Howell Toy was forced out of the Southern Baptist Theological Seminary, and he was appointed Hancock Professor of Hebrew and Other Oriental Languages at Harvard. He wrote *Judaism and Christianity* (1890), and was to write *A Critical and Exegetical Commentary on the Book of Proverbs* (1899). He later served on the editorial board for *The Jewish Encyclopaedia*

(1901-06). A quotation from Toy's speech at the Parliament opens Chapter Eight in this book.

Toy had been a chaplain in the Confederate army during the Civil War. Col. Thomas Wentworth Higginson had engaged in combat on the Union side. Higginson had been a Unitarian minister and a leader in the abolitionist movement, and in the war he commanded the first company of Negroes. His campaign experiences were recorded in a book called *Army Life in a Black Regiment*, published in 1870. Col. Higginson produced a novel *Malbone*, biographies of Margaret Fuller, Longfellow, and Whittier, reminiscences of political and literary friends, and he edited two volumes of poems by Emily Dickinson. An episode regarding a religious service in a Portuguese cathedral from his Parliament report on "The Sympathy of Religions" figures in Chapter Six.

Also a former Unitarian minister and prolific writer was Edward Everett Hale. His popular short novel *The Man Without a Country* first appeared anonymously in the *Atlantic Monthly* in 1863. Other works include *Franklin in France* (1887-88), *Memoirs of a Hundred Years* (1902), and the autobiographical *New England Boyhood* (1893). At Chicago he spoke on "Spiritual Forces in Human Progress," in which he foresaw social equality making "men as chaste as women. Nobody drunk, nobody stifled by this or that poison, given with this or that pretense, with everybody free to be the engine of the almighty soul." He concluded, "The twentieth century is to build a civilization which is to last forever, because it is a civilization founded on an idea."

The nature of much that is called religion — especially in the West — tends to make people visionary, whether looking backward at their origins and development, at themselves at the present time, or forward into the future. As will be seen, there are elements within these religions that discourage realistic observation.

The final speaker on the last day of meetings at the World's Parliament of Religions was Elder Daniel Offord from Mount

(New) Lebanon, New York, who gave a short account of "The Doctrine and Life of the Shakers." Their doctrine was belief in "the new earth and two orders. These comprise the natural order, for the worldly; and the spiritual order, for those worthy to attain the resurrection." The latter meant the Shakers. Their life was industrial, spent in producing marketable goods. Not mentioned by Elder Daniel was that the sect had had a remarkable history: their entire membership of thirteen persons (including three or four children) had migrated from England to America in 1774-75, and they acquired 15,000 converts here. The Shakers were distributed among twenty communities. Their heyday had been during the middle of the nineteenth century, but due to their injunction against procreating, and to deaths and desertions, they were on a marked decline. Three colonies already had dissolved, and others were soon to follow. Only eight were to survive World War I. That the Shaker spokesman had been assigned to the terminal position (and in the secondary "Scientific Section," not in the main meeting hall) was grimly foreboding. It accorded with Elder Offord's belated nostalgia: "Our organizations have demonstrated the practicability of Christian communism."

INTRODUCTION — notes

1 Barry Fell, *America B.C.*, New York 1977, and *Bronze Age America*, Boston, 1982.
2 Charles G. Leland, *Fu-sang or the Discovery of America by Chinese Buddhist Priests in the Fifth Century*, London, 1875.
3 Hjalmar R. Holand, *Norse Discoveries and Exploration in America 982-1302*, New York, 1940; Frederick J. Pohl, *The Viking Explorers*, New York, 1966.
4 John Henry Barrows (ed.), *The World's Parliament of Religions*, Chicago, 1893, p. 26.
5 *Ibid.*, p. 18.
6 Sketches about the speakers in this section and later in the introduction are taken from the "Biographic Notes" given on pages 1584 through 1590 in *The World's Parliament of Religions* and from other sources of general information, including library catalogs.

1

AIM AND SCOPE OF THE PARLIAMENT

THE WORLD'S PARLIAMENT OF RELIGIONS was not the first convocation of its kind in the world. According to Dharmapala, in his address of welcome during the introductory session, the earliest on record was that sponsored by the Indian Emperor Aśoka in the second quarter of the third century B.C. A thousand scholars convened in the city of Patna for seven months. Although predominantly Buddhist, included were those of other religions, as numerous sects were under the patronage of the enlightened ruler (Chapter Eight). On a limited scale and restricted membership were certain early Christian meetings, like the Council of Nicaea, held in Asia Minor in 325 A.D., which fixed the sacred books and creeds of Christianity. The best known interfaith convention was that of the sixteenth-century Mugal Emperor Akbar, mentioned by the Rev. E.L. Rexford and Rev. Joseph Cook of Boston during meetings on the fourth day of the Parliament, and by Prof. J. Estlin Carpenter of England four days later. Akbar ordered built in his capital, Fatehpur Sikri, a great hall known as the House of Worship, in which were held disputations by representatives of the many sects of Islam, and Brahmans, Jains, Zarathustrians, Jews and Christians. Prof. Carpenter noted that there grew in Akbar's heart the conviction that there were "sensible men in all religions." The Chicago Parliament differed from its predecessors in that it issued invitations to participants all over the earth, and its doors were open to the general public.

The World's Parliament of Religions held its principal meetings in the Hall of Columbus at the Art Institute of Chicago, a newly-erected stone building in restrained Classic

26

style, featuring arches and a pedimented central pavilion, on Michigan Avenue. Overflows and secondary meetings occupied the Hall of Washington, and lesser groups met elsewhere in the building. The major meetings were divided into morning, afternoon, and evening sessions from September 11 through 27, followed by an eight-day session on missions. A special scientific section convened in Room II on September 15, 20, 21, 22, 23, 24 and 27. Only on one day, September 20, were discussions on the relation of religion to science presented, the balance of the time being spent on ethnic cults, detailed accounts of non-Christian contemporary religions, and special sects, like Mormonism, the Dev Dharm, and Shakerism. In addition there were individual denominational congresses, lasting from a day to more than a week. The Evangelical Alliance Congress spanned eight days; the Catholic, five; Jewish, four; Lutheran and Evangelical Association, each three; Unitarianism and Theosophical Society, each two; and the others, mostly Protestant sects, one day. The Baptists turned down a congress because the Exposition opened on a Sunday. Some of the congresses transpired before the Parliament began, as in the case of the Jewish meeting, which took place from August 27 to 30; and the Lutheran, Catholic, and Congregational meetings were held before September 11. Several were in progress at the same time. Also provided were small rooms where the main speakers could meet people from the audience and answer questions.

Most of the two hundred participants were Americans. Strangely enough, the largest delegations from foreign lands came from India and Japan, eighteen and seventeen; then England, twelve; the Near East, ten; Europe, eight; and several from China, Ceylon, Siam, and Canada. The preponderance of lectures was on religion and the humanities, including ethics, and having to do with national and special groups — a total of some sixty talks. Closely allied were the dozen addresses on religious unity and speculation on what man's future religion would be. Another dozen were comparing religions, especially Christianity with the Farther Asian group. Fourteen talks were on gods and theology, eight on scriptures, four on immortality, and three each on philosophy and science and their bearing upon religion. Four speakers dealt with religion in a general way. A few dealt with tolerance and the attainment of peace. A good many talks were on missions, of which a large percentage were critical if not damning. Most of the talks on Christianity were delivered in the denominational gatherings, being too specialized to be of interest to the general assembly. Of specific religions, the largest number concerned Hinduism; then, in diminishing numbers, Judaism, Christian denominations, including the Greek Orthodox and Armenian churches, and Buddhism, Catholicism, Islam, Shinto, Confucianism, Parseeism, Taoism, Jainism, and certain ethnic groups. It must be understood that the subjects given above could be further broken down into numerous subtopics, and that many other aspects of religion were touched upon, such as faith, temperance, the family, the day of rest, the incarnation, man's divinity, sacraments, crime, and love and compassion. In responding to invitations sent by the Parliament, undoubtedly most of the speakers proposed the subjects and titles for their addresses. There was much overlapping. And there is evidence that some topics were requested by the committee for the congresses, a marked number falling to professors and divines in the Chicago area, by way of expanding into neglected fields and rounding out the coverage. Even so, important subjects were overlooked which would have thrown additional light upon topics included that were handled too narrowly.

The representation of outside religions at the Parliament was said to be in "precisely the spirit . . . with which a Christian missionary invites a Moslem and a Brahman into his own home — the spirit of love, inquiry, a desire for mutual understanding, a desire to learn as well as to teach." According to some of the things brought out about Christian missionaries at the Parliament, it might have been better to admit that other religions were listened to more out of social courtesy than as an expression of warm feelings or liberalism. At least at the Parliament itself apparently all who applied were given a hearing, though not all at the general meetings, and not all were written up in full in the two-volume publication containing the speeches. The directors assumed that their own broadest concepts were as expansive as those of every other religion participating. The slogan of the gathering was a quotation from the Old Testament, Malachi II, 10: "Have we not all one father? Hath not one God created us?" which was stamped on the front covers of the books containing the talks. The sentiment is strictly Near Eastern and tribal, "God" being defined six verses on as the Lord of Israel, the "we" and "us," therefore, referring only to Jews. Representatives of the more advanced religions of Farther Asia were offended by the childishness of considering God a father image, and by the primitiveness and backwardness of alluding to the creation myth.

The initial definition of religion offered at the Parliament came from the Hon. Charles Carroll Bonney, president of the World's Congress Auxiliary, in his opening address on September 11. He characterized it as "the love and worship of God and the love and service of man." Bonney endeavoured to buttress and enlarge upon his statement by quoting scripture: "of a truth God is no respecter of persons, but in every nation he that feareth God and worketh righteousness is acceptable to him." Undoubtedly Peter's declaration was selected because it seems to make every man eligible, but the qualification of working "righteousness" is narrow (Chapter Eight), and that a man must be terrified by God is diametrically opposed to the feeling of love contained in Bonney's definition. It is an archaism; but the speaker's next remark was more timely: "As the finite can never fully comprehend the infinite, nor perfectly express its own view of the divine, it necessarily follows that individual opinions of the divine nature and attributes will differ."

On the ninth day of meetings, Prof. J.P. Landis of the
Dayton Theological Seminary quoted an "eminent philosophical Christian writer" as giving a definition that is virtually
a paraphrase of Bonney's: "Religion is the union of man with
God, of the finite with the infinite, expressed in conscious
love and reverence." Landis was discussing the science of
religion, his word science here meaning "systematized knowledge." He went on to say that this implies "more than an
orderly arrangement of facts. It includes the discovery of the
principles and laws which underlie and pervade the facts.
Science seeks to reach the highest principles, those which
have given shape and character to the facts, and among these
principles even aspires to grasp the central one, so as to give
rational unity to the subject. . . . The religious phenomena of
the world and human experience are just as real as any with
which physical science has to deal. In the sense in which
he means it, James Freeman Clark is right when he says,
'The facts of consciousness constitute the basis of religious
science. . . . Faith, Hope, and Love are as real as form, sound
and color. The moral *laws* also, which may be deduced from
such experience are real and permanent, and these laws can
be verified in the daily course of human life. The whole realm
of spiritual exercises may and *ought* to be carefully examined,
analyzed and verified.'" Landis considered the "three most
prominent subjects" of the science of religion to be (1) "God,
his being and attributes," (2) "Nature, or the works of God,"
and (3) "Man in his relation to the Deity." The inclusion of
nature is unexpected for a Western theologian, and characterizing it as "the works of God" is beyond the pale of scientific
terminology or speculation.
    The Rev. Walter Elliott, of the Order of St. Paul in New
York, construed that the "end and office of religion is to
direct the aspirations of the soul toward an infinite good, and
to secure a perfect fruition. Man's longings for perfect wisdom, love and joy are not aberrations of the intelligence, or
morbid conditions of any kind; they are not purely subjective,

blind reachings forth toward nothing. They are most real life, excited into activity by the infinite reality of the Supreme Being, the most loving God, calling his creature to union with himself." As had Landis, Elliott went on to talk about sin, becoming deeply involved due to the restrictions of a highly dogmatized denomination. There is no place for nature in the Paulist's discourse: he is the playwright, whose business it is to direct the actors portrayed through his plot to the inevitable climax personified as God, the stage vacant of scenery.

The Rev. Lyman Abbott, of Plymouth Church in Brooklyn, brought the relationship of man and God to what he considered its logical conclusion through the thesis that religion constitutes the human uniqueness. "Man is a wonderful machine. This body of his is the most marvelous mechanism in the world. Man is an animal, linked to the animal race by his instincts, his appetites, his passions, his social nature. He has all that the animal possesses, only in a higher and larger degree; but he is more than a machine, more than an animal. He is linked to more than the earth from which he was formed; he is linked to the divine and the eternal." Like Landis, he considered the human traits making religion to be faith, hope, and love. Faith is that which "if it does not always see the Infinite, at all events always tries to see the Infinite;" hope "beckons him as to higher and higher achievements"; and love begins "in the cradle, binding him to his mother, widens in ever-broadening circles as life enlarges, . . . at last reaching out and taking in the whole human race, and in all of this learning that there is still a larger life in which we live and move and have our being, toward which we tend and by which we are fed and inspired."

Outward manifestations of religion admittedly are exclusively man-made — meaning such formalities as rituals, communion, preaching, reading sacred texts and demonstrative worship of all kinds — but these are the less subtle, the less essential aspects (Chapter Six). As Abbott observed, man has more complexities than the other species. One must concede that they are of degree and not of kind. If he has more of the desirable traits, like kindness, consideration, helpfulness, piety, and love, man also has greater capacities for the undesirable — cruelty, indifference to others' suffering, delight in thwarting his fellows, anger, and hate. What is faith and hope but devising a formula for appeasing man's inordinate anxiety, of which all conscious beings have some? In what way does man's love differ essentially from the inherent affection many creatures feel for other members of their kind? What more esteem, trust, and desire to serve has any being greater than that of a mongrel dog for a worthy (and sometimes for even an unworthy) master? The dawn of civilization created gods in the image of man, and the first glimmer of sacred literature flattered man as being in the image of the gods. Man's "larger life," as viewed in this reversible proposition, is a remote possibility, considering the purported paramountcy of the gods and the asserted insignificance of man.

It was the focus upon humanity and its intercourse with the created deity or deities that fabricated a lopsided definition of religion at the Parliament. This was amended by the delegates from Farther Asia, though what they said was not understood generally by the American audience.

In the afternoon session on September 25, directed to the subject of "The Importance of Philosophy to the Science of Religion," Swami Vivekananda spoke on "The Essence of the Hindu Religion." Although his remarks held fast to the letter of the system, they nevertheless were conciliatory to his audience. Hinduism, he said, is theistic, unlike Buddhism, which is agnostic, and Jainism, which is atheistic. He called God the "Almighty and All-merciful," which sounds Islamic. He noted that the *rishis* of the Vedic texts sang, "Thou art our father, thou art our mother; thou art our beloved friend; thou art the source of all strength." And a Hindu prayer ran, "Lord, I do not want wealth, nor children, nor learning. . . . but grant me this, that I may love thee without the hope of reward — unselfishly love for love's sake." On the subject of man, Vivekananda said, "the human soul is eternal and immortal, perfect and infinite, and death means only a change of center from one body to another. The present is determined by our past actions, and the future will be by the present; that it will go on evolving up or reverting back from birth to birth and death to death." In his selection from that vast body of Indian scriptures, which can supply just about any religious idea ever conceived, presenting God as mother as well as father, and as friend, loving God for love's sake, and eliminating any cause for fearing him by proclaiming man himself responsible for the afflictions that befall him, Vivekananda surpassed the Christians in using their own terms. His technique was found sufficiently appealing to incite a response that encouraged him to remain in the United States as a missionary. However much he accomplished here over the next four years, it remained for others to make more definite statements about Hinduism from the platform of Columbus Hall.

One was another Indian, Manilal Mabhubhai D'vivedi, a Brahman from Nadiad, whose paper on Hinduism was read a week before Vivekananda's. Questions posed afterward prompted D'vivedi to prepare ten short essays in response. The following sets forth the Hindu view on the "End and Office of Religion."

"In India religion has a triple aspect. It comprises cosmology, ontology and ethics. Religion, then, is not that something which satisfies the emotional nature of man, by setting up for admiration some ideal of all that is good and virtuous. Religion is that rational demonstration of the universe which explains the aim and object of existence, shows the relation of man to man, and supplies that real criterion of being which satisfies reason and ennobles emotion.

"In its passive aspect religion addresses itself to reason and explains the nature and relation of God, man, and universe, shows the real aim of existence, and lays down the rules of right conduct. In its active aspect it reveals to the heart of man the supremest idea of love and bliss, — an ideal which it ever strives to approach. Religion by the satisfaction of both these essential parts of the nature of man leads to mental peace, spiritual exaltation, universal good, all culminating in absolute self-realization." As in his pronouncements on so many topics brought up at the Parliament, D'vivedi did not merely surpass the remarks of other speakers, he made statements so conclusive that they could not be surpassed.

Virchand A. Gandhi, who outlined "The Philosophy and Ethics of the Jains" on the fifteenth day, gave in the wording of his title the contents of his religion, which is an offshoot of Hinduism. One part is "Shrute Dharma, *i.e.*, philosophy," and the other "Chatra Dharma, *i.e.*, ethics." Jain philosophy "inquires into the nature of nine principles, six kinds of living beings and four states of existence." Of the nine principles the first is soul, the second nonsoul, and the rest "are but the different states produced by the combination and separation of soul and nonsoul." The six kinds of living beings are divided according to the number of sense perceptions they possess, those with one having only touch, to which are added taste, smell, sight, hearing, and thinking. Gandhi said that he "would refer those who are desirous of studying Jain biology, zoology, botany, anatomy and phsiology to the many books published by our society." The four states of existence range from what Gandhi called denizens of hell, through lower (starting with plant) and higher (up to human) forms of life, to denizens of the celestial world. Jain ethics is directing one's conduct so as "to insure the fullest development of the soul. . . . Jainism teaches to look upon all living beings as upon oneself." The two parts of Gandhi's religion, one sees, differ from those of the Parliament's formula — as the love and worship of God and love and service to man — in that the first is attaining knowledge about the world in which one lives, and the second extends service beyond mankind to all sentient life. Vivekananda was mistaken in saying that

Jainism is atheistic, as Gandhi defined what God is (see Chapter Two); but God is not topmost in its religious orientation, which is more inclusive and more practical in its application than the theistic notion adopted by the Parliament.

The chief spokesman for Buddhism at the Parliament was Anagarika Dharmapala, of Ceylon, in whose speech, "The World's Debt to Buddha" he defined his religion as "a comprehensive system of ethics, and a transcendental metaphysic embracing a sublime psychology. To the simple-minded it offers a code of morality, to the earnest student a system of pure thought. But the basic doctrine is the self-purification of man. Spiritual progress is impossible for him who does not lead a life of purity and compassion. The rays of the sunlight of truth enter the mind of him who is fearless to examine truth, who is free from prejudice, who is not tied by the sensual passions and who has reasoning faculties to think. One has to be an atheist in the sense employed by Max Müller: 'There is an atheism which is unto death, there is another which is the very life-blood of all truth and faith. It is the power of giving up what, in our best, our most honest moments, we know to be no longer true; it is the readiness to replace the less perfect, however dear, however sacred it may have been to us, by the more perfect, however much it may be detested, as yet, by the world. It is the true self-surrender, the true self-sacrifice, the truest trust in truth, the truest faith. Without that atheism, no new religion, no reform, no reformation, no resuscitation would ever have been possible; without that atheism, no new life is possible for any one of us.' " If D'vivedi's verbal circumspection stretched to the limits of a religion as many-faceted as Hinduism, the résumés of Gandhi and Dharmapala as well accounted for Jainism and Buddhism, and neither was deterred by the fact that his differed considerably from the Parliament's definition.

On the next to last day of the meetings Kinza Riuge M. Hirai presented a brief but penetrating analysis of what he called "Synthetic Religion." Hirai had won his audience's esteem in his earlier talk on Japan's position toward Christianity and missions, and he approached the second topic with equal tact. Here, however, his technique was on the abstract rather than on the specific side. "Religion is *a priori* belief in an unknown entity, and no human being or lower animal can evade or resist this belief." He continued: "Knowledge by reasoning is the process of deriving conclusions from premises. If we trace back our premises to anterior premises, and try to reach the source of them, we come to the incomprehensible. Shall we then reject the first premises of our belief because they are inexplicable? No. We are forced to believe them. We believe something which we do not know. This is what I call *a priori* belief in an unknown entity." Some would look upon this entity as a creator god, who is "absolute, infinite, omnipotent," and who can "create by methods beyond our human intellect." But, "Creation implies relativity, and if God is creator he loses the attribute of absoluteness." Because we humans are not "unlimited and omnipotent, we cannot prove the divine infiniteness." Hirai's conclusion is that inasmuch as the reasoning for both go back to the same unknown, "theism and atheism mean the same thing, or both are misnomers of the same thing." His observation that religion is belief in an unknown "no human being or lower animal" can resist refutes the Rev. Lyman Abbott's thesis about religion being the exclusive property of man. Kinza Hirai's thinking had been nurtured by Zen in the Island Empire, where many different religions had come and where they had taken root and flourished side by side unmolested by the others. He had given deep consideration to what it was that held them together, and, as the title of his talk suggests, he wished to pass this idea along: "All the religions in the world are synthetized into one religion, or 'Entitism,' which has been the inherent spirit in Japan, and is called Satori, or Hotoke, in Japanese. The apparent contradictions among them are only the different descriptions of the same thing seen from different situations, and different views to be observed in the way to the same termination."

The Oriental mind may have become proficient in seeking out essences of agreement in the various religions, but such an accomplishment had not yet been achieved by the Occidental brain. As the latter dominated the scene, the Parliament "proved" exactly what it had set out to prove, which was, as worded by Dr. Theodore T. Munger: "The Parliament shows that the world moves, and on the whole moves Christward." The quotation, inserted in the final or summary chapter of the volumes recording the talks, was followed by the comment, "It showed a great confidence on the part of the critics of Christendom that they should stand up in the Parliament, as did the eloquent Hirai [in his first appearance], and protest not against real, but against false, Christianity. The only spoken prayers at the Parliament were the Lord's Prayer ... but in the daily repetition of the Universal Prayer men saw a divine finger pointing to the universal and ultimate religion. 'That religion,' as Prof. Goodspeed has said, 'is not so much Christianity as Christ. Such was the deepest voice of the Parliament.' "

But this was not very deep. As will be seen in Chapter Three, Christ was a mythical being imposed upon the historic figure Jesus, who had ability as a sorcerer but was a failure in his avowed religious mission. Yet in the centuries following Jesus' lifetime, the myth became a cult focus among numerous sects hostile to one another on the divine status of Christ, and on his relationship to other members of the hierarchy. Attending the Parliament were members of the rigid camps of Unitarians, Trinitarians, and Tetrarians (in Shakerism, Mother Ann was sister and bride of Jesus Christ) and none would budge. One of the few things they seemed to agree on was that outside religions "had nothing to add to the Christian creed." This was a flexible quantity. That the World's Parliament of Religions was conceived and assembled by the group and that attendance was as responsive as it was are indications of their striving in the right direction. A lot that was said was irrational and opinionated, banal and even pathetic, whereas also there were many provocative and interesting points brought out by the speakers, some against their own faith. Except for the steadfast narrowness of a few of the principal organizers, whose profession was at stake (Chapter Ten), most of the people attending the Parliament must have gone away with something greater than they brought to it.

2

CONCEPTS CONCERNING THE NATURE OF GOD

NO SUBJECT at the Parliament of Religions drew forth more divergent and contradictory statements and opinions than that on the nature of God, or the gods. Usually it was the latter, as often it was those who most vehemently protested their faith to be in the singular who proclaimed the plural. As we already have seen, the Parliament defined religion as the worship of God and service of man, in this order. Following the assembly and addresses of welcome, the first day of scheduled talks (September 12) was devoted mainly to theistic teachings and theories. Of the eight authors or speakers in the morning and afternoon sessions, one was a Roman Catholic, one an English Anglican, two were American educators, one an American missionary to India, one a Jewish rabbi, one a Hindu, and the last a German non-sectarian. From the Christian standpoint, the parliament was getting off on a safe start: talks by three of the first four mentioned above were on God considered from the rational or philosophical angle, the other looked at other religions from a Christian prospect; the rabbi's was analytical; one of the two on Hinduism was handled by a missionary, the second being of an outline nature; and the noncommittal wordiness of the last — Dr. Adolph Brodbeck's "Idealism the New Religion," which strove for self-improvement and took its tenets from science rather than existing religious dogmas — gave the chairman the opportunity of commenting that "the hospitality of this platform has been vindicated, . . . the aim of the Parliament of Religions to study all exhibits of the spectrum has been realized today."

The first of the speeches was written by the Very Rev.

Augustine F. Hewitt, of the Community of Paulists, and read by a confrere; it was on the "Rational Demonstration of the Being of God" as presented in Catholic philosophy. This philosophy, he explained, is not "a system derived from the Christian revelation and imposed by the authority of the Catholic Church," it is that taught in Catholic schools "adopted in great part from Aristotle and Plato." Hewitt drew upon their metaphysics in presenting God as the "first cause," later amplified in the statement: "The design and construction of the whole world order must proceed from an Author of supreme and divine intelligence." Further on he said, "we have no intuition of the essence of God. God is to us inscrutable, incomprehensible, dwelling in light, inaccessible." And at another point he declared, "In God alone essence and existence are identical." This is somewhat contradicted by his conclusion: "It is the highest achievement of human reason to bring the intellect to a knowledge of God as the first and final cause of the world," which separates the Infinite from the finite. The latter is more orthodox to his faith. As he had observed among his early remarks, "Christians, Jews, Mohammedans and philosophical theists are agreed in professing monotheism as their fundamental and cardinal doctrine." Christians and Jews *profess* monotheism, but their scriptures and theology indicate otherwise; Mohammed's religion recognizes celestial beings other than God but is virtually monotheistic; whereas philosophical theists think of God quite differently than do traditional religions, as indicated in Hewitt's talk.

The Rev. Dr. Alfred Williams Momerie, of King's College, London, who followed the Paulist, entitled his address "Philosophic and Moral Evidence for the Existence of God." The Englishman echoed his predecessor's pantheistic tendency by saying: "We must cease to believe in a finite God, outside of nature, who capriciously interferes with her phenomena, before we can begin to believe in an infinite God, immanent in nature, of whose mind and will all natural phenomena are the various but never-varying expression." He substantiated the concept by scientific observation, citing the law of gravity, the attraction of objects proportionate to their magnitude and proximity, indicating that this force is an inherent part of nature's design; and evolution accords with the idea, wherein "The Creator saw the end from the beginning." The last agrees with his attempt to reconcile scripture with reason, later corroborated by his indicating the astronomical figures of improbability "of the world's having been evolved by chance"; but the connection between the innate and creator gods eludes one. The moral evidence for God is apparent in the many instances wherein the wicked are punished. Considering moral justice, he poses the question, why should a mother "lose her darling child by accident or disease, and . . . she cannot by any agony of prayer recall the child to life?" His reply is a bit strange: "The child has died through a violation of some of nature's laws, and if such violation were unattended with death men would lose the great inducement to discover and obey them." It is not consistent with his thesis either, which he sums up as: "All knowledge . . . implies the existence of a Mind which is omnipresent and eternal, while the tendency toward righteousness, which is so unmistakably manifest in the course of history, together with the responses which this tendency awakens in our own hearts, combine to prove that the infinite Thinker is just and kind and good."

The third speech on September 12 related to those of the Paulist and British divines was that of Dr. W.T. Harris, United States commissioner of education, billed as "Proofs of the Existence of God." Harris' talk was the most knowledgeable of the Western speakers, showing that he was well read in the Greek philosophers and early Christian annotators. He held closer to the presentation and terminology of the Greeks than had Father Hewitt. Dr. Harris recalled Plato's two modes of acquiring knowledge, one through sense perceptions and the other by "logical presupposition." For the latter he referred to the Metaphysics, wherein "Aristotle unfolds his doctrine that dependent beings presuppose a divine being whose activity is pure knowing." Such notions were mulled over by theologicans of the first six centuries of our era, their object being "to give unity and system to the new doctrine of the divine-human nature of God taught by Christ." "The Greeks," he observed, "had seen the idea of the Logos . . . the Word that was in the beginning, and through which created beings arose in time and space. But how the finite and imperfect arose from the infinite and perfect the Greek did not understand as well as the Christian." The omitted phrase in the quotation after the word "Logos" is "or Eternally Begotten Son," of which the Greeks, of course, knew nothing; it was the insertion and contemplation of theologians, not philosophers. "Christian thinking," said Harris, "adds two new ideas to the two already found by Plato. It adds to the divine first and the second (the Logos), also a divine third, the Holy Spirit, and a fourth not divine, but the process of the third — calling it the *processio*. This idea of process explains the existence of a world of finite beings, for it contains evolution, development or derivation." Further on he said, "Nature is eternal, but not self-existent; it is the procession of the Holy Spirit, and arises in the double thought of the first Person and the Logos, or the timeless generation which is logically involved in the fact of God's consciousness as eternal reason." He concluded, "The idea of God is, as Kant has explained, the supreme directive or regulative idea in the mind. It is, moreover, as Plato and St. Anselm saw, the most certain of all our ideas, the light in all our seeing."

Using the Logos as an argument for the acceptance of Jesus is no more valid than the Nazis' extolling the amenities of the Fatherland for the support of Hitler, the savior of the nation. Neither a generalization nor an abstraction advocates a particular without extensive qualification. Harris confused two dissimilar elements — the philosophical and the mythical. The latter is the older, having come into being in the crude attempts of primitive man to explain the existence and operation of the physical world. He invented gods, resembling himself, to create and preside over it. Some of these gods related to man's environment, to the hills, forests, streams, lakes, sun, moon, and stars; and some looked after his affairs, including his household, harvest, business, wars, and fortune. The gods controlled nature but existed apart from it, and when man started worshipping them to make them better disposed toward improving his conditions, religion was born. Jesus, with his father-god, belongs to this tradition. Elsewhere, when man began to think rationally, he perceived principle inherent in nature as the cause of all happenings, and philosophy came into being. Beginning with Heraclitus, who lived in a Greek colony in Western Asia about 500 B.C., the primal agent was called Logos. As Father Hewitt pointed out, Catholic schools taught a modified Greek philosophy, but Christianity itself clung steadfastly to its archaic mythical core. However, other religions advanced to the philosophical stage, and their presentations at the Parliament will be taken up in due course.

One of the world's oldest religions is Hinduism. Its early form was discussed by a missionary to Madras, the Rev. Maurice Phillips, whose talk preceded that of Dr. Harris and was entitled "The Ancient Religion of India and Primitive Revelation." He pictured the ancient Aryans as "worshiping the elements of nature as *living persons*," which type of "worship is denominated 'Physiolatry.' . . . were it all nature," he added, "there would be no room for personification, for personification implies the knowledge of a person, and the personification of a natural object as an *object of worship*, implies the concept, more or less clear, of what we call God." Being a Christian clergyman, Phillip's standard for a fully-developed concept of God has to be identified with the self, and he berated "the ancient Hindus [for] never [having] grasped the idea of God as a *personal Being distinct from nature*." But though the Indians did not know "God as a

personal being distinct from natural phenomena, they possessed a wonderful knowledge of the actions and attributes
which preeminently belong to him. They ascribed to the
personified elements of nature the functions of Creator,
Preserver and Ruler; and the attributes of infinity, om-
niscience, omnipotence, immortality, righteousness, holiness
and mercy." Phillips emphasized the "error of identifying
the Monism of the Upanishads with the Monotheism of the
Bible — that is, the subtle powers resident in nature of the
Hindus' sacred books with the anthropomorphic overlord,
extraneous to creation, of the Jewish scriptures.

The Rev. Maurice Phillips was neither the only nor the first
person to disagree with the ancient Indians' views on gods.
Their contemporary Aryan kinsmen in Persia had, as voiced
by their prophet Zarathustra, better known by his Greek
name Zoroaster, who lived during the sixth century B.C. His
was the state creed under the Achaemenid and Sassanian kings,
but Zarathustrianism received a severe blow by Alexander's
conquest in 331 B.C., and a thousand years later the Moslem
Jihad sent adherents not wishing to convert to Islam fleeing
to India, where they became known as Parsees — Persians.
Jeanne Sorabji read Jinanji Jamshedji Modi's paper on "The
Religious System of the Parsees" before the Parliament, in
which Zarathustrianism is called "a monotheistic form of
religion. It believes in the existence of one God, whom it
knows . . . [as] Ahura-Mazda." Modi translated the name as
the "Omniscient Lord," and he mentioned that the early
Iranians rejected the ancient Aryan word for God, *daeva*
from *div* ("to shine"), because instead of being used for God
alone, it was being applied to many of his created objects. He
observed that many cultures adopted the older word: "Thus
the Greeks called their God, Deos or Zeus; the Romans,
Deus; the Germans, Teus; the Lithuanians, Diewas, and so on."
The Hindus rendered it Deva, and reserved Asura for demons.
As the Persians used this last word for gods (Ahura), they
called devils dives. The Parsee theological system recognized

the complementary powers of two primeval causes, Good and Evil, Spenta-mainyush, the increasing spirit (good), and Angra-mainyush, the decreasing spirit (evil), leaders of a host of ahuras and dives. The hierarchy also included guardian spirits to the number of 99,999. Accused of being dualistic and/or polytheistic, Modi said that Parseeism is no more so than is Christianity. Despite Modi's protests against dives, "shining ones," Ahura-Mazda is a god of light, after whom Thomas Edison named the incandescent bulb, the Mazda.

The living religion that is the rival of Hinduism for age, older than Zarathustrianism and still on home ground in the Near East, is Judaism, spared from the depredations of the Jihad by being considered a forerunner of Islam. At the Parliament, immediately preceding Mr. Phillips, Rabbi Isaac M. Wise of Cincinnati presented "The Theology of Judaism." He began by announcing that there is no theology in Judaism, which he characterized as "a religion of deeds without dogmas." For his auditors' consideration he presented the proposition, "Religion unites and theology divides the human family not seldom into hostile factions." However, Dr. Wise enumerated what he called four dogmas that figure in most religions: (1) the existence of deity, (2) the communication or revelation of this deity to and his worship of man, (3) the finer sensibilities (conscience, ethics and esthetics), and (4) "a state of felicity or torment beyond this . . . mundane life." He defined Judaism as "the complex of Israel's religious sentiments rationcinated to conceptions in harmony with its Jehovistic God cognition," and enlightened us no more as to the Jewish concept of God.

We are given a capsule sketch of the subject by Dr. Eliza R. Sunderland of Ann Arbor on the fifth day in her "Serious Study of All Religions." Mrs. Sunderland noted that all early Semitic religions had "much in common. Their gods were all tribal or national gods, limited to particular countries, choosing for themselves special dwelling places." She divided them into two groups: "Among the Arabs this early religion developed into animistic polydaemonism, and never rises much higher than this; but among the Mesopotamian Semites the nature beings rise above nature and rule it, and one among them rises above all the others as the head of an unlimited theocracy." The ancient god of the Jews, she said, was "El-Shaddai, but his worship had given place under their great leader, Moses, to a new cult, the worship of Yahveh, the dreadful and stern god of thunder, who first appeared to Moses at the [burning] bush under the name 'I am that I am.'" This cult was accompanied by a higher moral law unlike any the Semites knew at that time. However, Mrs. Sunderland pointed out, "Nineteenth-century research has discovered an equally high moral code in Egypt, and the very name 'Nuk pu Nuk,' 'I am that I am,' is found among Egyptian inscriptions." The old deity, Ed-Shaddai, began to be called Baal, and worship included Ashera, the goddess of fertility. But gradually Yahveh became supreme, and Judaism became "henotheistic, a belief in the existence of many gods, though worshiping only the national god," which is something quite different from monotheism.

The god that appeared to Moses in Midian was complex. He was spiteful, lavishing afflictions upon Pharaoh and his people, and, in Exodus, he is referred to as "a man of war," one who "dashed in pieces the enemy" (XV, 3, 6). Later, David similarly described this deity as the "Lord of hosts, the God of the armies of Israel" (I Samuel XVII, 45). At the beginning of Moses' first book, Genesis, he is also the creator of the universe, a role difficult to equate with that of a petty tribal god. It is fairly well agreed among scholars that the creation myth originated in Sumer and from there spread throughout the Near East. It might have been brought from Sumer by Abraham; it might have been adopted by the Jews in Babylon during the captivity, at about which time the Bible was being compiled; but it seems most likely that it was brought from Egypt by Moses, who allegedly recorded the legend.[1] All open with the watery chaos. The Egyptian makes the creator male, Atum, who conceives among the first things Nūt and Geb, Heaven and Earth. The Babylonians, however, instituted the day of rest.[2] After the glorious week of creating, Yahveh sinks into the narrow role of bloodthirsty tribal deity. Three centuries after "giving" the Israelites the Promised Land (it was their job to kill or drive off the rightful owners), Yahveh still was demanding and getting wholesale human sacrifices, as in the case of the seven "sons" of Saul whom King David turned over to the Gibeonites to be hanged that a drought would be terminated (II Samuel XXI, 1-10).

In another three centuries, or about 450 B.C., the prophets presented God in a new light. Prof. George S. Goodspeed of the University of Chicago, in setting forth "What the Dead Religions Have Bequeathed to the Living," claimed that, "the prophets released Israel's God from the fetters of nationality and from the bonds of selfish morality, and preached the doctrine of a transcendent righteous God of all the earth." But Jeremiah identified him as "the Lord that brought us up out of the land of Egypt" (II, 6); Ezekiel's god proclaimed "the house of Israel, are my people" (XXXIV, 30); Daniel praised the "God of my fathers" (II, 23); Hosea foresaw Israel seeking "the Lord their God" (III, 5); similarly Joel had Israel finding joy and gladness in the "house of our God" (I, 16); Amos had God identifying himself as he who "brought you up from the land of Egypt" (II, 10); Obadiah's god was localized on holy "mount Zion" (I, 17); to Nahum god extolled the "excellency of Israel" (II, 2); Habakkuk said that "God came from Teman, and the Holy One from Mount Paran," near Sinai (III, 3); Zephaniah's deity was the "God of Israel" (II, 9); Haggai was used as the mouthpiece of the "Lord of Hosts" (I, 2); Zechariah's god was "jealous for Jerusalem and for Zion" (I, 14), and Malachi's was the "God of Israel" (II, 16). Three prophets extended Yahveh's jurisdiction beyond Jews. Micah's god was concerned over Jerusalem and Samaria, the latter a town halfway between Jerusalem and Nazareth, but not Jewish (I, 1). Jonah was charged with going to the Semitic city of Nineveh, a three-days' journey (III, 3). God "repented of the evil, that he had said that he would do" unto the people of Nineveh for their wickedness, after Jonah had forewarned them of God's intended destruction of the city, and they had put on sackcloth and fasted forty days, which was a disappointment to Jonah. Isaiah, although calling God "the Holy One of Israel" (I, 4), later proclaimed that "he shall judge among the nations, and shall rebuke many people: and they shall beat their swords into plowshares, and their spears into pruning hooks: nation shall not lift up sword against nation, neither shall they learn war any more" (II, 4). Except for possibly the last, where he judges *among* the nations, there is no justification for calling Yahveh "a transcendant righteous God of all the earth." God was still tribal to the prophets, though he acquired a more personal relationship. Isaiah addressed him as "thou, O Lord, art our father, our redeemer" (LXIII, 16); and, as expressed in the Parliament's slogan, Malachi proclaimed that the Jews had "all one father . . . one God created us" (II, 10). A father god is as anthropomorphic and individualized, and hence, by definition, just as mythical as a war god.

Jesus adopted the father god of the prophets who had preceded him, as stated in the Lord's Prayer, beginning, "Our Father which art in heaven." In the Sermon on the Mount he admonished his listeners to swear "neither by heaven; for it is God's throne; Nor by the earth; for it is his footstool; neither by Jerusalem; for it is the city of the great King" (Matthew V, 34-35). Thus Jesus pictured God as Israel's giant ruler, quoting Isaiah (LXVI, 1). Later in Matthew he called God "Lord of heaven and earth" (XI, 25), which may mean an overlordship that extends beyond. Two verses later, he related himself to God as the son, saying "no man knoweth the Son, but the Father; neither knoweth any man the Father, save the Son," then he added that to any man who came to him weary he will give rest, meaning he had the authority to save. Unproved, insofar as the Jews were concerned, this was considered blasphemous; when brought before the high priest as a prisoner and asked whether he claimed to be "the Christ, the Son of God," Jesus replied, "Thou hast said; nevertheless I say unto you, Hereafter shall ye see the Son of Man [himself] sitting on the right hand of power, and coming in the clouds of heaven" (XXVI, 63-64). In seeking for Jesus' concept of God in the Bible, we get involved in claims about himself, which had best be left for a separate discussion (Chapter Three).

In the seventh century, the Arabs, who had been worshipping an "animistic polydaemonism," were stirred to a higher form of religion by the self-acclaimed prophet Mohammed. As Dr. George Washburn, president of Robert College, Constantinople, noted in his speech on "The Points of Contact and Contrast between Christianity and Mohammedanism," Mohammed was particularly aroused against "the worship of the stars, of *Lat* and *Ozza* and *Manah*, and of the 360 idols in the temple at Mecca," in place of which he endeavoured to institute monotheism. He recognized the Bible as the word of God, though he was illiterate and could not read it himself, Mohammed was obsessed with the idea that the Judgment Day was at hand, and it was imperative that man should make peace with (submit to) God. This god, Allah, was modeled more on the early Jewish concept than upon the later Old or New Testament modification. He was attended by archangels (of whom Gabriel appeared to Mohammed in his natural form), angels of both sexes, and in opposition to which there was Satan, who sometimes caused the prophet to say things he did not mean and yet were recorded in the Koran. Jesus was considered a prophet; he was not divine, though he was called "The Messiah" (IV, 169). Prof. Washburn likened the Moslem view of Allah to "an absolute Oriental monarch, and his unlimited power to do what he pleases makes entire submission to his will the first, most prominent duty." He referred to the "ninety-nine names of God which the good Moslem constantly repeats." The last part of Chapter

LIX in the Koran describes Allah: "He is God than whom there is no god; who knows the unseen and the visible; He is the merciful, the compassionate! He is God than whom there is no god; the King, the Holy, the Peace-Giver, the Faithful, the Protector, the Mighty, the Repairer, the Great! . . . He is God, the Creator, the Maker, the Fashioner; His are the excellent names! His praises, whatever are in the heavens and the earth do celebrate; for God is the mighty, the wise!"[3] Mohammed had much more to say about God than had Jesus.

In other passages of the Koran, Allah accords more with Dr. Washburn's "Oriental monarch." His merciful aspect is modified in Chapter V: "He pardons whom he pleases and punishes whom he pleases." His compassionate and protector attributes are limited, as in Chapter VIII: "Verily, the worst of beasts in God's sight are the deaf, the dumb who do not understand. Had God known any good in them, he would have made them hear." And the "worst of beasts in God's eyes are those who misbelieve"; and the recommended treatment is, "If ye be believers, kill them!" (Chapter IX). Such exclamations by Mohammed became the battle cry of the Jihad, the war of extermination waged by Islam against infidels. Allah is rather similar to Yahveh, a "man of war" and pleased by those who fear him. The difference between Islam's and Christianity's gods, Washburn stated, is that the latter "is a moral being, doing what is right because it is right, and that he can no more pardon sin arbitrarily than he can make a wrong action right; that he could not be just and yet justify the sinner, without the atonement made by the incarnation and the suffering and the death of Jesus Christ." Washburn seems to be saying that there are two moral beings in Christianity — God cannot forgive transgressions but Jesus can; whereas both God and the prophet in Islam are amoral beings — Allah can forgive iniquities but Mohammed cannot.

More than a century before the Hebrew prophets modified the idea of God from the stern Yahveh to a father image, there was a complete changeover in the way gods were regarded in India. The early nature gods, which Phillips found not personal enough, either became exceedingly personal as *avatāras* (see Chapter Three), or else they became completely impersonal and illusive. Under the old order the concept of the gods held the germ of deity as inherent principle. As an example, formerly, the male god Brahmā was the first member of the Hindu trinity, the Creator. After Śiva (the Destroyer) has ended a world cycle and Vishnu (the Preserver) has nursed the essence of the future world through countless eons on a sea of chaos, Brahmā comes forth and performs the act of genesis, and a new universe is born. The later Brahmā, properly rendered Brahma or Brahman (neuter), is the Supreme Soul, an other-than-material generator, who begets spirit, ātma. This last term may be applied to the individual soul belonging to an insect, bird, or man, or the Universal Soul, the cosmic life, and it may be written Ātma or Ātman. This is the God immanent in nature of which Dr. Momerie spoke during the morning session of the Parliament on 12 September 1893.

In the afternoon session, Virchand A. Gandhi read Manilal M. D'vivedi's paper on "Hinduism," in which he reviewed the overwhelming works of Indian religious literature (Chapter Five). Asked about the Hindu concept of God, D'vivedi responded according to the outlook of the Advaita philosophy taught in the Upanishads. In part his response stated, "God in the sense of an extra-cosmic personal Creator is unknown to this philosophy. It distinctly denies such Creator as illogical and irrelevant in the general scheme of nature. God is formless and all-pervading. This however requires to be explained. The world of forms as we see it is unreal, for we do not know *per se* what any given thing is made of. We only know certain names and forms, and we deal with these as subject and object. The persistent fact in all experience is the fact that implies thought [or absolute mind] and bliss.

"Existence, thought, and bliss are common to all things; what varies are name and form. These three are then the invariable and eternal attributes of all things. . . . Thought is the universal form of all experience, and being implies thought which can never be transcended . . . This universal intelligence is the soul of nature; it is the aggregate of all that is. It is in fact the All, the conditions of experience — time, space, causation — do not limit it, for their very being depends upon it. This is the God of the *Advaita*, known by several names, such as *Brahman, Atman, Chit*, and so on. It is present in all and every particle of the universe, in the thoughts and arts of all things. It is all light, all bliss, all existence."

One is struck by D'vivedi's use of the neuter pronoun "It," instead of the masculine "He," in referring to God as an unlimited concept. Of course! "He" is used for male animals (man included) and may be applied to a god of mythology ("She" for a goddess), but the word is inadequate and misleading in referring to the philosophical concept of God. We speak of the universe itself as "it," and the same word should be used for that power which permeates and activates it, spelled with a capital "I" as "It."

Represented at the Parliament were four religions from Farther Asia that had come into being during the early period of philosophy, all of them in the sixth century B.C., and whose concept of God was of a metaphysical nature from the beginning. Two originated in India. Their founders were not of the Brahman (priest) but of the Kshatriya or ruling caste. One of these religions remained in the homeland and became a branch of Hinduism; it is known as Jainism. The second, Buddhism, long the state religion, spread throughout Asia yet declined in its native country. After the Moslem invasion of India it did not recover, as did Hinduism, because its liberalism was no longer looked upon with favor by a caste-conscious society. The other two philosophy religions were Chinese, Confucianism and Taoism.

Virchand A. Gandhi, who had read D'vivedi's paper on Hinduism on September 12, thirteen days later delivered his own on "The Philosophy and Ethics of the Jains." Its unique characterization of religion was considered in Chapter One. Gandhi defined God as "a subtle essence underlying all substances, conscious as well as unconscious, which becomes an eternal cause of all modifications." The "eternal cause" is an attribute wholly different from that of the single incident of creation.

Coeval with the origin of Jainism was Buddhism. At the time of the Chicago Fair, Buddhism was the world's largest religion, estimated to have about 75,000,000 more adherents than Christianity.[4] Its foremost protagonist at the Parliament was Dharmapala, of Colombo, Ceylon. "Dharmapala" was an epithet meaning "guardian of the Dharma or Buddhist law," and he who bore the name not only guarded but expounded that "law." Dharmapala spoke six times at the Parliament meetings, his principal address being on the eighth day and called "The World's Debt to Buddha." In it was given a résumé of the teaching of the founder, Siddhartha Gautama, a prince who renounced occupying a temporal throne for obtaining the eternal verities. The Buddhist notion of God is tied up with its world view, and in a paragraph on Buddhist theism, Dharmapala said, "Accepting the doctrine of evolution as the only true one, with its corollary, the law of cause and effect, he [the Buddha] condemns the idea of a creator and strictly forbids inquiring into it as being useless." The important goal is the attainment of enlightenment and release from the shortcomings and miseries of the physical world. The gods, at least the "supreme god of the Brahmans and minor gods are accepted; but they are subject to the law of cause and effect" no less than other beings. The speaker from Ceylon concluded by saying, "there is no difference between the perfect man and his supreme god." This means that a person who has expanded his finiteness to its utmost has attained identity with the Infinite. He has become Buddha.

Dharmapala belonged to the Theravādin ("Sect of the Elders") or Southern School of Buddhism. Only in some of its legends a few Hindu gods appear, such as the four *devas*, who attend Siddhartha's birth, and Mara, the Tempter, who tries to distract him at the time of his enlightenment, and there is recognition of Maitreya, the Bodhisattva of the Future. Mrs. Eliza Sunderland did not have this in mind when, in her study of ancient religions, she took a slam at Buddhism, "as it was atheistic in its origin it soon became infected by the most fantastic mythology and the most childish superstitions." Her use of the word "soon" is ill-advised, as what she alludes to is the amalgamation with some Asian animistic systems a millennium after Buddhism's inception. Native Tibetan Pönism, for instance, combined with Buddhism to become Lamaism, which, by the way, changed a hard and fierce primitive mountain people into a gentle, kind, and benevolent population. Its indigenous "fantastic" demons were retained as protectors of the Buddhist Dharma. Some of them are indeed terrifying, dressed in skins and bone aprons, with skulls on their crowns and fashioned into cups and drums in their hands, together with clubs, choppers and thunderbolts, their grimacing faces with fangs exposed, a halo of flames enveloping their bodies. What Mrs. Sunderland calls "childish superstitions" may refer to what generally throughout Mahāyāna or Northern Buddhism is the Bodhisattva ideal. The term means "Buddha essence" and applies to a being who has purified himself to the degree whereby he might pass into Nirvāna (identify with the Infinite), but instead he chooses to remain within reach of the earth plane to assist its inhabitants. Among the Bodhisattvas are Manla the healer; Avalokiteśvara, whose compassion is universal; Mañjuśri, the bestower of wisdom; and Jizō, patron of travelers and he who leads the bewildered souls of little children to the security of Amida's Paradise. As they deal with the physical world, Bodhisattvas have the rank of gods; Buddhas, which have passed the stage of *parinirvāna*, are pure spiritual entities and therefore belong to a higher category. They become the All in One. This is what Dharmapala called the "supreme god," a conciliatory term.

Of the other two religions originating in the sixth century B.C., and which are Chinese, the better known is Confucianism. There were two papers about it read at the Parliament by William Pipe. The first was the longest on any subject, and it was composed by the Hon. Pung Kwang Yu, first delegate of the Chinese Delegation; the other was by his countryman Kung Hsien Ho of Shanghai. Yu threw the topic into its proper perspective by presenting the *San-kao*, the "Three Teachings" accepted by the Chinese generally. The first, or *Yu-kao*, is Confucianism, which is basically a social and political system. Except that the emperor and other directors of state take their authority from *T'ien* (Heaven) and respect for elders and forebears diverges into ancestor worship, *Yu-kao* has little to do with religion. The second teaching, which Yu calls *Foh-kao*, is Buddhism, an import to China and just reviewed. The third teaching is indigenous, *Tao-kao*, or Taoism. *Tao* means "reason," and the system is derived from an essay written by a sage known as Lao-tzu, titled *Tao-te*, "Reason-virtue," to which later was suffixed the word *Ching*, "Precept." The nearest the work comes to mentioning what is generally called God is absolute *Tao*, Ultimate Reason. It is a sort of Platonic ideal or perfect model. The opening sentence in Lao-tzu's essay goes, "The Reason that can be reasoned is not the eternal Reason."[5] Prof. Milton S. Terry of Northwestern University, Evanston, Ill., gave John Chalmers' translation of the twenty-fifth paragraph of the *Tao-te Ching*, which suggests a sort of spiritualized creation myth and brings out the diametrically opposed theistic views of Yahveh and Tao. It reads:

"There was something chaotic in nature which existed before heaven and earth. It was still. It was void. It stood alone and was not changed. It pervaded everywhere and was not endangered. It may be regarded as the mother of the universe. I know not its name, but give it the title of Tao. If I am forced to make a name for it, I say it is Great; being great, I say that it passes away, passing away, I say that it is far off; being far off, I say that it returns. Now Tao is great; heaven is great; earth is great; a king is great. In the universe there are four greatnesses, and a king is one of them. Man takes his law from the earth; the earth takes its law from heaven; heaven takes its law from Tao; and Tao takes its law from what it is in itself." Terry's comments include, "Students of Laotsze's book have tried to express his idea of Tao by other terms. It has been called the Supreme Reason, the Universal Soul, the Eternal Idea, the Nameless Void, Mother of Being and Essence of Things. But the very mystery that attaches to the word becomes an element of power in the literary features of the book. That suggestiveness of something great and yet intangible, a something that awes and impresses, and yet eludes our grasp, is recognized by all great· writers and critics as a conspicuous element in the masterpiece of literature."[6] Its philosophical-religious connotation is even more staggering.

The contribution of ancient Indian and Chinese philosophy concerning the reigning power of the universe was a transformation from the magnified human being of early times into a limitless abstraction. It dematerialized the form of God into an all-pervading spirit. This was a complete ideological turnover, elevating God to a vastness that was entirely impersonal. In a sense it made God inaccessible even to religion, which focused more upon ethics than speculation, yet a morality no more limited to man than God was limited to man (Chapter Eight). The philosophy religions increased in mutual harmony and serenity each with the others.

By contrast, the particular aspects and affiliations of the "He" gods were sources of recurring contention between nations that looked upon them differently, as in the case of the devas/divs and ashuras/ahuras in the pair of ancient Aryan religions, Hinduism and Parseeism, derived from a common source. What they show is that the attributes of the mythological beings may be twisted arbitrarily in various directions, and each will be believed by as many persons as can be convinced of their "revealed truths." It is a playing with suppositions, the "theology [that] divides the human family not seldom" of Dr. Wise. It is the useless flights of fancy with which circumscribed religions occupied themselves in the Near East and West long after such were abandoned as futile in Farther Asia. Christianity was only one of the mystery religions that was bred and thrived on the chaos and oppression proper to the decaying Roman empire. The others came from the same general area, the arc at the eastern end of the Mediterranean. Among them were the Orpheus cult from Greece, the Cybele cult from Anatolia, the Atargathis cult from Syria, the Mithra cult from Persia, and the Osiris and Isis cult from Egypt.[7] They took advantage of those already excessively insecure to instill feelings of sinful guilt, offering them, through their exotic gods, promises of bliss and contentment in their fantasized worlds on the other side of death. They differed from earlier forms in the degree with which worshippers became intimately involved with and possessive of the worshipped. Although they were similar in purpose and makeup, the mystery religions varied in particulars. Each jealously guarded its secret doctrines and liturgies that assuredly gained for the votary, or the votary's soul, a permanent abiding place in its heavenly spa, the fee for which was exclusive devotion and unqualified faith. Each proclaimed itself the only true religion, directed to the worship of the only true deity. They offered a semblance of serenity, constantly requiring renewing, in place of serenity itself.

Dr. Milton Valentine, president of the Theological Seminary, Gettysburg, Pa., in his paper on the "Harmonies and Distinctions in the Theistic Teaching of the Various Historic Faiths," proclaimed that, "The human feeling of helplessness and need called for a God who could hear and understand, feel and act. And whenever thought rose beyond the many pseudo-gods to the existence of the one true God as a creator and ruler of the world, the ten thousand marks of order, plan and purpose in nature, speaking to men's hearts and reason, led up to the grand truth that the Maker of all is a thinker and both knows and wills."

Viewed from the other side of the earth, D'vivedi took exception to the basic assumption Valentine expressed, saying, "I humbly beg to differ from those who see in Monotheism, in the recognition of a personal god apart from nature, the acme of intellectual development. I believe this is only a kind of anthropomorphism which the human mind stumbles upon in its first efforts to understand the unknown. The ultimate satisfaction of human reason and emotion lies in the realization of that universal essence which is the All."

CHAPTER TWO — notes

1 There are two versions of the creation myth given in Genesis: the first is told in Chapter I and is entirely the work of "God," whereas the second, related in Chapters II and III, is performed by "LORD God," the word of four capitalized letters identifying with the original YHVH (or JHVH), Moses' Yahveh (or Jehovah). The opposing views regarding sexual relationships in the two versions suggest different authors or periods (see Chapter Four), and perhaps Moses (or a later editor) was inserting an older Jewish myth before relating his own. See Exodus VI, 3.

2 Compare Jack Finegan, *Light from the Ancient Past*, Princeton, 1951, pp. 50-54, with Lloyd M. Graham, *Deceptions and Myths of the Bible*, New York, 1975, pp. 29-30.

3 E.W. Palmer (translator), *The Koran*, Oxford University Press, 1900, p. 479 (1947 reprint).

4 At the first assembly of the Parliament (11 September 1893), Dharmapala opened his speech by extending the "good wishes of four hundred and seventy-five millions of Buddhists." In the talk of Dr. George Washburn on "The Points of Contact and Contrast between Christianity and Mohammedanism," he said that "After nineteen hundred years Christianity numbers 400,000,000, and Islam, after thirteen hundred years, 200,000,000."

5 As translated into English in Paul Carus, *The Canon of Reason and Virtue*, Chicago, 1927, p. [73].

6 The Chinese separation of the Universal from ordinary spirits created a problem for Christian missionaries as to what term to use for God. Dr. Henry Blodgett, Protestant missionary to Peking, offered a paper

to the Scientific Section of the Parliament suggesting *"Tien-chu"* be accepted as standard. Confusion arises, he said, from Christians' use of three renditions: (1) *Shen*, which "many Protestant and all Roman and Greek missionaries use for Spirit when speaking of the Holy Spirit;" (2) *Shang-ti*, a term already obsolete among the Catholics and falling into disfavor among Protestants; and (3) *Tien-chu*, then currently favored by the Latin and Greek churches. *Tien* (actually *T'ien*), he says, means "Heaven" and *chu* means "Lord."

7   Franz Cumant, *Oriental Religions in Roman Paganism* (1911), Dover reprint, New York, 1956.

3

THE INCARNATION

A DISCUSSION OF GOD or of the gods logically is followed by comments about demigods. These beings belong to groups of mixed parentage, one half of which is human, like centaurs and satyrs (whose other half is horse or goat), which are supernatural creatures embued with the gift of prophecy. Demigods are of a higher order, inasmuch as the second parent is a god. The type of god is self-evident: the universal god is without sex and does not particularize, so the parent has to be a finite, mythical or "He" god. Also, this parent must be the father, that the offspring may be born of a human mother on earth. The god may approach the woman in a disguised form, as Zeus came to Leda in the shape of a swan. Leda thereafter bore twin sons, Castor, who was mortal, the seed of her human husband, and Pollux, the immortal scion of the god. Pollux, it will be remembered, secured from his heavenly father immortality for his brother. In the Book of Luke, the two boys John and Jesus are born at approximately the same time but have different mothers, Elizabeth and Mary, who are cousins. The winged Gabriel appears to Elizabeth's husband with the news of the conception, and John is born a mortal. Gabriel contacts Mary directly, whose son, Jesus, is born a demigod and is immortal. The latter legend belongs to the period of mystery religions and therefore had to establish a personal relationship with its auditors. Thus Jesus offers immortality to all of his brothers, meaning all those who recognize him and obey his commandments.

The folk literature of just about every country contains stories about demigods. They have the proper parentage for the earliest heroes. So long as their feats exalt themselves,

these heroes remain secular; it is when their exploits benefit
the tribe or the world in general that they become religious
figures. Prof. J. Estlin Carpenter of Manchester New College,
Oxford, England, in his comparative thesis called "The Need
of a Wider Conception of Revelation, or Lessons from the
Sacred Books of the World," reviewed a number of incarnation
legends resembling that of Christianity. In Central America,
he said, "the beautiful story of the Mexican Quetzalcoatl
may be taken as a type — the virgin-born one, who inaugurates
a reign of peace, who establishes arts, institutes beneficent
laws, abolishes all human and animal sacrifices, and suppresses
war — they all revolve around the idea of disclosing among
men a higher life of wisdom and righteousness and love,
which is in truth an unveiling of heaven. Or consider a much
more highly developed type, that of the Buddha in Theistic
Buddhism, as the manifestation of the self-Existing Everlasting God." It is possible that the legend of Quetzelcoatl is
an embroidered account of an Asian missionary and follower
of the Buddha, who had crossed the Pacific to spread the
Dharma in the New World.[1]

The Rev. T.E. Slater, of the London Missionary Society
stationed at Bangalore, India, in a paper entitled "Concession
to Native Ideas, Having Special Reference to Hinduism," called
attention to an old Hindu myth. "The idea exists in the three
chief Vedas and in the Brahmanas and Upanishads that
Prajapati, 'the lord and supporter of his creatures' — the
Purusha (primeval male) — begotten before the world, becoming half immortal and half mortal in a body fit for sacrifice,
offered himself for the devas (emancipated mortals) and for
the benefit of the world; thereby making all subsequent sacrifices a reflection or figure of himself. The ideal of the Vedic
Prajapati, mortal and yet divine, himself both priest and victim,
who by death overcame death, has long since been lost in
India." Slater concluded, "No other than the Jesus of the Gospels . . . has yet appeared to fulfill this primitive idea of
redemption by the efficacy of sacrifice."

An American Congregationalist missionary, the Rev. Robert A. Hume, examining "The Contact of Christian and Hindu Thought: Points of Likeness and Contrast," suggested another connection. Many people in India looked upon Christ as "none other than Krishna," and although he said there is "no historical evidence for this, . . . it seems comprehensive and ideal." Krishna is an *avatāra*, a "descent" or incarnation of the god Vishnu, of which there have been many. The *Bhāgavata Purāna* lists twenty-two. The first was Purusha, the progenitor of man, mentioned by Slater, and the last will be Kalki, who is to appear at the end of the Iron Age on a white horse "with a drawn sword blazing like a comet, for the final destruction of the wicked, the renovation of creation, and the restoration of purity."² Kalki corresponds to the Christ at the Last Judgment, and with Purusha, the two incarnations become the alpha and omega of the present world cycle. In order to achieve certain ends, some of Vishnu's incarnations are zoomorphic. Several of the human *avatārds* are called Krishna, the "dark colored", one of which is Govinda, the cowherd. With his name sometimes pronounced "Krishta" and his worship including an infant cult (Bala-Krishna), he becomes a likely model for the Good Shepherd, he who was born in a stable. The most beloved Krishna is the charioteer and counselor to Arjuna in the renowned epic the *Mahābhārata*. Here Krishna recites the *Bhagavadgītā* the "Song of the Celestial One," which is the heart of Hindu religious writings. The *Purāna* describes Vishnu's (or Krishna's) incarnations as being "Like rivulets flowing from an inexhaustible lake." Krishna refers to them as he instructs the prince on the morning before plunging into battle:

> When righteousness
> Declines, O Bharata! when Wickedness
> Is strong, I rise, from age to age, and take
> Visible shape, and move a man with men,
> Succouring the good, thrusting the evil back,

And setting Virtue on her seat again.
Who knows the truth touching my births on earth
And my divine work, when he quits the flesh
Puts on its load no more, falls no more down
To earthly birth: to Me he comes, dear Prince![3]

Thus long before Jesus the Krishta of India proclaimed his visits to the world to set things right, not once but innumerable times, and those who recognize him will be received by him.

The cosmic views of Farther Asia and the Mediterranean area differ in perspective, both as regards the perceiver and the field perceived. The latter is exceedingly limited, placing priorities on the human personality and its perceptibility as approximating the maximum potential. The Farther Asian takes a more impersonal and critical stand, realizing the limitations of the finite observer, restricted to a fixed point in space and time. His world exceeds the greatest distances and longest duration that he can see or imagine, and this world, he reminds himself, is only one of many that are as countless as the stars. According to the Hindu sages, a single mahayuga, or world period, lasts 4,320,000 solar years.

According to the seventeenth-century Christian pedant Dr. John Lightfoot, who based his calculations on the Bible, the Holy Trinity created the world at 9:00 o'clock in the morning on 23 October 4004 B.C. Nothing existed before that time, and with the end of the world due, or even overdue, compared to the Indian concept, the Christian universe is restricted to the point of being insignificant. The single act of its creation (whether by Yahveh or the Holy Trinity) is incidental alongside the astronomical number of times Brahmā has performed the feat. And with the staggering continuance of each cycle, is it any wonder that Krishna found it necessary to manifest himself myriad times, "Succouring the good, thrusting the evil back"? Only once did the equivalent of evil come into the Judeo-Christian world; it occurred soon after the creation, when the first human couple disobeyed an injunction given by a god whose concept of the difference between good and bad is his own caprice. Nevertheless, the act doomed Adam's issue to mortality. The situation was remedied by the appearance of the single incarnation Jesus Christ, who offered fallen man restitution and about whom the credulous have rhapsodized unstintingly.

In holding forth on "Christ, the Saviour of the World," the Rev. B. Fay Mills of Rhode Island declared, "he was a new and complete revelation of God's eternal suffering for the redemption of humanity. He showed that God was pure, and unselfish, and meek, and forgiving, and that he had always been suffering for the sins of men. He revealed the meaning of forgiveness and the deliverance from sin. It had been costing God to forgive sin all that it had cost man to bear it and more. This had to be in God's thought before he made the world. ... We are told that Adam was created in the image of God, and if he had been an obedient child it may have been that he would have grown up to be a full-grown son of the Eternal; but he sold his birthright for a mess of pottage. The second Adam was the Son of Man, revealing to us that the perfect man differs in no respect from the perfect God. He was God. He became man, not *a* man, but *man*. He was God and man, not two persons in one existence, but revealing the identity of man and God, ... The third great thought in connection with the salvation of Jesus Christ is, that through the completeness of his redemption there is no necessity nor reason for any form of sin in the individual. ... For a man who ... believes in the love of God, in the forgiveness of sins and the redemption of the world; and surrenders himself to the mastership of Jesus; this [salvation] is not only a possibility but a certainty."

Here curious inventions have been devised to make a crude, irritable, and conglomerate tribal deity appear an appealingly simple personality through the offices of a spotless son. In driving Adam and Eve from Eden, God was acting as much like an Oriental monarch as Allah was accused of behaving by Washburn, and proclaiming him "pure, and unselfish, and meek, and forgiving" is distorting the Biblical account. The damnation of intervening man between the Expulsion and the Nativity, timed as some four thousand years, is a trite expedient to accentuate the grace of the savior who then appeared; and it lacks the magnanimity of Krishna's gathering to His heaven uncountable worthies throughout some four million years of innumerable world cycles. In this connection we must not overlook Dr. Wise's point regarding the "state of felicity ... beyond this ... mundane life," presented as a valid system of salvation inherent in Judaism and religions in general, and which has nothing to do with Jesus, as the Jews did not recognize him officially, and those stragglers who did become ostrasized.

Exactly what about Jesus is fact and what fancy? The Episcopal Bishop of Kentucky, T.U. Dudley, discoursed on "The Historic Christ," and his first two sentences declared, "Beyond a controversy in or about the year 750 of the building of the city of Rome, a man named Jesus was born in the province of Judaea. Equally beyond a controversy this man was crucified under Pontius Pilate, a Roman governor at Jerusalem, in or about the year of the city, 783." Dudley gave no source. His dates correspond to within a few years of those traditionally accepted, though the year 750 would put Jesus' birth a little after the death of King Herod, which disagrees with the accounts in Matthew and Luke.[4] Matthew is the only gospel writer acceptable as having been a living witness of Jesus, but the book did not appear until the second quarter of the second century A.D. No known contemporary report mentions Jesus, though several historians born soon afterward at least indicate that there was such a person.[5] After the bishop's opening remarks and for the next 7,000 words, he recounted what "millions of men believe." From here on he was neither "historic" nor narrative, but sermonish and explosive. A typical passage runs, "and upon this world, hopeless and dead, bursts the cry of the Nazarene.

Hear, O Israel — nay, hear ye men of every region, race and age — the Lord thy God, the Omnipotent, the Infinite, the Eternal, is One, is Person, is Spirit, is *Father*, and like as a father pitieth the little children about his hearthstone, so this Creator and Ruler of the universe loveth and pitieth every man!"

The story of Jesus is told in the first four books of the New Testament, those of the evangelists. As stated above, Matthew, supposedly the publican, is the only one who could have known Jesus. Mark gives a résumé of what Matthew has said. Luke is the most fluent storyteller. The first verse in John indicates that he belonged to the Alexandrian Gnostic school, which existed before the Christian era and applied its pre-existing ideas to the new faith. Matthew, though a believer and not a disinterested observer, and much edited, may be considered reliable insofar as his narrative goes. His claim that Mary "was found with child of the Holy Ghost" is a fantasy. He tells of the visit of "wise men of the east," at the time of the nativity, suggesting a link with the Krishna (especially Bala-Krishna) myth of India; else they are Magi, Persian priests, establishing a connection with Zarathustra or Mithra. Jesus' public life begins with his baptism by John the Baptist, which was a purification rite proper to the Essene brotherhood. This is followed by his fasting forty days in the wilderness and being tempted by the devil, a unique austerity for him, perhaps suggested by the well-known Buddha story. That his mission concerned only the Jews and followed the laws of Moses is made clear in Matthew V, 18; VIII, 4; X, 6; and elsewhere, and he believed that he had been born to save the nation (X, 23; XVI, 28). Thus he considered himself the Jewish messiah, whose coming was predicted by the prophets. He lived up to this image by relating parables and performing miracles, and Chapters XXIII-XXV are devoted to prophetic exhortation. The Sermon on the Mount, Chapters V-VII, however, goes beyond the Hebrew law and shows a warm humanity (Chapter Eight). Jesus demonstrates the messianic intent by coming from Nazareth and entering Jerusalem riding on an ass. The "multitude spread their garments in the way; others cut down branches from trees, and strawed them in the way." Jesus thus arrives triumphantly at the temple, where he distrupts the money changers, heals the infirm, and displeases the priests. From here on things go awry. The priests take vengeance by having him seized. The chosen "disciples" show that they have no discipline, as one betrays him, one denies him, and they all desert him. The "more than twelve legions of angels" that he claimed would defend him at the time of his capture (XXVI, 53) do not appear, and Jesus is crucified, pathetically crying, "My God, my God, why has thou forsaken me?" A rich follower, Joseph of Arimathaea, goes to Pilate and asks permission to remove the body, which he orders placed in his sepulcher. Matthew speaks of an earthquake, of an "angel" coming out of heaven and rolling away the stone at the entrance, of his telling the women that Jesus "is risen," and of Jesus' appearance to the eleven apostles; but Matthew says nothing about an ascension. The eschatological fulfillment, which failed to materialize at that time, as Jesus had predicted (XVI, 28), was postponed by his followers to some future date. Matthew compensates by having Jesus enjoin the apostles to "teach all nations, baptizing them in the name of the Father, and of the Son, and of the Holy Ghost." This being the only time that teaching outside of the Jewish tribe is mentioned, coupled with the injunction about baptizing — which Jesus never performed — would indicate a later interpolation. Magnifying Jesus as the foreordained, suffering, dying god is a concept suspiciously close to earlier legends not only about the Indian Prajapati, but the Egyptian Osiris, the Phrygian Attis, and the Greek Adonis.[6]

At the World's Parliament of Religions the Rev. James W. Lee of Atlanta, holding forth on "Christ the Reason of the Universe," touched on the subject of the high attainment of Christian culture: "the facts of Christ's life and death and resurrection and ascension underlie western civilization, and have been the potent factors in its creation. If the men made a mistake who supposed they saw in Christ the fulfillment of all prophecy, the harmony of all truth, the perfection of all righteousness, the solution of all problems, and the sum of all beauty, then . . . this is the most marvelous mistake in all history, for following the light of this mistake men have come to the most enlightened and rational civilization of ancient or modern times."

The facts of this civilization are that Christianity was an obscure mystery cult among many; it had been somewhat persecuted and deprived of some of its property until it found a champion in Constantine, who gave it royal patronage, leading to its becoming the state religion. Early in the fourth century, Constantine inherited his father's realm of Britain and Gaul, and he became one of six rulers of the expiring Roman empire. He determined to become sole emperor by killing or conquering his rivals. During the march on Rome he dreamed of victory through having the cipher of Christ emblazoned on the shields of his soldiers. This accomplished, his army won the battle of Milvian Bridge, enabling him to enter the city as its master. Constantine was a devotee of the sun god, Apollo, but because his priests refused him remission of sin for the murders of his second wife, eldest son, and eleven-year-old nephew, he turned to the Christian bishops, who offered him absolution in return for repentance and baptism. In 325 he convened and presided over the Council of Nicaea, famous for its creed that has kept orthodox Christianity at a mythological plateau for sixteen-and-a-half centuries. Five years later Constantine moved his court to the old Greek town of Byzantium, located on the Bosphorus between the Black and Mediterranean seas, where tariff advantages could be extracted from the rich trade passing between Asia and Alexandria. The new capital was called Constantinople. The namesake emperor dressed in sumptuous robes, resided in a magnificent palace and demanded the reverential attentions of a Babylonian potentate. Like lavishness was reflected in the Byzantine Church, under whose arches of richly-grained marbles, vaults, and domes of glittering gold and mosaics, priests in costly brocaded vestments officiated at the pagan-like sacrifice using jewel-encrusted sacramental vessels. This dazzling form of worship was the Christianity that Europe inherited, becoming official in the year 383. Meanwhile, Constantine died in 337, allowing himself to be baptized on his deathbed. He was proclaimed a Roman god by act of the senate, and he was made a Christian saint by the church, although his sainthood, attested to by ancient church images (linked with Pope Sylvester), has been declared a matter of false identity.[7] The deification of later Roman emperors equaled them to Egyptian pharaohs, only the latter had to do with their birth, each being a son of the god Re-Atum, and the former (as in the case of Constantine) was conferred after death. The divine affiliation claimed for Jesus was of the order of the pharaohs'. The crystallization of the Christian religion under Constantine was certainly a totally different phenomenon from what it started out to be under its founder.

Constantine's lingering preference for Apollo, the Roman sun god, and Apollo's link with Mithra, the Persian god of solar light whose cult was popular among the troops upon whom the emperor depended for his temporal power, resulted in his proclaiming Sunday a day of rest, and he or his influence designated the winter solstice (the yearly nativity of the sun) Christ's birthday. The Mithraic practice of sacrificing a bull and partaking of its blood and flesh may have been the source of the Christian eucharist.[8] The earliest representations of Jesus were modeled on existing beardless Apollo figures, only clothed. The suffering, bearded Christ image was imported later from Syria.

The authority of the church derived from the passage in Matthew XVI, 18-19, wherein Jesus made a wordplay on Peter's name, "rock," and says that upon it he will build his church and to Peter he will give "the keys of the kingdom of heaven; and whatsoever thou shalt bind on earth shall be bound in heaven; and whatsoever thou shalt loose on earth shall be loosed in heaven." With the shepherd himself allegedly investing in the church so much jurisdiction over the sheep, these mild beings dare not but follow his emissary pastors or fail in their attendance at the sheepfold.

The church gained great precedence from the supernatural events at the end of Jesus' life and their attributed significance, as told by the later evangelists. Bishop Dudley summarized them in the third sentence of his "Historic Christ" sermon: "Of this man, Jesus, millions of men believe that, according to his own sure word of promise, he came back from the grave on the third day after his crucifixion; that forty days thereafter, in the presence of chosen witnesses, he visibly ascended into the heavens; that there he now liveth to make perpetual intercession with the one God, his own Father, for us men whom he did redeem; that in the fullness of time he shall come again with glory to judge both the quick and the dead; and that of his kingdom there shall be no end." The fanciful dénouement of an ascension runs counter to that of certain Asian sects, which does not disagree with Matthew's. It is related that Jesus left the land that had abused him for that which gives asylum to refugees of all religions, that he settled and taught for many years in Kashmir. Evidence is furnished by the tomb containing his remains. It is in Srinagar, the "Holy City."⁹

Wrangling over events and their significance is inevitable where proofs are as spurious as the episodes. That its salvation system depends on such makes Christianity the world's foremost arena for internal religious controversy. Hirai's "a priori belief in an unknown entity" may be acceptable as a religious foundation, but Christianity carries it all the way up to the eaves. Such unrealistic absurdity in theology was linked with a totalitarian government in which the imperial household stood with the churchmen at the apex of a social pyramid, and everybody below them was reduced to a state of servitude and ignorance. The order implanted by Christendom in Europe appropriately has been labeled the Dark Ages. Once the term was applied to the entire epoch up to the Renaissance, but now the later phase, after the year 1000, is divided into the Romanesque (the poorly understood Roman) and Gothic ("barbarian") periods. The Renaissance, "rebirth" of classic learning and culture, when even popes became collectors of antiquities and patrons of secular arts, challenged the authority of the church. It was accompanied by numerous heresy uprisings, which were quelled by church-sponsored men-at-arms, wholesale murder and executions, and the Inquisition. The Reformation's success among the wealthy merchants in the cities of Northwest Europe during the sixteenth century accomplished a complete withdrawal from the old institution, though Protestantism retained fundamentally the same narrow beliefs. The "most enlightened and rational civilization of ancient or modern times," of which Lee spoke, had taken over the New World and annihilated most of its occupants, and those natives of the fertile Eastern forests who had survived had been escorted to arid Western wasteland and dumped by the United States army six decades before the Chicago Fair; it had abolished slavery at the expense of long, bitter, and bloody fighting less than thirty years prior to the fair; it still had unjust exclusion laws against ethnic groups, and it was then struggling with women's rights; it suffered from acute alcohol, crime, and poverty problems, and within a quarter of a century it was to be embroiled in World War I, to be followed after a similar span of time by World War II, the two most disastrous holocausts mankind has ever known, and the opposing forces were formed principally, if not exclusively, of Christian nations.

The mystery religions brought forward a concept of deity that adds a third pronoun to our list of the "He" type particularized in narrative and "It" type universalized in philosophy. As we have seen, the mysteries were a belated outgrowth of mythologies but slanted in a new direction, toward the votaries, soliciting their patronage, appealing to their egos, offering the utmost in benefits — an eternity of selfness. The god accepted by the mystery adepts was, therefore, the "I" god, the god that they wanted to have being, that which would provide them with what they most wanted provided, and they raised this "I" deity to supremacy. The "I" god differs from the "He" and "It" types, which are objective, in that this third type is subjective. If the myth god is in the image of man collectively, the ego god is in the likeness of man personally. The power of the "I" gods is manifested in the wonderful accomplishments that their votaries achieve. Some duplicate the favors proper to the mythical "He" predecessors, such as victory in battle. An instance is that of Cybele, whose abode, the black areolite stone, when brought to Rome and installed on the Capitoline hill, enabled Scipio to defeat the Punic terror Hannibal at Zama.[10] The Puritan Christians in America exalted over the decimation of the Indians by the epidemics contracted from themselves, referring to them as "The Wonderful Preparation the Lord Christ by His Providence Wrought for His People's Abode in the Western World."[11] Most characteristic were those personal benefits that were unknown to the earlier mythologies, purification and salvation. Judaism had long before anticipated the former by appointing itself the chosen people, but it was the later prophets — already in the mystery-religion era — who introduced immortality (Chapter Four). As such, Judaism took its place in Rome among the other exotics, and Yahveh or the Lord became an "I" god alongside the other Eastern Mediterranean deities. But the principal one on whose shoulders fell the supreme mantle of I-ness was the founder of the mystery religion that won out over all others. The Jews had acknowledged prophets as spokesmen of the Lord, but they had not conferred divinity on earthlings. This was a Greek-Phrygian-Egyptian-Chaldean practice that was bestowed upon Jesus during the better part of a century that interlay his lifetime and the earliest known recording of the New Testament. The Christology then established became the most important dogma of the church. Thus is became Jesus, hailed the Christ, son of the god "I am that I am," who stands preëminent in the spotlight of "I" resplendence.

On the last day of the Parliament talks the Rt. Rev. John J. Keane, rector of the Catholic University in Washington, climaxed his topic "The Ultimate Religion" with, "We have seen that Jesus Christ is not a myth, not a symbol, but a living personal reality. He is not a vague, shadowy personality, leaving only a dim, vague, mystical impression behind him, he is a clear and definite personality, with a clear and definite teaching as to truth, clear and definite command as to duty, clear and definite ordaining as to the means by which God's life is imparted to man and by which man receives it, corresponds to it, and advances toward perfection."

There were those at the Parliament who strove to dispel such fetishism. Col. Thomas Wentworth Higginson, a former Unitarian minister talking on "The Sympathy of Religion," stated that the sympathy element is common to "all vast structures of spiritual organization ... It lies not in what they know, for they are alike, in a scientific sense, in knowing nothing. Their point of sympathy lies in what they have sublimely created through longing imagination. In all these faiths are the same alloy of human superstition; the same fables of miracle and prophecy, the same signs and wonders, the same preternatural births and resurrections. In point of knowledge, all are helpless; in point of credulity, all puerile; in point of aspiration, all sublime. All seek after God, if haply they might find him. All, moreover, look around for some human life, more exalted than the rest, which may be taken as God's highest earthly reflection. Terror leads them to imagine demons, hungry to destroy, but hope creates for them redeemers mighty to save."

From the Chicago environs Dr. Paul Carus, editor of the Open Court Publishing Company, which was just launching its fleet of translations of East Asian texts of wisdom that were to transport many stagnant minds to more lucid waters, in his talk entitled "Science a Religious Revelation" came directly to the point: "Reverence for our master makes us easily forgetful of our highest duty, reverence for an impartial recognition of the truth. The antipathy of a certain class of religious men toward science, although natural and excusable, should nevertheless be recognized as a grievous fault; it is a moral error and an irreligious attitude.

"Our religious mythology is so thoroughly identified with religion itself that when the former is recognized as erroneous, the latter also will unavoidably collapse."

CHAPTER THREE — notes

1   Henriette Mertz, *Pale Ink, Two Ancient Records of Chinese Exploration in America*, Chicago, 1972, pp. 47-50, 73, 85-6. See also note 2, introduction of present book.

2   John Dowson, *A Classical Dictionary of Hindu Mythology*, London, 1950, p. 38.

3   Edwin Arnold (translator), *The Song Celestial or Bhagavād-gītā*, Philadelphia, n. d., pp. 24-5.

4   The census, which took Joseph and Mary to Bethlehem, occurred in the year of Rome 747 or 6 B.C. *Encyclopaedia Britannica*, Chicago, London and Toronto, 1970, Vol. 12, p. 1016.

5   "References either to Jesus of Nazareth or to Christus in Josephus, Tacitus, Suetonius, Pliny the Younger and certain passages of the Talmud and Midrash do not increase our knowledge of Jesus materially, but they confirm by non-Christian testimony that he caused a ferment among Jews by his miracles and teachings and was condemned and put to death under Pontius Pilate. Agreement on the latter point fixes the period of Jesus' activity fairly conclusively between 28 and 30 A.D." Horace L. Friess, Herbert W. Schneider, *Religions in Various Cultures*, New York, 1932, p. 200. See also: Albert Schweitzer, *The Quest of the Historical Jesus*, New York, 1954. The latter book reviews the German biographers of Jesus inclusive of the third quarter of the eighteenth to the early twentieth century; it was published originally in German in 1906.

6   Franz Cumant, *Oriental Religions in Roman Paganism* (1911), Dover reprint, New York, 1956, pp. 30, 59, 69, 93.

7 A. Jameson, *Sacred and Legendary Art*, London, 1891, pp. 686-93 (Vol. II).

8 Esmé Wynne-Tyson, *Mithras, the Fellow in the Cap*, London, 1958, pp. 128-30, 176-8.

9 Mrs. Gloria Gasque told the author that when she first visited the site there was only an engraved plaque in the pavement. The tomb concept was espoused by Mirza Ghulam Ahmad at the beginning of this century, and evidently his sect, called the Ahmadiya, erected the present Mughal-style mausoleum. See: *The Globe*, 24 June 1980, p. 15.

10 Cumant, *op. cit.*, pp. 46-7.

11 William Brandon, *The American Heritage Book of Indians*, New York, 1961, p. 171.

4

IMMORTALITY

THE SANCTITY OF THE BIBLE was accepted by the majority of participants at the World's Parliament of Religions. It was their source of solace, offering them a fuller and eternal afterlife in Heaven. They imagined Heaven as a place free of worries, free of anxieties, free of problems, provided with every necessity, every want, every comfort, where they were united with their loved ones, on equal terms with angels, and close to their maker, God, and their personal savior, Jesus Christ. The concept had been presented to them as ideal, and they believed in it. A place in Heaven was a promise, made to them in the Bible, requiring only that they live a righteous existence and maintain sufficient faith; it would be their just reward.

The future domain will be idyllic. It will be like that first Garden of Eden, which God provided for the progenitors of the human race. They, too, were in a state of bliss. Adam possessed the three perfections, "the perfection of nature, the body and the soul," according to the Rev. Dr. D.J. Kennedy of Somerset, O., who gave the Catholic interpretation in a talk called "The Redemption of Sinful Man through Jesus Christ." For his sin Adam was not only expelled from Paradise but was inflicted with the "three wounds of ignorance, weakness and passion." His afflictions were passed on to his progeny, which was the world's entire population. God decided to remedy the situation by choosing of all possible solutions that which "was best for man" (Kennedy here quoted St. Athanasius), this being to save man "through the suffering and merits of Christ, because . . . he [God] gave to the world the greatest manifestation ever known of his own

76

goodness, power, wisdom and justice. . . . the saving influence of Christ is to be found principally in his death; because by his death he reconciled us with God, freed us from sin and satisfied God's justice, restored us to grace and justification, freed us from the power of Satan, and made us once more the children of God."

Christianity has the one story that firmly links original sin, the incarnation, and salvation. Having looked at the second factor in the preceding chapter, we may now concentrate on the first and last. We had best begin by getting down to the basic elements, as presented in the Bible itself. In Genesis, Chapter I, after God has made the beasts he made man and woman simultaneously and told them to "be fruitful and multiply." As not mentioned otherwise, he made them out of the same nothing as everything else, the only difference being that they resembled him. In Chapter II God fashioned the man alone out of "the dust of the ground and breathed into his nostrils the breath of life," then "planted a garden eastward in Eden" and placed man in it "to dress it and keep it." After this God "formed every beast of the field, and every fowl of the air" and brought them to Adam to be named. Finally he made woman out of one of Adam's ribs. The second version of the story introduced the two wondrous trees in the garden, one of life and the other of knowledge. The tree of life was immortality. The other, of "knowledge," employs the word used throughout the Bible to signify copulation. The tree of knowledge was strictly forbidden to Adam and Eve. In Chapter III the woman was tempted by the serpent phallic symbol to taste of its fruit and shared it with the man (how could she do otherwise?), for which deed God drove them out of Eden. The short, more primitive version of the story in Chapter I, in which God commanded the couple to procreate, ended with the Creator surveying everything "that he had made, and, behold, it is very good." The longer, later, moralizing version, in which God cautioned the couple against "knowing" one another, terminated in

Chapter III by his stationing cherubim with flaming swords around the garden to prevent Adam and Eve from returning "to take also of the tree of life, and eat, and live for ever." No explanation was given as to what happened afterward to Eden with its two trees, or, whatever that fate may have been, why it could not have occurred at the time of the expulsion, which would have saved bringing in the cherubim, whose existence had not been accounted for in the preceding creation myth.

In both renditions of the legend man came out a mortal, like every other creature. The idea did not accord with the later ideology in the Bible having to do with the build-up of Jewish national pride, having Yahveh as the tutelary. Man had to be something more than beast. The prophet Isaiah proclaimed that "Israel shall be saved in the Lord with an everlasting salvation," for God who "formed the earth and made it; he hath established, he created it not in vain." Isaiah quoted the deity as saying that there is "no God else beside me; a just God and a Saviour" (XLVI, 17-18, 21). Elsewhere the promise of salvation was extended to individuals. Psalm Ninety One, which begins, "He that dwelleth in the secret place of the most High shall abide under the shadow of the Almighty," shifts in the last three verses to God as the speaker, declaring: "with long life will I satisfy him, and shew him my salvation." As Prof. D.G. Lyon of Harvard mentioned in "Jewish Contributions to Civilization," it is the Book of Daniel wherein is made the concise declaration of an afterlife. Daniel beheld a supernatural being "clothed in linen," whose body "was like the beryl, and . . . his arms and feet like in colour to polished brass," who gave the promise that the "people shall be delivered . . . and many of them that sleep in the dust of the earth shall awake, some to everlasting life, and some to shame and everlasting contempt" (X, 5-6; XII, 1-2).

At the Advent Christian Church meeting, in the Denominational Congresses, on September 14 the Rev. Miles Grant of Boston spoke on "Conditional Immortality." He observed: "The word, soul, in the Bible, is the rendering of three Hebrew words and one Greek word, the chief Hebrew being *nephesh*. This latter term has three meanings, (a) life, (b) living creatures, (c) desire. A careful study of the passages proves that it is impossible to have an immortal soul without an immortal body ... Passages like Eccles. ix, 5; Ps. vi, 6; I Cor. xv, 16, 18 indicate that personal consciousness is not immortal. When life departs from a body all consciousness and intelligence cease." He ends with, "After a careful study of the Bible for nearly fifty years, I am compelled to believe that it uniformly teaches that only the righteous will live forever and the necessary conclusion is that conditioned immortality is a Bible doctrine."

As Prof. William Wilkinson noted at the Parliament in his paper on "The Attitude of Christianity toward Other Religions," God's function of saving souls, as set forth in the Old Testament, is taken over exclusively by Jesus in the New Testament (Introduction). What Jesus proposed as his system of immortality is quite different from the many variations that Christians hold. Either one accepts the gospels as reliable, insofar as they report reasonable facsimiles of Jesus' sayings, or else one is launched on a trackless voyage of suppositions that lead to nowhere. One has to accept the fact that Jesus was an illiterate provincial, living in a remote section of the ancient Roman empire. He probably never heard of Socrates, Plato, and Aristotle; of Pythagoras, Siddhartha Gautama, and Lao-tzu; or any of the other earlier great philosophers who attempted to embrace a universal viewpoint. Jesus did not even have a clearcut concept of spirit as divorced from matter, although phrases suggesting such had crept into the texts that became the New Testament during the century intervening his lifetime and the compilation of the book. These insertions attempted to bring his teaching up to date with the other mystery religions, but inasmuch as they contradicted what Jesus had said, they merely add confusion to the matter.

Jesus was deluded by the errors he had learned from the Jewish Bible, namely, that Earth was stationary and paramount, and Heaven was a solid, domed firmament. He fancied himself as becoming the regal doorkeeper to the latter, empowered to admit those having the proper qualifications and subscribing to his novel presumption.

Commentators have called his system the Last Judgment. Matthew quoted Jesus as saying, "When the Son of man shall come to his glory, and all the holy angels with him, then shall he sit upon the throne of his glory: And before him shall be gathered all nations; and he shall separate them one from another, as a shepherd divideth his sheep from his goats: And he shall set the sheep on his right hand, but the goats on the left. Then shall the King say unto them on his right hand, Come, ye blessed of my Father, inherit the kingdom prepared for you from the foundation of the world" (XXV, 31-34). Elsewhere, referring to this coming into his glory, Jesus added, "Verily I say unto you, There be some standing here, which shall not taste of death, till they see the Son of man coming in his kingdom" (XVI, 28). The expression "son of man" was generally used throughout the ancient Near East to add lustre to the first person pronoun; and it is here in character for a man who thinks of himself as the son of the tribal god, and who will "save" his people. There can be no doubt but that Jesus believed this separating of the sheep (Jews faithful to himself) from the goats (others) would take place during his present lifetime. After selecting his "disciples" and telling them to spread his word (to Jews only), he concluded: "Ye shall not have gone over the cities of Israel, till the Son of man be come" (X, 23). That Jesus considered redemption solely for Jews is verified by his statement to the Samaritan woman, "Ye worship ye know not what: we know what we worship; for salvation is of the Jews" (John IV, 22). The Samaritans were descendants of Syrians and Mesopotamians who settled in Palestine after the Jews had been deported to Babylon; they had adopted most of the Hebrew religion. Jesus makes the fine distinction that although they worship the same god as himself, because they were not Hebrew by birth they could not obtain salvation. Jesus' ministry came to an end when he was crucified; he recovered to bid farewell to his "disciples" and then disappeared — to die somewhere — and that should have been the end of his fantastic, self-aggrandizing Last Judgment. But the apostles, ignoring what Jesus had said about when it would occur, concocted the supposition that it had been postponed. Furthermore, they extended the benefits beyond the narrow flock of "sheep" to include some of the "goats." Failing to get what he considered adequate Jewish support, Peter sought to snare the Gentiles by promising them salvation, testifying that he *believed* it would be granted "through the grace of the Lord Jesus Christ" (Acts XV, 11). The church also abandoned Jesus' original claim and adopted the broader and delayed spectacular. In the fifteen thirties, Michelangelo depicted the Last Judgment in fresco on the principal wall of the Sistine Chapel in the Vatican at Rome as the counterpart of the Creation and Old Testament scenes that he had executed earlier on the ceiling. One notes in this masterwork not the rising of souls but of buried bodies coming out of the ground to be sorted by a herculanean Christ, which is as visualized in Matthew. In our day, Christendom, which has been divided into innumerable splinter groups, has been reaffirming the still pending Last Judgment for two thousand years; but, inasmuch as it has not yet taken place, nobody has been saved — certainly not on Christ's authority, and with no more likelihood on what others *assume* to have been his authority. The apostles did not claim to offer deliverance on their own, and although Roman churchmen sell indulgences and purport to make intercession, neither do they. Protestantism offers redemption on faith, but faith is merely another term for self-deception (Chapter Seven), and its authority is attested to be the Bible, whose limited view on the matter has been stated. The evidence for the Christian Heaven is as remote as its likelihood. Except for the weird, unsatisfactory, and unacceptable descriptions given in Revelation (IV-X, XXI-XXII), what Heaven is supposed to be like is left to anybody's conjecture.

In his talk on "Conditional Immortality" the Rev. Miles Grant had prefaced his comments on scripture with the observation, "Science declares on the subject that from our knowledge of the functions of the brain it is difficult to believe in immortality of the personal consciousness, that there is no consciousness without a brain whereby to think."

That anybody would consider either the Bible, with its ambiguous use of terms, vital contradictions, and dubious factuality (see Chapter Five), stereotyped for fifteen centuries, or science at its late-nineteenth-century stage of development, not yet aware even of extra-sensory perception and far from recognizing the findings of parapsychology, as the final word is limiting oneself to practically an irrelevant view of immortality. Papers presented at the Parliament had a great deal more to offer. Let us next glance at what was said about certain primitive beliefs and work our way up to more significant observations.

Alice C. Fletcher, sketching "The Religion of the North American Indians," summed up their view: "Personal immortality was universally recognized. The next world resembled this with the element of suffering eliminated. There was no place of future punishment; all alike started at death upon the journey to the other world, but the quarrelsome and unjust never reached it; they endlessly wandered."

Prof. George S. Goodspeed, of the University of Chicago, discussed "What the Dead Religions Have Bequeathed to the Living." His description of the Egyptians in this regard was that they were "the most joyous of creatures, and yet seem to have devoted themselves to building tombs. . . . The man of Egypt never looked outside of his own land without disdain. It contained for him the fullness of all that heart could wish . . . and the favorite picture which he formed of the future life was only that of another Egypt like the present." Certainly no other civilization has left so many graphic representations of what they thought the realm of the dead to be, and, as Goodspeed suggested, it looks like their pictures of Egypt itself.

Jeanne Sorabji, reading Jinanji Modi's paper on Parseeism, touched on Zarathustra's concept of immortality, upon which groundwork, he said, "the whole edifice of our moral nature rests." Unlike the non-committal mention of the afterlife in the Bible, the "Avesta writings of Hādokht Nushk and the nineteenth chapter of the Vendidād and of the Pehlevi books of Minokherad and Virāf-nāmeh treat of the fate of the soul after death. ... for three days after a man's death his soul remains within the limits of this world under the guidance of the angel Srosh. ... On the dawn of the third night the departed souls appear at the 'Chinvat Bridge' [which leads to heaven]. This bridge is guarded by the angel Meher Dāver, *i.e.*, Meher the Judge. He presides there as a judge assisted by the angels Rashné and Astād, the former representing Justice and the latter Truth. At this bridge, and before this angel Meher, the soul of every man has to give an account of its doings in the past life. Meher Dāver, the judge, weighs a man's actions by a scale-pan. If a man's good actions outweigh his evil ones, even by a small particle, he is allowed to pass from the bridge to the other end of heaven. If his evil actions outweigh his good ones, even by a small weight, he is not allowed to pass over the bridge, but is hurled down into the deep abyss of hell. If his meritorious and evil deeds counterbalance each other, he is sent to a place known as 'Hamast-gehan,' corresponding to the Christian 'Purgatory' and the Mohammedan 'Aeraf.' His meritorious deeds done in the past life would prevent him from going to hell, and his evil actions would not let him go to heaven." Thus, centuries earlier, Zarathustra taught of released *souls* going to heaven, whereas Jesus "saved" revived bodies. Destruction of a corpse would preclude Christian salvation.

Concerning that other major religion of the Near East, Islam, President Washburn of Robert College, Constantinople, remarked in his comparative study delivered on the fifth day: "Both Christians and Moslems believe that God has sent *prophets and apostles* into the world to teach men his will; both believe in the *judgment day* and the *resurrection of the dead*, the immortality of the soul and rewards and punishments in the future life."

The Koran gives vivid descriptions of both Heaven and Hell. Vignettes about the latter include: "Verily, hell is an ambuscade; a reward for the outrageous, to tarry therein for ages. They shall not taste therein cool to drink, but only boiling water and puss; — a fit reward!" And, "Hell is flaming . . . those who disbelieve in our signs, we will broil them with fire; whenever their skins are well done, then we will change them for other skins, that they may taste the torment. Verily, God is glorious and wise." The next verse gives us a glance into an all-male Paradise, "But those who believe and do right, we will make them enter gardens beneath which rivers flow, and they shall dwell therein for ever and aye." A longer passage, in a later Sūrah, adds: "God . . . will cast on them brightness and joy; and their reward for their patience shall be Paradise and silk! reclining therein upon couches they shall neither see therein sun nor piercing cold; and close down upon them shall be its shadows; and lowering over them its fruits to cull; and they shall be served round with vessels of silver and goblets that are as flagons — flagons of silver which they shall mete out! and they shall drink therein a cup tempered with Zinjabil [ginger], a spring therein named Silsabil! and there shall go round about them eternal boys; when thou seest them thou wilt think them scattered pearls; and when thou seest them thou shalt see pleasure and a great estate! . . . Verily, this is a reward for you, and your efforts are thanked."[1]

Prof. Goodspeed's analysis of the ancient Egyptians' realm of the dead as "another Egypt" may be applied to Mohammed's paradise as another Arabia, only the latter's dry heat has become sufferable by the provision of plenty of shade and drinks. The same unpleasant natural feature provides the cue for hell, fiery hot and nothing but boiling water as an inadequate thirst-quencher. The renewal of skins, upon the old ones being broiled, is a clever device for prolonging the agony of the damned, but it represents a tremendous expenditure of creative energy and materials if it is to go on indefinitely, especially with new inductees arriving hourly at the ambuscade.

Art forms of the various cultures are revealing in their concepts of the hereafter. Mention has been made of Michelangelo's Last Judgment in the Sistine Chapel, wherein Jesus separates the blessed from the condemned. The latter are in despair, but, as in other Italian Renaissance paintings, the saved have little better prospects, as they face a boring eternity with nothing to do but stand around and give thanks for their idleness. By comparison, the chosen among the Moslems can be grateful for their couches and beverages. The judge of the dead is a personage found at the entrances of heaven and hell in all systems of personal rewards and punishments. Islam accepts Jesus, at least as returning before the end of the world. Zarathustra stations Meher Dāver at Chinvat Bridge; and later, in Persia, Mithra assumes the post. Such judges figure at the folk level among all of the Farther Asia religions. Throughout the sphere of Hindu culture are the many forms of Yama, by some considered to have been given this position because he was the first man to die, and by others because Yama accumulated great merit, then sinned in anger, and the gods did not know what else to do with him.[2]

All religions that have made their deity a specific "He" god, through having him create a world with a defined beginning and an imminently expected end, and yet have had him provide an everlasting abode for the deceased faithful are guilty of gross inconsistency. Besides, the concept of personal salvation is inherently contradictory, because a finite being cannot exist in an infinity of time. An "It" god, which is all-pervading, conceivably provides an unbounded abode, but it is not a particular place and it does not contain particular inhabitants. As there seems to be no reconciliation between the individual and the cosmic in those religions we have examined, the matter stands at a stalemate in them.

One looks for a clearer understanding of immortality in the East, where the universe itself and the Spirit that animates it are both known to be unlimited. Finite objects are but imperfect particles of the cosmos and are referred to as illusions. Finite conscious beings are but reflections of the Universal Spirit, and their individual existences are ephemeral. Swami Vivekananda, who made a noble effort to explain Hinduism to Americans in their own terms, said, in part, "the Hindu believes that he is a spirit. Him the sword cannot pierce — him the fire cannot burn — him the water cannot melt — him the air cannot dry. And that every soul is a circle whose circumference is nowhere, but whose center is located in a body, and death means the change of this center from body to body. Nor is the soul bound by the conditions of matter. In its very essence, it is free, unbounded, holy and pure and perfect. But some how or other it has got itself bound down by matter, and thinks itself as matter.'Why should the free, perfect and pure being be under the thraldom of matter, is the next question. How can the perfect be deluded into the belief that he is imperfect [?] ... we have been told that Hindus shirk the question and say that no such question can be there, and some thinkers want to answer it by the posing of one or more quasi-perfect beings, and big scientific names to fill up the gap. But naming is not explaining. ... the Hindu is more sincere. He does not want to take shelter under sophistry. He is brave enough to face the question in a manly fashion. And his answer is, I do not know. I do not know how the perfect being, the soul came to think itself as imperfect, as joined to and conditioned by matter. But the fact is a fact for all that. It is a fact in everybody's consciousness that he thinks himself as a body. We do not attempt to explain why I am in this body. The answer that it is the will of God, is no explanation.

"Well then, the human soul is eternal and immortal, perfect and infinite, and death means only a change of center from one body to another. The present is determined by our past actions, and the future will be by the present; that it will go on evolving up or reverting back from birth to birth and death to death." Vivekananda is speaking here of metempsychosis, of the soul being reborn in various bodies, according to its desires, attractions and merits. It works itself back up to perfection, which "will be reached when the bond shall burst, and the word they use is therefore mukto — freedom, freedom from the bonds of imperfection, freedom from death and misery. . . . And what becomes of man when he becomes perfect? He lives a life of bliss, infinite. He enjoys infinite and perfect bliss, having obtained the only thing in which man ought to have pleasure, God, and enjoys the bliss with God."

D'vivedi, who gave the comprehensive account of Hinduism during the afternoon session on the first day of speeches, would take exception to some of Vivekananda's verbal compromises. Briefly, in his own words: "The being is the absolute under conditions of relativity, whence every being is eternally immortal. But to speak of the immortality of the being as such is absurd. The form of the being is only transitory; and by form I do not mean the physical form, but the spiritual one which makes it a *jiva* — a soul. . . . the soul must cease to be a soul at the supreme moment of self-realization. If the soul were immortal, there would be no liberation." Looking back, it will be seen that although Vivekananda said "the human soul is eternal and immortal," he only meant the latter, "immortal" — meaning not-mortal, that is, surviving the mortal body — passing on to successive incarnations until it reaches perfection. Here it loses its selfness through absorption into the Universal; then It becomes eternal. D'vivedi also would object to Vivekananda's calling *mukto* "bliss with God," but the budding missionary undoubtedly felt that this was an expression people with liberal Christian backgrounds would be able to grasp. At another place Vivekananda spoke

of it as being "one with Brahma," which, using the explicit
term for the Supreme Soul, immanent in nature, undoubtedly
passed muster with D'vivedi.

Buddhism goes a step farther than Hinduism in eliminating
the gods from the process. As Dharmapala remarked in his
talk on "The World's Debt to Buddha," mentioned in Chapter
Two, the gods themselves are subject to the law of exigent
consequences. Here they are not only stripped of the power
to create but of the power to save. Because Buddhism began
as an independent speculative system, it was not burdened
with inherited gods to be compromised with reason. The
world's structure and the world's workings could be looked
at with unbiased scrutiny. From this simple and direct viewpoint unfolded the premise that there is order in the world
wherein that which evolves is determined by that which
preceded. The Law of Cause and Effect. A chick and not a
lizard hatches from an egg because it was laid by a hen. A
house frame stands because it has been hewn from good
wood and fitted together properly with pins. A vacation can
be enjoyed because money for its expenses has been procured.
A man becomes dissipated after inebrious revelries. One is
reborn because he willed it in his previous life, and all aspects
of the situation are resolved out of previous conditions: the
choice of parents, family and social relationships, environment, opportunities, and whatever else has to do with the
desired goal — conditioned by what is deserved, of course. A
vital factor is the Law of Karma, the balance of one's good
and bad deeds, which determines the status the person
occupies or will occupy. A man has free will and he can, to
some degree, define his station; his positive actions in the
past will advance it, his negative exploits will impede. As his
selfishness binds, and his ego limits, his reaching out by
helping others enlarges himself and his prospects, aiming at
the Universal. And what, then, is the "Universal" if it is not
God? In this connection it is a state of perfect peace and
ecstasy. Because entering into this state requires giving up all

of one's petty individuality, there are those who call it extinction. It is, but it is the extinction of distinctions, the attainment of completeness, identification with the All. As Buddhism looks upon those interests and pleasures that keep us in the mundane world as ignorance, the thinking one seeks, through the Dharma, the way that leads to the final achievement, is enlightenment, and that goal attained is Enlightenment. The historic figure who founded the system, Gautama, attained it; he is called the Buddha, the "Enlightened One." Many have attained it. But Buddhahood is not transmitted; it is earned. Buddhas can only show others the way; salvation must be worked out for oneself.

The Western ego, which gave birth to and in return has been nourished by the "I" religions, has difficulty seeing how giving itself up is anything but annihilation. The Rev. Dr. George C. Lorimer of Boston, speaking on "The Baptists in History," on September 27, said that the Anabaptists in the sixteenth century "were more than satisfied to sacrifice and suffer for man, that the individual, instead of becoming unconscious in God, might become fully conscious of the perfection of God in the individual." For all of its personal appeal, the statement is lacking in basic logic. The Infinite's perfection cannot be grasped by the finite, but only an imperfect portion, only temporarily, and only to the capacities of the individual. The aggregate of all such consciousness in the world could never approximate anything more than a complex of finiteness — which is neither God nor the Infinite. Another statement similar to Lorimer's was made by a fellow Boston cleric, Dr. Philip S. Moxon, who on the third day of the regular meetings spoke on "The Argument for Immortality." He said, "Men cheat themselves with phrases who talk about the re-absorption of the finite soul in the infinite soul, and call that immortality. The finite and the infinite coexist in this world; that of itself is proof that they may co-exist in the next world, and forever." The point overlooked is that the Infinite existed through unmeasured time before and therefore may be expected to persist likewise in the future, whereas the finite that came into being will have to give up its selfness in the same manner. The Rev. Samuel M. Warren, of the New Church at nearby Cambridge, Ma., in discussing "The Soul and Its Future Life," presented the idea that, "It is a gross fallacy of the senses, that there is no substance but matter, and nothing substantial but what is material. Is not God, the Divine Omnipotent Creator of all things, substantial? ... Is it reasonable that this material world should be so full of life and loveliness and beauty, ... and not the spiritual world wherein the soul is to abide forever?" He asserted, "Not only is that world substantial, but it must be a world of surpassing loveliness and beauty.... And the life of that world is human life. The same laws of life and happiness obtain there that govern here, because they are grounded in human nature. Man is a social being, and everywhere in that world, as in this, desires and seeks the companionship of these that are congenial to him, that is, who are of similar quality to himself. Men are thus mutually drawn together by spiritual affinity." The substance of the "Divine Omnipotent Creator" is the substance of gravity that makes the apple drop, and if the spiritual world is "full of life and loveliness and beauty" such was not mentioned in the Biblical authority. The "spiritual affinity" of man is an egotistical staccato.

Grant's "Conditioned Immortality" paper noted that science had declared that there "is no consciousness without a brain whereby to think." The argument was presented that even if one were reborn, or reincarnated, the later would be an entirely different consciousness from the one that had been. Insofar as this consideration is concerned, a man is a different person at forty than he was at four, or at eighteen for that matter. What, then, is so repelling about changing? Is not the eternal-idleness extremity worse? The Rev. Joseph Cook began his "Strategic Certainties of Comparative Religion" talk with these words: "It is no more wonderful that we should live again than that we should live at all. It is less wonderful that we should continue to live than that we have begun to live. And even the most determined and superficial skeptic knows that we have begun." Another quotation that fits in here was included in Moxon's talk on immortality and comes from John Fiske, who labored to reconcile religion and science: "The only thing which cerebral physiology tells us, when studied with the aid of molecular physics, is against the materialist, as far as it goes. It tells us that, during the present life, although thought and feeling are always manifested in connection with a peculiar form of matter, yet by no possibility can thought and feeling be in any sense the products of matter. Nothing could be more grossly unscientific than the famous remark of Cabanis, that the brain secretes thought as the liver secretes bile. It is not even correct to say that thought goes on in the brain. What goes on in the brain is an amazingly complex series of molecular movements, with which thought and feeling are in some unknown way correlated, not as effects or as causes, but as concomitants. . . . The materialistic assumption . . . that the life of the soul accordingly ends with the life of the body, is perhaps the most colossal instance of baseless assumption that is known to the history of philosophy." These two statements were incorporated in talks advocating the Christian-heaven theme, yet they clearly refute the Christ and Church salvation system, while supporting reincarnation.

The work that Edgar Cayce engaged in for about forty-three years prior to his death in 1945 supplied considerable evidence of conveying many elements from one life to another. In some 14,000 readings given to over 6,000 persons in a self-induced sleep, or trance, each one transcribed in writing, Cayce delved into personal matters related to his subjects, most having to do with physical disabilities and how to rectify them. However, about 2,500 were what came to be called "life readings," dealing with why people are at their present status. He made numerous references to their current illnesses and afflictions resulting from demeritorious deeds committed in previous lives, to the renewing of former interests and accomplishments in this life, the resuming of friendships and family relationships, and various other connections. The highly technical knowledge inherent in the reports and the sometimes miraculous results from its application, as well as predictions of a worldwide nature that have been fulfilled, verify a source far superior to any that can be found in the medium's limited background. The records are kept in the archives of the Association for Research and Enlightenment at Virginia Beach, Va.; they may be examined by serious-minded applicants, and many interesting books have been written about Edgar Cayce as a person as well as about the statistical data contained in the readings.[3]

Recent investigations in the realm of multiple personalities also have turned up subjects in whom are found entities with characteristics entirely different from their real selves, which entities can do things with their bodies that they themselves cannot do, and can speak languages fluently which the core self never heard, indicative of some kind of an independent experience.[4] Whatever the scientific investigator may call it, "incarnation" is as good as any other word.

An ubiquitous oversight among Western religions, due to their concentration on God and the human animal, is their failure to include other sentient beings in the scheme of things. Those whom St. Francis called the "little brothers" may be less developed than man, but the differences between them are of a quantitative and not of a qualitative nature. Under the mythopoeic viewpoint animals are dismissed as not being in the image of the deity, which is only another way of saying that they do not look like humans, and therefore it does not mean anything. In the Near and Middle East religions, animals are considered to have no souls; they neither are nor ever can be immortal. In Farther Asia they have a soul proportionate to man's, and they pass from life to life just as people do. Edgar Cayce and others before him spoke of fauna as having "group souls," a term considered inadequate by Dr.

Gina Cerminara, who has studied the Cayce readings most in depth and devoted a section in one of her books to this topic.[5] Cayce declined to give readings for subhuman applicants, but he sometimes identified them with their present masters or mistresses as having been pets in former incarnations. One falls into abysmal error in looking at things too narrowly. Philosophic, religious, and scientific principles stand a better chance of being true the broader the prospect from which they are deducted, and the freer the observer from previous conceptions, or misconceptions. Dr. Paul Carus, in discussing "Science a Religious Revelation," said that "The science of mechanics does not come to destroy the mechanical inventions of the past, but on the contrary, it will make them more available. In the same way a scientific insight into religious truth does not come to destroy religion; it will purify and broaden it." What is the idea of a continuing world arrived at by untrammeled ancient Indian sages but the indestructibility of matter and the conservation of energy of modern physicists? And what is reincarnation but the operation of a similar law on the conscious or spiritual level? The scientific laws regarding matter are no more to be limited to one substance than those having to do with living beings to one nation or species.

If there is acceptable evidence for reincarnation, is there also comparable confirmation for Heaven or Enlightenment? The answer is: not on the same grounds. That for the former is revelation, and that for the latter is meditation, one being associated with faith, the other with reason. The Bible revelation regarding immortality was reviewed early in this chapter. The technique for meditation will be taken up in Chapter Seven.

CHAPTER FOUR — notes

1   E.H. Palmer, *The Koran*, Oxford University Press, 1900, pp. 513, 72, 510 (1947 reprint). References are to Sūrah LXXXVII, 21-25; Sūrah LXXVI, 11-23.
2   "Pander in his *Pantheon des Tschangtscha Hutuktu*, gives the following legend in regard to Yama: There was once a holy man

who lived in a cave in deep meditation for fifty years, after which he was to enter into Nirvāṇa. On the night of the forty-ninth year, eleventh month, and twenty-ninth day, two robbers entered the cave with a stolen bull, which they proceeded to kill by cutting off its head. When they discovered the presence of the ascetic, they decided to do away with him as witness of their theft. He begged them to spare his life, explaining that in a few moments he would be entering into Nirvāṇa, and that if they killed him before the time he would lose all the benefit of his fifty years' penance. But they refused to believe him, and cut off his head, whereupon his body assumed the ferocious form of Yama, King of Hell, and taking up the bull's head, he set it on his own headless shoulders. He then killed the two robbers and drank their blood from cups made of their skulls." Alice Getty, *The Gods of Northern Buddhism*, Oxford, 1028, p. 152.

3   The definitive biography is by Thomas Sugrue, *There Is a River, the Story of Edgar Cayce*, New York, 1942, revised 1945. Also recommended are Gina Cerminara, *Many Mansions*, New York, 1950, and *The World Within*, New York, 1957; Jesse Stern, *Edgar Cayce, the Sleeping Prophet*, New York, 1967; Noel Layley and Hugh Lynn Cayce, *Edgar Cayce on Reincarnation*, New York, 1967; Mary Ann Woodward, *Edgar Cayce's Story of Reincarnation*, New York, 1971.

4   Daniel Keyes, *The Minds of Billy Milligen*, New York, 1981; Flora Rheta Schweiber, *Sybil*, Chicago, 1973.

5   Gina Cerminara, *Many Lives, Many Loves*, New York, 1963, Chapter Seven, "Our Little Brothers: Reincarnation and Animals," Paperback edition, 1981, pp. 160-215.

5

SACRED SCRIPTURES

A DISTINCTION MUST BE MADE between books that are considered sacred and those that are merely religious. A sacred book has a totalitarian implication that the religious has not. Its contents are not to be disputed: that which is descriptive is to be taken for truth; that which is narrative is to be considered fact; that which is instructive is to be followed to the letter; and that which is presented as esoteric is to be believed implicitedly. Writings having to do with sacred rites, by association, become sacred. Works that discuss concepts of God or theories about the operation of the world are religious. One may agree with them or not; their acceptance is not demanded. Normally, accounts or histories of noble and pious figures are religious, but there are exceptions in the "I"-oriented cults. Religious writings, therefore, are exoteric and rational. Sacred scriptures are esoteric and passionate. Two images come to mind. The first is a modern American courtroom in which a witness, about to give testimony, is made to swear to tell the truth while placing his right hand upon a Bible, as though it contains some magic to assure veracity. The second is a twelfth-century Chinese Ch'an monk tearing up sutra scrolls; once he has absorbed their intrinsic contents and made them part of his life, the documents are no longer anything more than ink marks on paper.

The vast and varied religious literature of India was reviewed at the Parliament in Manilal M. D'vivedi's dissertation on "Hinduism." The volumes have to do with the different schools of thought, and in order to make them comprehensible D'vivedi grouped them by period. "At least six different and well-marked stages are visible in the history of

Indian philosophic thought . . . (1) The *Vedas*; (2) the *Sutra*; (3) the *Dars'ana*; (4) the *Purāna*; (5) the *Sampradāya*; (6) the *Samāja*. Each of these is enough to fill several volumes, and all I can attempt here is a cursory survey, imperfect and incomplete . . ."[1]

1. "Let us begin with the *Vedas*. The oldest of the four *Vedas* is admittedly the *Rigveda*. It is the most ancient record of the Aryan nation, nay, of the first humanity our earth knows of. . . . We find in the *Vedas* a highly superior order of rationalistic thought pervading all the hymns, and we have ample reason to conclude that the gods involved are each and all more than the childish poetry of primitive hearts. . . . In their spiritual aspect all gods are one, for well says the well-known text: 'One only essence the wise declare in many ways.' . . . In the *Vedas* there are marks everywhere of the recognition of the idea of one god, the god of nature manifesting himself in many forms. . . . This idea of the formless All . . . is the central idea of the *Vedas*, . . . the root idea of the *Hindu* religion in general. . . . If we grasp this central idea of the *Vedas* we . . . may come at once to the second phase of religious thought, the *Sutras* and *Smrtis* based on the ritualistic portion of Vedic literature.

"Between the *Vedas* and the *Sutras* lie the *Brāhmana* with the *Upanishads* and *Āryanakas* and *Smrtis*. The books called *Brāhmanas* and *Upanishads* form part of the *Vedas* . . . the former explaining the ritualistic use and application of *Vedic* hymns, the latter systemitizing the unique philosophy contained in them. What the *Brāhmanas* explained allegorically, and in the quaint phraseology of the *Vedas*, the *Smrtis*, which followed them, explained in plain systematic modern *Sanskrit*."

2. "*Sutra* means an aphorism. . . . The *Sutras* deal with the *Brāhmanas* and *Smrtis* on the one hand, and with the *Upanishads* on the other. . . . The *Sutras* are divided principally into the *Grhya*, *S'ranta* and *Dharma Sutras*. The first deals with the *Smrtis*, the second with the *Brāhmanas*, and the

third with the law as administered by the *Smrtis*." D'vivedi goes into some detail as to how these apply to the Hindu social system, then comes to the next group of writings.

3. "*Dars'anas*, which enlarge upon the central idea of *ātman* or *Brahman*, enunciated in the Vedas and developed in the Upanishads. . . . The six *Dars'anas* are *Nyāya, Vais'eshika, Sānkhya, Yoga, Mimānsā* and *Vedānta*, more conveniently grouped as the two *Nyāyas*, the two *Sānkhyas* and the two *Mimānsās*." The two *Nyāyas* have to do with the "nature of knowledge and the instruments of knowledge" and advocate "the atomic theory of the universe" in which "atoms move in accordance with the will of an extra-cosmic personal creator, called *Is'vara*. Every being has a soul, called *Jiva*," and the "highest happiness lies in the *Jiva's* becoming permanently free from its attribute of misery. . . . The *Sānkhyas* differed . . . in that they repudiate the idea of a personal creator of the universe. . . . God himself could not create something out of nothing. And as to intelligence, the *Sānkhyas* maintain that it is inherent in nature. These philosophers, therefore, hold that the whole universe is evolved, by slow degrees, in a natural manner from one primordial matter called *Mulaprakrti*, and that *parus'a*, the principle of intelligence, is always co-ordinate with, though ever apart from, *Mulaprakrti*. Like the *Naiyāyikas*, they believe in the multiplicity of *purus'as* — souls, but, unlike them, they deny the necessity as well as the existence of an extra-cosmic God." Another part "expands the ethical side of the teaching by setting forth several physical and psychological rules and exercises capable of leading to the last state of happiness called *Kaivalya* — life according to nature. This is the theistic *Sānkhya*. The two *Mimānsās* . . . are the orthodox *Dars'anas par excellence*, and as such are in direct touch with the *Vedas*, and the *Upanishads*, which continue to govern them from beginning to end. *Mimānsā* means inquiry, and the first or preliminary is called *Purva-Mimānsā*, the second *Uttara-Mimānsā*. The object of the first is to determine the exact meaning and value of the injunctions

and prohibitions given out in the *Vedas*, and that of the second is to explain the esoteric teaching of the *Upanishads*. . . . [it is] popularly known as the *Vedānta* . . . [and] emphasizes the idea of the All, the universal *Ātman* or *Brahman*, set forth in the *Upanishads* and maintains the unity not only of the Cosmos, but of all intelligence in general. . . . The *Vedānta* is a system of absolute idealism in which subject and object are welded into one unique consciousness, the realization whereof is the end and aim of existence, the highest bliss — *moks'a*." This last term corresponds to Swami Vivekananda's *mukto*, mentioned in the preceding chapter. D'vivedi defined it as "the very being of all existence, but experience stands in the way of complete realization by creating imaginary distinctions of subject and object." Inasmuch as "The subtleties of the *Dars'anas* were certainly too hard for ordinary minds," a simpler means of presenting their salient points "was indeed very urgently required." This was the purpose of the following group.

4. "the *Purānas* are closely connected with the *Vedas* and *Sutras*, and the *Dars'anas*, and all they claim to accomplish is a popular exposition of the basic ideal of philosophy, religion and morality set forth in them. In other words the *Purānas* are nothing more nor less than broad, clear commentaries on the ancient teaching of the *Vedas*." D'vivedi cites several such interpretations, goes into the Hindu concept of world cycles (touched upon in Chapter Three), and mentions that the theistic image (idol) of ancient mythological figures came into use at this time, characterizing it as "a convenient object for purposes of concentration," which has "an exact parallel in the worship of the Tau in Egypt, of the cross in Christendom, of fire in Zoroastrianism, and of the *Kāba* in Mohammedanism."

5. The next period is called *Sampradāya*, which "means tradition, the teaching handed down from teacher to pupil." It flourished during the eleventh and twelfth centuries, and introduced "the *Dvaita*, the *Vis'uddhādvaita* and the *Vis'-ishthādvaita* schools of philosophy, , , The first is purely dualistic, postulating the separate yet coordinate existence of mind

and matter. The second and third profess to be unitarian, but in a considerably modified sense of the word. The *Vis'uddhād-vaita* teaches the unity of the cosmos, but it insists on the All having certain attributes which endow it with the desire to manifest itself as the cosmos. The third system is purely dualistic though it goes by the name of modified unitarianism. It maintains the unity of *chit* (soul), *achet* (matter), and *Is'vara* (God), each in its own sphere, the third member of this trinity governing all and pervading the whole though not apart from the cosmos. . . . These three *Sampradāyas* teach a system of ethics entirely opposed to the [earlier] . . . called *Dharma* in the *Advaita*. They displace *Jnāna* [knowledge] by *Bhakti* [devotion]; and *Karma* [deeds] by *Prasāda* [grace]." Here, said D'vivedi, "we see the last of pure Hinduism;" it is followed by teachings called *"Panthas* — mere ways to Religion, as opposed to the traditional teaching of the *Sampradāyas.*"

6. The last or modern period, termed *Samāja*, is eclectic, an attempt to reconcile traditional Hinduism with foreign religions, giving rise to societies like the Ārya Samāja, the Brahmo Samāja and the Theosophical Society. The last two were represented at the Parliament.

From this condensation of an already brief account of the multitudinous writings of the Asian subcontinent, it will be noted that Hinduism presents many interpretations of the cosmic scheme other than the two principal concepts of God mentioned in Chapter Two. The "physiolatry" of missionary Phillips and the "formless and all-pervading" of D'vivedi represent the earliest known and the culminating ideas on the subject, with other speculations, regardless of period, interlaying them.

Certainly the *Vedas* and probably the other classics of Hindu religious literature are considered sacred scriptures. As we come down to the present time, works produced are only religious treatises.

When the Chicago Fair was in progress, the Hindu classics were just being made available as English translations edited by

Prof. Max Müller (whose paper on "Greek Philosophy and the Christian Religion" was read on the ninth day at the Parliament), in the Sacred Books of the East series. Included were some of the *Vedas* (Volumes XXXII and XLVI), twelve *Upanishads* (Volumes I and XV) and some of the *Sutras* (Volumes II, XIV, XXV, XXIX and XXX) by G. Buhler and H. Oldenberg. Others were being brought out in English at Bombay and Calcutta.

Virchand A. Gandhi might have given a review of Jain books numerically almost as impressive as those of Brahmanical literature. The ancient Jain writings include twelve *Angas*, the *Prathamānuyoga*, fourteen *Pūrvagatas*, five *Chūlikās*, and fourteen *Prakīrnakas*.² Some of these books, known to have existed, had been lost. H. Jacobi translated some of them in Volumes XXII and XLV of the Sacred Books of the East series. Others must have been produced in India, as Gandhi referred those interested in the subject "to the many books published by our society."

Buddhism produced a voluminous literature in Pali, Sanskrit, Chinese, Japanese, Tibetan, and many other languages, and its books began to be printed almost a thousand years before Gutenberg brought out the Bible. Buddhism itself is divided into two schools, the Theravādin ("Sect of Elders") or Southern, and Mahāyāna ("Greater Vehicle") or Northern. The principal writings of the Southern School are the *Tipitaka*, the "Three Baskets," about which Prof. Milton S. Terry, in his discourse on "The Sacred Books of the World as Literature," noted that: "In bulk these writings rival all that was ever included under the title of the Vedas, and contain more than seven times the amount of matter in the Scriptures of the Old and New Testaments." The "Three Baskets" are: the *Vinaya Pitaka*, containing the rules of monastic discipline; the *Sutta Pitaka*, consisting of four *Nikāyas*, or collections of discussions on doctrine, and a fifth *Nikāya* of devotional verses; and the *Abhidhamma Pitaka*, made up of scholastic commentaries and elaboration on doctrine, particularly in the field of psychological ethics.

The *Khuddhamma Nikāya* ("Smallish Collection") includes the *Jātaka* tales, a compilation of 547 stories culled from older Indian fables (such as are found in the *Panchatantra*), in which the Buddha, in former lives, is identified with the righteous hero. He is often an animal, like the hare in the *Sasa Jātaka*, back to which — and the footprint cult of the Buddha — the old American superstition of carrying a rabbit's-foot charm has been traced. Many American Indian and Negro folk tales descended from the *Jātakas* (or other East Indian equivalents), such as the Uncle Remus stories recorded by Joel Chandler Harris.[3]

The fifth *Nikāya* contains the *Dhammapada*, a treatise of 423 verses said to have been pronounced by the Buddha and which some consider the heart of his teaching.

Another early work is an interrogation of the monk Nāgasena by King Menander, one of the rulers who continued the dynasty implanted by Alexander the Great in Baktria during the latter part of the second century B.C. The book is called *The Questions of King Milinda* (his Buddhist name).

To the Southern scriptures the Mahāyāna or Northern School added many books. Those of the early period were in Sanskrit. The most influential were the *Saddharmapundarika*, the "Lotus of the Good Law," the *Mahāprajñāpāramita Sutra*, the "Great Transcendental Wisdom Treatise," and the *Vajracchedikā*, "Diamond Cutter," which established the essential doctrines. The *Buddhacharita* and *Lalitavistara* give the legendary life of the Buddha.

Dharmapala prepared a bibliography of Buddhist books available in English at the time of the Parliament. G. Beal had translated the *Dhammapada*, a *Catena of Buddhist Scriptures*, and *Chinese Buddhist Literature*, and he had written other books about Buddhism. Prof. T.W. Rhys-Davids had translated the *Jātakas*. And the Sacred Books of the East provided Volumes X and XI on early Buddhist doctrine, Volumes XIII,

XVI and XX on the *Vinaya* texts; Volume XXI was the *Lotus of the Good Law*, and Volumes XXXV and XXXVI were the *Questions of King Milinda*.

Zenshiro Noguchi, the emissary of four Japanese Buddhist sorios and who himself gave a paper on "The Religions of the World," brought "many thousand copies of English translations of Buddhist works, such as *Outlines of the Mahayana, as Taught by Buddha, A Brief Account of Shin-shu, A Shin-shu Catechism*, and *The Sutra of Forty-two Sections and Two Other Short Sutras*, etc. Besides these, four hundred volumes of complete *Buddha Shaka's Sutra*," which were presented to the Chairman of the Congress. Shin-shu is the name of the Pure Land sect of Japanese Buddhism; and Shaka is the Japanese form of Shakya (Sanskrit) or Shakiya (Pali), which refers to the Buddha by his clan name.

As indicated by the episode of the Ch'an monk rending the sutra scrolls told at the beginning of this chapter, in Buddhism, especially in the meditation sects, writings are considered mere aids to the serious business of attaining Enlightenment, which is gained through one's own efforts. Therefore, no matter how refined, inspiring, and beautiful the Buddhist sutras may be, technically they cannot be called sacred. The *Jātaka* fables are for the ethical instruction of beginners and children, and are not considered factual; and in accounts of the gods, like the *Bardo Thodol*, the Tibetan Book of the Dead, the reader is reminded that deities and demons exist only within "thine own intellect."[4]

The anonymous "Prize Essay" on Taoism, recorded as having been one of sixty on Chinese religions submitted by scholars of "the Celestial Empire," was read at the Scientific Section either on September 15 or 20. It refers at the beginning to the core text, Lao-tzu's *Tao-te Ching*. Lao-tzu was an older contemporary of Confucius and the Buddha, and he wrote the 5,000-character essay during his seventy-third year. The occasion was his leaving China to retire in solitude, and it was written at the request of the warden at the western gate, one Yin Hsi, himself a scholar. The *Tao-te Ching* was composed spontaneously and is a collection of aphorisms, which, as its title ("Reason-Virtue") suggests, deals with intellectual and moral concepts. The term *Tao*, interpreted as "Ultimate Reason," has been related to the immanent God (Chapter Two). Although the term *fa* is used in Chinese to translate Dharma, Lao-tzu's Reason and the Buddha's Way are much the same thing. The perfect *Tao*, whether God, Reason, or the Way, cannot be reasoned and is therefore raised to the transcendental. So also are beauty and goodness, whereas when they are made a display of they become ugliness and badness. In the eleventh paragraph Lao-tzu defines the function of emptiness, the usefulness of the void within the solid; examples are the hole in the nave of the wheel enabling it to turn on its axle, the hollowness of a ceramic vessel that can be filled with whatever it is meant to contain, and the cutout doors and windows in walls and empty space within a house that make it livable. This last was the principle of organic architecture, as conceived by Louis Sullivan, which when encountered as having been anticipated 2,500 years earlier by Lao-tzu, prompted Sullivan's protégé Frank Lloyd Wright to exclaim that he felt like a balloon that has been punctured. Other important thoughts in the *Tao-te* are the superiority of simplicity over complexity, the desirability of being content with contentment, and achieving without striving. The last constitutes the final remark in the essay, and it is the antithesis of the materialistic, grasping attitude.

The author of the "Prize Essay" mentions three secondary Taoists books, *The Great Beginning, The Great Peace, The Great Purity*. The last is the *Ch'ing Kang Ching*, which, with the *Tao-te Ching* and essays by Lao-tzu's early follower, Chuang-tzu, appeared in Volumes XXXIX and XV as The Texts of Taoism in the Sacred Books of the East series in 1891.

Turning westward, we pause in the Middle East to consider the sacred scriptures of the Parsees. Jinanji Modi, in discussing the Zarathustra concept of the destiny of the soul, mentions "The Avesta writings of Hādokht Nushk and the nineteenth chapter of the Vendidād and of the Pehlevi books of Monokherad and Virāf-nāmeh." The oldest of these scriptures are characterized Avesta from the antique language in which they were conceived, the body of literature being referred to as the Zend-Avesta, *Zend* meaning "commentary." Of the twenty-two treatises, or Nasks (Nushks), most were destroyed by Alexander's depredations at Persepolis in 331 B.C.; only five have survived. One of these is the *Vendidād*, a priestly code of purifications and penalties. Ervad Bharuchā, in a "Sketch of Zoroastrianism" at the Parliament, said that the only Nask originating with Zarathustra was the *Gathas*, or Psalms, the rest being "the composition of priests after his death, but not later than B.C. 559." Subsequent scriptures, written in Pehlevi, date from about the fourth century A.D., of which the responses of the High Priest Monokherad to ninety-two queries and the book of the "account of the journey of Ardai-Virāf through the heavenly regions" were mentioned by Modi. The 'Jewish Bible and canonical New Testament roughly correspond in period to the Avesta and Pehlevi books of Parseeism.

The next stop on our journey investigating holy writ is in the region of scriptures of unqualified sanctity, wherein each faith considers its writings to be the exclusive revelation made by God. Included are the three great Semitic manifestations, Judaism, Christianity, and Islam. Each, to some degree, acknowledges a relationship with the other two, yet each declares itself superior. Judaism proclaims its priority, pointing out that Christianity could not have existed without it; Christianity looks upon Judaism as a mere substructure, of little consequence alone; and Islam pays both token recognition while considering itself of ultimate uniqueness.

Dr. Alexander Kohut, Rabbi of the Congregation Ahawath Chesad in New York City, on the sixth day of the Parliament talked about "What the Hebrew Scriptures Have Wrought for

Mankind." He began by saying that "God is the anchor of new-born hope, the electric quickener of life's uneven current." The last metaphor was topical inasmuch as the Columbian Exposition was the first of the major world's fairs to be illuminated by electricity. Rabbi Kohut continued: "To the innate comprehension of the rudest soul, God and the Bible are synonymous. Both are effulgent with the glory of one truth, with the majesty of one sublime conception." Having established the basic worth and connection between God and Bible, Kohut plunged into a doxology on faith — to everybody but those in accord with it an instrument of uncertain reliability (Chapter Seven) — calling it "the creed of Israel . . . who bequeathed the precious legacy to Semitic and Aryan nations." Then he lauded Israel itself against other ancient kingdoms in the Near East. "Chaldea wrought magic, Babylonia myth, Assyria monuments, Egypt science, Greece art, Rome war and chivalry — of Judea let it be said, that she founded a hallowed faith, spread a pure religion, and propagated the paternal love of an All-Father." He characterized the last as "a creed undominated by cumbrous tyranny, unembarrassed by dogmatic technicalities, unstrained by heavy self-sacrifice and extravagant ceremonialism — a religion sublime and unique in history, free from gaping superstitions, appalling idolatries, and vicious immoralities . . . originating in a monotheistic conception." Judaism may show little inclination for self-sacrifice, but it contains plenty of tyranny, dogmatism, ceremonialisms, superstitions, idolatries, and vicious immoralities; and it is only conditionally monotheistic, as one can read in the Bible. The rabbi praised this book with equal fervor: "Bible ethics, justice, morality, righteousness and all the mighty elements embodied in virtuous life, are summed up in Judaism's great truths, faithfully portrayed and preserved to mankind in that ponderous volume of poetic inspiration."

Also on the sixth day of the Parliament Rabbi G. Gottheil stated in the last paragraph of his talk that, "For two centuries of the Christian Church, no other Bible was known but the

Old Testament." He was followed by the Rev. Theodore T. Munger of New Haven, Conn., speaking on "Christianity as Interpreted by Literature." In analyzing the background of his subject he said, "The Jew was too primitive and simple-minded as a thinker to analyze his thought or his nature; but in history, in ethics, in imaginative fiction and in certain forms of poetry his literature well endures comparison with any that can be named. No sympathetic reader will deny that the Hebrew Scriptures are full of inspiration, but the thoughtful reader resents putting that inspiration into a rule or form, and he refuses to read them under a notion of authority that bars up the avenues of the mind, and turns every mental faculty into a nullity." Munger changed his tune in turning to his own religious field: "It is not ... wholly true to say the Hebrew Scriptures gave shape and direction to Christ; he was too unique, too original, too full of direct inspiration and vision to justify such an assertion, but he stood upon them not as an authoritative guide in religion but as illustrative of truth, as valuable for their inspiring quality and as full of signs of more truth and fuller grace."

The Old and New Testaments make odd bedfellows. The Christian minister called the partisans of the former "primitive and simple-minded," except in that domain used to sow seeds for cultivating his own Christ figure. Yet the two books have been acclaimed together in the highest possible terms by Catholic and Protestant alike. Mgr. Robert Seton called attention to the Vatican Council held in 1870, which decreed: "If any one shall not receive as sacred and canonical the books of Holy Scripture, entire with all their parts, as the Holy Synod of Trent has enumerated them, or shall deny that they have been divinely inspired, let him be anathema." Later Seton said, "The church has always taught that God is the one author of the Old and New Testament; but the Vatican Council more clearly declared immediate inspiration ... having been written by the inspiration of the Holy Ghost." The Rev. Joseph Cook, Boston Congregationalist, affirmed,

"The self-evident truths in scripture, as everywhere else, are not only unchangeable, unassailable and trustworthy; they are actually infallible, and they are the spiritual summits on which the cathedral of the Holy Word, with all its columns, architraves and pinnacles, have been built."

Prof. Charles A. Briggs took exception to the Bible's perfection, noting that "the best text, versions and citations of these Holy Scriptures that we can get, have numerous and important discrepancies. . . . most of them were composed by unknown authors . . . have passed through the hands of a considerable number of unknown editors, who have brought together the older material without removing discrepancies, inconsistencies and errors. . . . God himself did not speak according to the Hebrew Scriptures, more than a few words from Theophany, which are recorded here and there in the Old Testament. God spoke in much the greater part of the Old Testament through the voices and pens of the authors of the Scriptures. Did the human voice and pen in all the numerous writers and editors of Holy Scripture prior to the completion of the Canon always deliver an inerrant word? Even if all the writers were so possessed of the Holy Spirit as to be merely passive in his hands, the question arises, can the finite voice and the finite pen deliver and express the inerrant truth of God? How can an imperfect word, sentence and clause express a perfect divine truth? It is evident that the writers of the Bible were not as a rule in the ecstatic state."

Perhaps in answer to Dr. Briggs' point concerning the "finite voice and finite pen," the Rev. Frank Sewall, general pastor of the Maryland Association, said in his discourse later in the same session, "The nature and the degree of the inspiration which thus characterizes the Bible can only be learned from the declaration of the Holy Scriptures themselves, since only the divine can truly reveal the divine or afford to human minds the means of judging truly regarding what is divine." This is like admonishing customers not to heed any statements about the product except those contained in its own commercials, as only those who make and market it know how superior it is to all others. If the material in the Bible were all, or even mostly, on a high level, as in so many of the treatises of India and China, Sewall's pronouncement would be worthy of consideration. But when one is confronted by such material as the two discordant creation myths, the genealogies of fallen man, some noting when each was circumsized, King Saul's demand as dowry for his daughter the foreskins of one hundred Philistines, King David's rape of Bathsheba and order that her husband be killed, his later problem about being able to "gat no heat," the introduction of the virgin into his bed and contest over her between his two sons, resulting in fratricide, King Solomon's love of "many strange women" (and his indiscriminate worship of their foreign gods), and the inventory of gold treasures in his possession, one begins to feel that assigning the authorship of the Bible to God is the greatest blasphemy that Jews or Christians ever committed.

The Jewish Bible is complemented by the Talmud (Aramaic for "learning"), a compilation of oral laws as opposed to the scriptural written laws, though nevertheless in textbook form. In authority they are equal and together compose the Torah (Hebrew for "law"), the complete law. The two divisions of the Talmud are the Mishna, a codified collection of legal interpretations of the Pentateuch, in Hebrew, and the Gemara, commentary on the material in the Mishna, in Aramaic. The former deals with six orders: (1) laws pertaining to agriculture and the seasons, (2) laws for the Sabbath and festivals, (3) laws regarding vows, marriage, and divorce, (4) laws concerning civil and criminal matters, (5) laws regarding ritual slaughter, sacrifice and holy objects, and (6) laws regarding ceremonial piety, The Mishna dates from the first and second centuries A.D. The Gemara resorts to considerable hairsplitting and diverges into such subjects as astronomy, geography, domestic and historical gossip and folklore. There were both Palestinian and Babylonian Talmuds; because of the fragmentary preservation of the former, the latter became the authoritative work.

The Talmud is ignored by Christians, whereas the Hebrew Bible became the stepping stone to the New Testament and inseparable from it. Mr. Sewall contended that the link is traceable back to the founder of the Christian religion. "In the very words of Jesus Christ, the Canon of the Word is established in a two-fold manner: First, intrinsically, as included those books which interiorly testify of him, and were all to be fulfilled by him (I say interiorly, because comparatively few of the prophecies regarding the Lord are apparent in the literal sense of the prophecy, and hence, when our Lord declared to the disciples the fulfillment of the Word of the Old Testament in himself, we read that 'He opened their understanding that they might understand the Scriptures'). Secondly, the Canon is fixed specifically by our Lord's naming three books which compose it under the three divisions: 'The Law, the Prophets and the Psalms.' The Canon, in this sense, comprises: ... The five books of Moses, or the 'law,' ... the so-called *Earlier Prophets* ... the *Later Prophets* ... and finally the book of Psalms. The other books of the Old Testament ... while losing nothing of the sacredness hitherto accorded to them, must nevertheless forever stand in a category apart from those writings specified by our Lord as having their fulfillment in himself."

Whether claimed by an historic Jesus or fabricated by one of his idolaters, the "interior' testimony of his coming became the bulwark for the Christology that developed. "The redemption of our Lord and Saviour Jesus Christ ... [became] the central idea of all Christian instruction," declared Mgr. Seton. Jesus prognosticated his own death and went resolutely to the slaughter to save mankind. The histrionics overshadow Jesus' teaching, which lasted only a year or two, or his good deeds, also limited, but they were pointed up by the miracles he wrought. It seems likely that there was some basis for accepting the miracles, as the Jewish historian Josephus, although born after Jesus' lifetime, heard of "wonderful things concerning him," without being specific as to what they were.[5] The one eyewitness gospel writer Matthew was prejudiced in favor of the supernatural and therefore was vulnerable to being deceived himself. It was the Rev. Theodore T. Munger who turned criticism upon his own party at the Parliament, saying that "the church has relied too exclusively upon the miracles, which led to its worship [of] the Bible as a fetish, and to fill it with all sorts of magical meanings and forced dogmas." The Rev. Luther F. Townsend of Boston mentioned that in the second century the "progressive" views of Clement of Alexandria led him to attempt "to make the teaching and example of Christ of more importance than his death and sufferings . . . [but] Clement was not able in any perceptible degree to disturb the foundations of apostolic Christianity." If the Old Testament formed the foyer of the Christian scriptures, the New Testament, as a collection of testimonials, became the shrine for the cult image.

The Jewish Bible became fixed as the Masoretic version and was adopted about 100 A.D. The Christian Old Testament was derived from an entirely different source, the Septuagint, a Hellenistic Jewish translation into Greek of the third century B.C. It contained seven more books than the Masora and became the first part of St. Jerome's Vulgate of the early fifth century. Almost a thousand years later, Protestants withdrew the books not included in the Masora from the body of the Old Testament, and these were assembled as an appendix called the Apocrypha. Today they are eliminated from printed versions of the King James Bible.

Early Christians knew and used many books that later churchmen rejected. Some of them no longer exist, and some that do have been all but forgotten; some have reappeared in relatively recent times. Many of these works were considered inspired yet were excluded from the canonical selection. Of this body, some were chosen on irrational grounds, such as for the symbolic necessity of having four gospels, which led to adding that of John to the Synoptic three. Some of the writings were eschewed as not being compatible to the Pauline

Epistles, favored by the church. Authors of the Patristic Literature of the first and second centuries included St. Clement I, St. Ignatius of Antioch, St. Polycarp, and Papias. Among the works is the Pseudepigraphy, meaning "Things Falsely Ascribed," of which several appear as part of the Apocrypha in the authorized version of the Bible. Among those not accepted is "The Shepherd of Hermas," written by the brother of Pius, Bishop of Rome, and which takes its name from the angel appearing in the garb of a shepherd. The book contains four "Visions," twelve "Commands" and ten "Similitudes," and the teachings are concerned with morals, penance and the condition of the church. The Didache is also in three parts; the first deals with moral precepts and the balance with rites and directions for the clergy. These two books may have been dismissed because of their institutional orientation, but the selection of the bizarre apocrypha that was included seems to have been a matter of group or personal taste.

Attributed to St. Matthew is "The Gospel of the Birth of Mary," which tells of her conception, training as a virgin in the temple, the voice from the Ark that requires her marriage, and the choice of Joseph as husband. It is followed, chronologically, by the Protevangelium, "An Historical Account of the Birth of Christ, and the Perpetual Virgin Mary, His Mother, by James the Lesser, Cousin and Brother of the Lord Jesus, Chief Apostle and First Bishop of the Christians in Jerusalem." With such a subject and recorder (questioned, of course, as is the authorship of most of the books that went into the Bible), this gospel would seem to have much to recommend it. Its text concentrates on Mary's pregnancy, Joseph's ordeal in the temple as to whether he had defiled Mary, the testimony of the midwife regarding the miracle of the virgin birth, and the order of King Herod to destroy all children in Bethlehem under two years of age. "The First Gospel of the Infancy" is ascribed to "Joseph the high-priest, called by some Caiaphas." It begins with an authentic note, not found in any of the Biblical gospels — namely, the date of Augustus' tax decree, which was "In the three hundred and ninth year of the aera of Alexander." The new-born babe speaks to his mother, "Mary, I am Jesus the Son of God, . . . and my father hath sent me for the salvation of the world." They are visited by the wise men, who come "according to the prophecy of Zoradascht" (Zarathustra). Chapters V through XXII, following the return from Egypt, are largely devoted to healings performed by Mary, and by his clothing and the boy Jesus himself. The book is succeeded by "Thomas's Gospel of the Infancy of Jesus Christ," of which only a fragment survives. Some of the miracles in the two infancy gospels are cruel and vindictive: in the first, Jesus curses the strict schoolmaster, who is about to strike him, so that his hand shrivels and he dies; and in the second a boy running in the street who brushes his shoulder suffers the same fate, and when the townspeople rebuke him, Jesus causes them to become blind. One is reminded of the fig tree Jesus encounters after the Triumphal Entry, which, because it bears no fruit to appease his hunger, he curses so that it withers (Matthew XXI, 19); or his lack of feeling for the disciple who asks permission to go bury his father, to whom Jesus replies: "Follow me; and let the dead bury their dead" (VIII, 22). "The Gospel of Nicodemus" is attributed to the lame man healed by Jesus at the Bethesda pool (John V, 5-8), and its twenty-two chapters cover the latter episodes of Jesus' life. It features the testimony of Nicodemus, who speaks up in Jesus' defense at the trial; relates the story of the crucifixion, resurrection, the descent of Jesus into Hell; and it concludes with the Jews' finding verification of Jesus as the messiah in their scriptures in the temple.

In 1886 the French Archaeological Mission, digging at Akhmim in the Valley of the Upper Nile, discovered a parchment codex, which was identified as "The Lost Gospel According to Peter." It is of about the length of the two books associated with his name in the New Testament, and it deals with the condemnation and execution of Jesus. This report differs in twenty-nine facts from that of the four gospels, among them that Jesus exclaims from the cross, "My power, my power, thou hast forsaken me"; and before daybreak, following the entombment, "The heavens opened, and two men descend from thence with great light;" they go to the sepulcher and emerge "supporting one, and a cross followed them." Agreeing basically with Matthew (Chapter Three), the undelayed "ascension" is attested to only by the guards — who give it as their excuse for fleeing — and when the women arrive in the morning, the tomb is empty except for the figure "clothed in a robe exceedingly bright," who tells them that "He is risen and gone."[6]

Not generally known and recognized in Christendom is the gospel given in an Aramaic manuscript in the Vatican Library, which, with a similar recording in Old Slavonic, was translated into English by Dr. Edmond Bordeaux Szekely and first published during the 1930s. The preservation of these two texts is attributed to Nestorian priests, who brought them to the West, fleeing before the hordes of Genghis Khan. The work is called *The Essene Gospel of Peace*, and in it Jesus is presented as teaching an ethics of Buddhist universality.[7]

Another, more ample account is *The Gospel of the Holy Twelve*. Supposedly Emanuel Swedenborg (died 1772), the Swedish seer and mystic, and Placidus, a fourteenth-century Carmelite monk, acted as spirit translators of an Aramaic text preserved in Tibet, which was transcribed by Edward Maitland and Dr. Anna Kingsford during the 1880s. The book was praised highly by Count Leo Tolstoy. It agrees with the Szekely gospel in assigning an Essene background to Jesus. Unlike it, *The Gospel of the Holy Twelve* is quite articulate regarding the events of his life. Jesus was married in his eighteenth year, and seven years later his wife, Miriam, "died, for God took her that he might go on to higher things which he had to do, and to suffer for the sons and daughters of men" (VI, 10).[8] After a ministry of eighteen years, Jesus was crucified on the eve of his fiftieth birthday (XCV, 9). In the *Essene Gospel*, Jesus talks of the Earthly Mother and Heavenly

Father, whereas in the *Holy Twelve* the deity is (as in its rendition of the Lord's Prayer): "Our Father-Mother Who art above and within" (XIX, 3). The Holy Trinity is "the Father, Spouse and Son" (XCVI, 18). The teaching is well integrated into the biographic narrative. At the wells near Tiberias, when "a certain young man brought live rabbits and pigeons, that he might have to eat with his disciples," Jesus said to him, "Thou hast a good heart and God shall give thee light, but knowest thou not that God in the beginning gave to man the fruits of the earth for food, and did not make him lower than the ape, or the ox, or the horse, or the sheep, that he should kill and eat the flesh and blood of his fellow creatures. Ye believe that Moses indeed commanded such creatures to be slain and offered in sacrifice and eaten, and so do ye in the temple, but behold a greater than Moses is here, and he cometh to put away the bloody sacrifices of the law, and the feasts on them, and to restore to you the pure oblation and unbloody sacrifice as in the beginning, even the grains and fruits of the earth" (XXVIII, 2-3). Another similar rebuttal of Moses' authority occurred at the Last Supper or Passover. Judas had brought a lamb, but Jesus refused to let it be slain, and Judas said to him, "Master, behold the unleaven bread, the mingled wine and the oil and the herbs, but where is the lamb that Moses commanded?" John then referred to Jesus as "the good Shepherd which giveth his life for the sheep." And Jesus replied: "If I am lifted up on the cross then indeed shall the lamb be slain; but woe unto him by whom it is delivered into the hands of the slayers: it were better for him had he not been born" (LXXXV, 6-8). Consistent throughout the text, Jesus stands firmly for humaneness and justice in opposition to the Mosaic Law, which gives his final sacrifice supreme meaning, and if the Maitland-Kingsford version is correct, then nobody was ever more maligned, by being made to advocate what he bitterly contested, than Jesus in Christianity's authorized gospels.

Among the antique writings excluded from the New

Testament are epistles similar to those admitted. Some are allegedly written by Paul, the purported author of twelve books of the present Bible.

The acceptance of some of the letters of Paul, the rejection of others, the inclusion of the first gospel by Matthew and the preclusion of his "Gospel of the Birth of Mary," and the approval of the two epistles of Peter but refusal of his "Lost Gospel" (though belatedly discovered) are puzzling matters. The writings of Peter, James, and Matthew constitute the only documents ascribed as being first-hand reports concerning Jesus, and — as has been noted — most of these have been repudiated by the church. One is reminded of the legendary incident regarding Constantine and the bishops seated in the dark at their "council," with the various books and letters strewn about on the floor, waiting for the Holy Ghost to levitate to the top of the table those documents that were to be included in the Bible as canonical.

As Mgr. Seton remarked before the World's Parliament of Religions, "Some ten generations of Christians lived and died before that collection of sacred books called the Bible was universally known and received." The familiar New Testament arrangement first appeared in the Festal Epistle of St. Athanasius, early in the fourth century. The selection was questioned (along with that of the Old Testament) during the Reformation. Martin Luther, for instance, eschewed the Book of James because it did not accord with his tenet of justification by faith alone. The Catholic Bible differs from that of the Protestant in having forty-six instead of thirty-nine books to the Old Testament (due to the elimination of the Apocrypha), and it is supplied with notes informing the reader how each part should be interpreted (the creation myth "is not to present a scientific picture but to teach a religious truth" — the dependency of man upon a mythical creator-god). These notes vary from edition to edition. As in the case of some modern Protestant Bibles, its text has been cleaned up somewhat, at times to the degree wherein it distorts the original meaning, as in the case of King David's bed companion, who in the new version administers to him as his "nurse."

When one thinks about the many formal controversies and the prolonged petty bickerings that transpired during the early centuries over Christian sacred scriptures, Christian doctrine, and Christology; that they were settled by arbitrary means, either by majority of votes in council or dictatorial decree on the part of the presiding officer (bishop or emperor), or perhaps by alleged miracles; that, though to a lesser degree, matters are still being disputed; that what was determined as orthodox at one period and place gave way to something else at another, each resulting in modifications to the text, one is overwhelmed by the transciency of the Bible, causing one to form serious reservations about accepting such frequently manipulated subject matter as being anything other than highly questionable.

Midway between the establishment of the Christian church and the Reformation schism arose the third member of the Near East trilogy of religions based on exclusive faith in its own legends and dogmas. This was Islam, which Dr. George Washburn of Robert College compared with Christianity on the fifth day of the Parliament talks. Both the Old and New Testaments were known in Arabia when Mohammed was living, during the late sixth and early seventh centuries, though the prophet could have known about them only through hearsay as he could not read. Dr. Washburn detected a greater influence from collateral sources: "The historical parts of the Koran correspond with the Talmud, and the writing current among the heretical Christian sects, such as the Protevangelium of James, the pseudo Matthew, and the gospel of the nativity of Mary, rather than with the Bible. His [Mohammed's] information was probably obtained verbally from his Jewish and Christian friends, who seem, in some cases, to have deceived him intentionally. He seems to have believed their statements that his coming was foretold in the Scriptures, and to have hoped for some years that they would accept him as their promised leader."

The "Introduction to the Parliament Papers," in the two-volume work recording them, quoted a passage omitted from the account proper of Prof. M.S. Terry's talk on "The Sacred Books of the World as Literature," which had to do with the recording of the Koran. It said that Mohammed "dictated his revelations to his disciples, and they wrote them on date leaves, bits of parchment, tablets of white stone and shoulder-blades of sheep. After the prophet's death the different fragments were collected and arranged according to the length of the chapters, beginning with the longest and ending with the shortest." As other scholars have pointed out, this was close to the reverse of the sequence in which they were spoken, as Mohammed became more verbose as time progressed. At least the system had the virtue of recording the prophet's sayings on the spot, not from faulty memory, or worse, from oft-repeated accounts long afterward, translated and retranslated. Mohammed's Arabic remains the official language of Islam. There are verses in the Koran equal to any in the earlier gospels. In a letter from Paris, J. Sanua Abou Naddara included several selections showing that "the Koran is tolerant, humane and moral." One of them was: "Surely those who believe, and the Jews and the Christians and the Sabians, whoever believeth in God and the Last Day, and doeth that which is right, they shall have their reward with their Lord. There shall come no fear on them, neither shall they be grieved." (II, 59.) Another: "Good and evil shall not be held equal. Turn away evil from that which is better, and behold, the man between whom and thyself there was enmity shall become, as it were, thy warmest friend." (LXI, 33.) Mohammed's own estimate of the book was: "If men and genii united themselves together to bring the like of the Koran they could not bring the like though they should back each other up."

Dr. Washburn's comment was: "The Koran claimed to be a new and perfect revelation of the will of God, and from the time of the Prophet's death to this day no Moslem has appealed to the ancient traditions of Arabia or to the Jewish or Christian

Scriptures as the ground of the faith. The Koran and the traditions are sufficient and final. I believe that every orthodox Moslem regards Islam as a separate, distinct, and absolutely exclusive religion; and there is nothing to be gained by calling it a form of Christianity." There would be nothing gained in calling Christianity a form of Judaism either. In their dogmatic exclusiveness, in their devotional isolationalism, and in their unswerving faith in themselves the three Semitic religions remain autonomous bodies.

As the Jewish Bible has its Talmud, the Koran has an appendage called the Sunna, which means the example of the Prophet. The Sunna is made up of moral sayings and anecdotes of Mohammed collected after his death, recorded in the late ninth century, some of which are borrowings from other religious teachers but presented as the Prophet's utterances. There are serious disagreements between quotations in the Koran and Sunna, to ease which situation Moslems cite Mohammed as having said, "My community will never agree in an error." The principle expressed is Ijima, the agreement of Islam, which allows for differences of opinion.

The compilation of the chronicles of Japanese Shinto was coeval with the recording of the Koran. At the Scientific Section meeting on September 25 the chairman read a paper by Prof. Takayoshi Matsuyama on "The Origin of Shintoism." It speaks of the native sect as being a reaction against foreign religions arising a thousand years after their introduction. "In 1700 a Shinto priest founded 'pure' Shintoism, declaring that his doctrine was the one given by the gods." Other reformers followed, and their theme was that "Shinto was transmitted through the first parents of the Japanese to the progenitor of the mikados; that the primitive faith should be studied in the *Kojiki* and the *Nihongi*; and that Buddhism and Confucianism, while useful in India and China, were man-founded, and useless in Japan, which the gods had from the beginning blessed peculiarly. . . . The *Kojiki* was completed in 712, the *Nihongi* in 720, and almost their every word is considered undeniable truth." Here, in the Far East, is another instance of a delayed compilation of ancient myths seized upon and presented as indisputable gospel.

The Rev. E.L. Rexford of Boston, in discussing "The Religious Intent," noted, Max Müller says that what the world needs is a 'a bookless religion.' It is precisely this bookless religion that the world already has, but does not realize it as it should. There is, I repeat, an experience in human souls that lies deeper than the province of any book — a religious sense, a holy ecstasy that no book can create or describe. The book doesn't create the religion — the religion creates the book."

After even a superficial perusal of the world's religious literature, one arrives at an altered definition of what portion can be called sacred with honest conviction. To apply the term to some books, no matter how widely acclaimed they are to being holy, is imprudent when they exhibit intrinsic evidence of not being what they are purported to be, and when their unstable identity renders impossible the singling out of a generally-agreed-upon candidate for consideration. As all are composed by human authors, and it is a matter of opinion as to how inspired they were during the writing process, if used at all the term "sacred" had best be limited to the meaning of "venerable" and employed to single out only the most ancient scriptures.

CHAPTER FIVE — notes

1   In the transcript of D'vivedi's paper in the two-volume report on the Parliament Talks, the transliteration of Sanskrit terms varies for the same word from place to place. In the quotations given here, they have been made consistent. However, the transliteration is not always correct. Notably the apostrophe following an "s", as in *Dars'ana*, should be written as an aigu accent mark over the "s", denoting a sibilant, thus *Darśana*. The "r" occurring between two consonants, as in *Smrtis*, is the lingual vowel properly transliterated "ṛ", thus *Smṛtis*. Later (sixth paragraph beyond in the text), in the word *Jnāna*, the first "n" is a palatal and should be written *Jñāna*.

2   Jagmanderlal Jaina, *Outlines of Jainism*, Chicago, 1940, pp. [135] - 145.

3   Joel Chandler Harris, *Uncle Remus, His Songs and His Sayings*, New York, 1880; *Nights with Uncle Remus*, Boston, 1883; *Uncle Remus and His Friends*, Cambridge, *ca.* 1892, etc. Ruth I. Clive, "The Tar-Baby Story," *American Literature*, 1930, Vol. 2, pp. [72]-78; Aurelius M. Espinosa, "Notes on the Origin and History of the Tar-Baby Story," *Journal of American Folklore*, April-June, 1930, Vol. 43, no. 168, pp. 129-209; Espinosa, "A New Classification of the Fundamental Elements of the Tar-Baby Story. . . ." *ibid.*, January-March, 1943, Vol. 56, no. 219, pp. 31-37.

4   W.T. Evans-Wentz (ed.), Lama Kazi Dawa-Samdup (translator), *The Tibetan Book of the Dead*, London, New York and Toronto, 1949, p. 122.

5   William Whiston (translator), *The Works of Flavius Josephus . . . to Which Are Added Seven Dissertations Concerning Jesus Christ . . . etc.*, Philadelphia, Standard Edition (original 2-volume edition, 1945), n. d., p. 535.

6   *The Lost Books of the Bible*, New York, 1979, pp. 282-286. Except for the Pseudepigraphy, this work also reprints translations of the books mentioned in the preceding paragraph, and the letters of Paul, mentioned four paragraphs below.

7   San Diego, 1977. Volume I consists of "about a third of the complete manuscripts which exist in Aramaic in the archives of the Vatican and in old Slavonic in the Royal Archives of the Hapsburgs (now the property of the Austrian Government)." From the 1937 foreword; the book then bore the title, *The Essene Gospel of John.*

8   *The Gospel of the Holy Twelve: Known also as the Gospel of the Perfect Life, Translated from the original Aramaic and Edited by A Disciple of the Master*, reprint by John M. Watkins, London, 1956.

6

THE RELIGIOUS ENVELOPMENT

FORMALIZED AND SOCIALIZED religion came into being during the organization process and coeval with the crystallization of tribal myths of the New Stone Age. The characteristic feature was the forming of a special class of priests, who ruled over aspects of the unseen world just as the chiefs ruled over temporal matters. Usually, once established, both orders became hereditary. The two worked out agreements for sharing the benefits of their respective authorities, but sometimes there was contest between them. Thus began a system of church and state that continued down into the present century. The overlay on religion often confused and stifled the religious essential, and it became mistaken for religion itself. It adopted the name of religion but not its spirit, and it clothed and often disguised religion until there was nothing left recognizable about it. This so-called religion had assumed the ways of the world even as it made liaison with the world. The classic example is Christianity of the Byzantine Church as opposed to what had been intended by the founder, the earlier manifestation subsequently being seen but dimly because of the glitter and splendor of the later development interposed between it and recent generations. It was the expropriation of religion by priests, the selfsame class from which Jesus attempted to rescue religion. The show they devised was the opaque envelopment that concealed the quickening heart within.

The core function of ancient priests was keeping those whom they served in good stead with the mythical gods by propitiating the latter, be it by sacrifices, magic, or symbolic means. The Parsee priests of India, formerly Iran, practiced a fire-refinement rite that goes back to the Achaemenid dynasty. Jinanji Modi incorporated into his talk at the Parliament an account of it as given in Dossabhoy Framjee's *History of the Parsees* (Vol. II, p. 212): "A new element of purity is added to the fire burning in the fire temples of the Parsees by the religious ceremonies accompanied with prayers that are performed over it, before it is installed in its place in a vase on an exalted stand in a chamber set apart. The sacred fire burning there is not the ordinary fire burning in our hearths. It has undergone several ceremonies, and it is these ceremonies, full of meaning, that render the fire more sacred in the eyes of a Parsee. We will briefly recount the process here. In establishing a fire temple, fires from various places of manufacture are brought and kept in different vases. Great efforts are also made to obtain fire caused by lightning. Over one of these fires a perforated metallic flat tray with a handle attached is held. On this tray are placed small chips and dust of sandalwood. These chips and dust are ignited by the heat of the fire below, care being taken that the perforated tray does not touch the fire. Thus a new fire is created out of the first fire. Then from this new fire another one is created by the same process. From this new fire another is again produced, and so on, until the process is repeated nine times. The fire thus prepared after the ninth process is considered pure. The fires brought from other places of manufacture are treated in a similar manner. These purified fires are all collected together upon a large vase, which is then put in its proper place in a separate chamber." Modi explained that, to a Parsee, fire is "the emblem of God's refulgence, glory and light, . . . the visible form of all energy." The ceremonial fires "are collected from the houses of men of different grades in society." As the fires are refined before being placed in "the exalted place in the vase, so before God all men . . . are equal, provided they pass through the process of purification, *i.e.*, provided they preserve purity of thoughts, purity of words, purity of deeds." The ritual is only symbolic to the Parsee: "Nature in all its grandeur is his temple of worship. The glorious sun, the resplendent moon, the mountains towering high into the heavens . . . draw forth from his soul admiration and praise for the Great Architect who is their author."

In ancient Judaism the primary service rendered by the priests was performing blood sacrifices. The practice began, according to the Bible, with the second generation of mankind, when the two sons of Adam and Eve brought their offerings to the Lord: "Cain brought of the fruit of the ground" and "Abel . . . the firstlings of his flock and of the fat thereof." The Lord had "respect" for the latter alone, which was the earliest incident of appeasement following the Fall, and it initiated a gruesome routine of slaughtering animals. The next mention of sacrifice is immediately after the flood, when Noah emerged from the ark, built an altar, and "took of every clean beast, and of every clean fowl, and offered burnt offerings on the altar. And the Lord smelled a sweet savour." It must have stunk like a fire at the stockyards. The first mention of a priest is in Genesis XIV, 18, in the person of Melchizedec, "king of Salem . . . and . . . priest of the most high God," who befriended Abraham. Sacrifices were still performed by laymen, as indicated in the abortive offering of Isaac, for whom a ram was substituted (XXII, 1-13). The Jews acquired a priest-leader in Moses, who led them out of Egypt and established the law. In Exodus he sacrificed in pharaoh's land to remove the plague of flies, and God instructed him how to build an altar of unhewn stones after dictating the Ten Commandments. On it Moses made "burnt offerings, and sacrificed peace offerings of oxen unto the Lord," in which the victims were bled, "and half of the blood he sprinkled on the altar" and another portion on the people.

It is in the third book of Moses, Leviticus, that Moses' brother Aaron and his sons are appointed priests, and the altar is set up "by the door of the tabernacle." Animals are bestowed voluntarily and are sacrificed before the congregation. Wood is placed on the altar, and after the bullock has been killed the priests "lay the parts, the head, and the fat, in order upon the wood," and the victim's "inwards and his legs shall be washed in water: and the priest shall burn all on the altar." Sheep and goats are treated similarly. A turtledove or other fowl is handled a bit differently: "the priest shall bring it unto the altar, and wring off his head, and burn it on the altar; and the blood thereof shall be wrung out at the side of the altar: And he shall pluck away his crop with his feathers, and cast it beside the altar on the east part, by the place of the ashes: And he shall cleave it with the wings thereof, but shall not divide it asunder: and the priest shall burn it upon the altar, upon the wood that is upon the fire: it is a burnt sacrifice, an offering made by fire, and a sweet savour unto the Lord." Not all of the flesh is consumed by the flames, as it is stated that a "remnant of the meat offering shall be Aaron's and his sons." This, of course, was sufficient incentive to insure frequent recurrence of the cruel practice, and the first ten chapters of Leviticus, are devoted almost exclusively to such sacrifices, with detailed reports on what was done with the blood, the fat, and such organs as the liver and kidneys.

In the balance of Leviticus accounts of sacrifices are shared with the record of God's "statutes and judgments and laws," which are to be kept on the bargaining system, with threats of calamitous consequences for failure to comply. Significantly, the peace offering is here supplemented by the "sin offering." Chapter XXVII begins with the scale of prices that priests are to put upon human beings and chattels resulting from "a singular vow" made unto the Lord, ranging from "fifty shekels of silver" for men aged between twenty and sixty down to "three shekels" for little girls from a month to five years old. Probably people were not sacrificed on the altar, as no instructions were given for killing them or cutting up their bodies. Later, during the reign of King David, humans were sacrificed by hanging. At the end of the chapter it is stated that the consecrated humans and chattels are redeemable for a fifth more than the estimated price, Also, the tithe system was inaugurated, whereby "of the herd, or of the flock, even of whatsoever passeth under the rod, the tenth shall be holy unto the Lord." The priests thereby became the administrators — virtually the owners — of ten percent of what the laity possessed. They no longer had to depend upon freewill offerings, as they could claim what had been turned over to them. The present system of rabbinical kosher slaughter, with its feature of bloodletting, is descended from the ancient practice of sacrifice.

In Numbers, Aaron and the priests further prosper. The Levites are given to them as guards and bearers of the tabernacle. They officiate at a new type of "offering of jealousy," in which they curse any woman brought to them accused of adultery and give her "bitter water" to drink, which, if she be guilty will cause that "her belly shall swell, and her thigh shall rot." And a new rule is made that any "offering . . . of the children of Israel, which they bring unto the priest, shall be his." Offerings were of gold, silver, and wine. Finally, the Lord's share of war plunder (amounting to one-fiftieth) is turned over to the priests. In Joshua they march with the army in the siege of Jericho, thus becoming the prototype of chaplains in World Wars I and II.

A type of religious organization different from that of professional priests came into existence in India during the sixth century B.C. Its members did not perform religious services for others but strove to achieve spiritual perfection in themselves. All that they sought from the world was simple nourishment, obtained from charitable householders as a single meal each day, and a plain garment with which to cover themselves; and they lived in caves or other natural shelters or in huts in enclosures, endowed by sympathetic lay members. They were called bhikshus, Sanskrit for "beggars." These bhikshus took vows to lead a pure and simple life, and they divided their time between listening to religious discussions, meditating, and performing altruistic acts and teaching, that is, engaging in missionary work. A paper submitted to the

Parliament by the Rt. Rev. H. Sumangala of the "Southern Buddhist Church of Ceylon," and read by Dharmapala, described Buddhism as "the oldest of missionary religions, the principle of propagation having been adopted by its promulgator at the very beginning and enforced by him in the dispatch of his immediate followers, 'The Brethren of the Yellow Robe,' shortly after his attainment of the state of perfect spiritual illumination, 2481 years ago [in 1893], under the Bodhi-tree at Buddha Gaya in Middle India. Traces of these ancient missions have been discovered in late years, and the influence of their teachings recognized by Western scholars in various directions. The spread of these ideas has invariably been effected by their intrinsic excellence, and never, as we rejoice to know, by the aid of force, or appeal to the superstitious weakness of the uneducated masses. No blood stains our temples, no profitable harvest have we reaped from human oppression. The Tathāgata Buddha has enjoined his followers to promote education, foster scientific enquiry, respect the religious views of others, frequent the company of the wise, and avoid unproductive controversy."

The Buddhist monastic and missionary systems served as models for Christian communities and apostolic endeavours some five centuries later. There was one fundamental difference: in Buddhism every member is allowed to think for himself, and not even the abbot of a monastery can tell the lately-arrived menial in the scullery what he is to believe, whereas in Christianity, universally, a fixed dogma is of mandatory acceptance, and it differs from one sect to another. In both Buddhism and Christianity there were varying schools of thought — or belief — but in the former no animosity existed among them.

In Nobuta Kishimoto's paper on the "Future of Religion in Japan," he spoke of Buddhism as having come "from India through China and Corea, and now [it] is the most popular religion in Japan. At present there are at least ten different sects which all go by the name of Buddhism, but which are often quite different from one another. Some sects are atheistic and others are almost theistic. Some are strict and others are liberal. Some are scholarly and others are popular. Some are pessimistic in their principles and teach annihilation to be the ultimate end of human existence. Others are optimistic and teach a happy life in a future existence, if not in the present world. But all unite at least in the one thing, viz., the law of cause and effect. 'One reaps what he sows,' is the universal teaching of Japanese Buddhism, although the application of the law may be different in different sects."

The religious overlay in Christianity displayed as much diversity as in Buddhism, but it offered not so many contrasting varieties as clashing oppositions. Dr. Alfred W. Momerie, Professor at King's College, London, in speaking on "The Essence of Religion in Right Conduct," recalled that Jesus said, "Not everyone that sayeth unto me, Lord, Lord, shall enter into the Kingdom of Heaven, but he that doeth the will of my Father." Momerie considered this "will" to be one of virtuous deeds. He pointed out that "Christ taught no dogmas, Christ laid down no system of ceremonialism. And yet, what do we find in Christendom? For centuries his disciples engaged in the fiercest controversy over the question, 'Whether his substance' — (whatever that may be — you may know, I don't) — 'was the same substance of the Father or only similar.' They fought like tigers over the definition of the very Prince of Peace. Later on Christendom was literally rent asunder over the question of 'Whether the Holy Ghost proceeded from the Father and the Son' (whatever that may mean). And my own church, the Church of England, has been, and still is, in danger of disruption from the question of clothes."

Discussing a similar topic, "The Reunion of Christendom," Dr. Philip Schaff of Union Theological Seminary, New York, reviewed the institutional vicissitudes of the church in chronological order: "The unity and harmony of the Christian Church were threatened and disturbed from the beginning partly by legitimate controversy, which is inseparable from progress, partly by ecclesiastical domination and intolerance, partly by the spirit of pride, selfishness and narrowness which tends to create heresy and schism. The church had hardly existed twenty years when it was brought to the brink of disruption by the question of circumcision as a condition of church membership and salvation. The party spirit which character- ized the philosophical schools of Greece manifested itself in the congregation at Corinth, and created four divisions, calling themselves respectively after Paul, Apollos, Cephas, and Christ (in the sectarian sense).

"1. Many schisms arose in the early ages before and after the Council of Nicaea. Almost every great controversy resulted in the excommunication of the defeated party, who organized a separate sect, if they were not exterminated by the civil power.

"2. In the ninth century, the great Catholic Church itself was split in two on the doctrinal question of the procession of the Holy Spirit, and the ecclesiastical question of the primacy of the Bishop of Rome. The Greek schism lasts to this day and seems as far from being healed as ever.

"In view of this greatest, and yet least justifiable, of all schisms, neither the Greek nor the Latin Church should cast a stone upon the divisions of Protestantism. They all share in the sin and guilt of schism, and should also share in a common repentance.

"3. In the sixteenth century, the Latin or Western Church was rent into two hostile camps, the Roman and the Protestant, in consequence of the evangelical reformation and the papal reaction.

"4. In England, a new era of division dates from the Toler- ation Act of 1688, which secured to the orthodox dissenters — Presbyterians, Independents, Baptists and Quakers — a lim- ited toleration, while the Episcopal Church remained the established or national religion in England, and the Reformed or Presbyterian Church remained the national religion in Scotland.

"The principle of toleration gradually developed into that of religious freedom, and was extended to the Methodists, Unitarians, and Roman Catholics.

"We find, therefore, the largest number of denominations in England and America where religious freedom is most fully enjoyed; while on the continent of Europe, especially in Roman Catholic countries, freedom of public worship is denied or abridged, although of late it is making irresistible progress.

"5. In the United States, all the creeds and sects of Europe meet on a basis of liberty and equality before the law, and are multiplied by native ingenuity and enterprise.

"The number is much too large, and a reproach to the Christian name. For these divisions promote jealousies, antagonisms, and interferences at home and on missionary fields abroad, at the expense of our common Christianity."

We might turn to the Eastern Church, in the land where the controversies started and the direct descendant of that early church, for a testimonial on how engrossed it had become in religious envelopments. The following excerpt comes from the talk on "The Armenian Church" by Prof. Minas Tcheraz of the School of Modern Oriental Studies, London. "The Armenian Church belongs to the Eastern Church, and its rites do not differ much from those of the Greek Church; but it is completely autonomous, and is ruled by its deacons, priests and bishops, whose ecclesiastical vestments recall those of the Greeks and Latins. It has a special hagiography which embraces the entire ecclesiastical year; a special ritual, a special missal, a special breviary, a special hymnary. It admits the seven sacraments, but administers extreme unction only to the ecclesiastics; does not recognize either expiations or indulgences; and celebrates the communion with unleavened bread and wine without water. It holds Easter at the date assigned by Christians before the Nicene Council, and the Nativity and Epiphany on the sixth of January. It prescribes fasting on Wednesday and Friday, and has a period of fasting and an order of saints which are peculiar to it. It believes that the Holy Spirit proceeds from the Father. It is not at all Eutychian, of which it has been falsely accused, for it explicitly professes the dogma of the two natures, of the two wills and of the two operations in Jesus Christ."

Such complexities are the fabrications of religious industrialism, indicative of the arguments and decisions made at backroom board meetings; they are the counterpart of the intricacies that have evolved into the front show itself. Col. Thomas Wentworth Higginson of Cambridge, Ma., told the Parliament about a worship service he attended in Europe which was reminiscent of mystery plays and confirmed its mystery-religion origin. "I was once in a Portuguese cathedral when, after the three days of mourning, in Holy Week, came the final day of Hallelujah. The great church had looked dim and sad, with the innumerable windows closely curtained, since the moment when the symbolical bier of Jesus was borne to its symbolical tomb beneath the high altar, while the three mystic candles blazed above it. There had been agony and beating of cheeks in the darkness, while ghostly processions moved through the aisles, and fearful transparencies were unrolled from the pulpit. The priests kneeled in gorgeous robes, chanting, with their heads resting on the altar steps; the multitude hung expectant on their words. Suddenly burst forth a new chant, '*Gloria in Excelsis!*' In that instant every curtain was rolled aside, the cathedral was bathed in glory, the organs clashed, the bells chimed, flowers were thrown from the galleries, little birds were let loose, friends embraced and greeted one another, and we looked down upon a tumultuous sea of faces, all floating in a sunlit haze. And yet, I thought, the whole of this sublime transformation consisted in letting in the light of day! These priests and attendants, each stationed at his post, had only removed the darkness they themselves had made." Col. Higginson's comment on the experience was: "Unveil these darkened windows, but remove also these darkening walls; this temple itself is but a lingering shadow of that gloom. Instead of its stifling incense, give us God's pure air, and teach us that the broadest religion is the best."

In Islam, the outward gestures of a good Moslem were given by Dr. Washburn in his paper comparing and contrasting this religion with Christianity. He called them "the first practical duties" and enumerated them as: *"Confession* of God, and Mohammed his prophet; *Prayer* at least five times a day; *Fasting* during the month of Ramazan, from dawn to sunset; *Alms* to the annual amount of two and one half per cent. on property; *Pilgrimage* to Mecca at least once in a lifetime. A sixth duty, of equal importance, is taking part in *sacred war*, or war for religion; but some orthodox Moslems hold that this is not a perpetual obligation."

Islam became as sectarian as Christianity, perhaps more so, as Mohammed is reputed to have said, "The Jews are divided into 71 sects, and the Christians are divided into 72 sects, and my people will be divided into 73 sects." The two principal groups are the Sunnites and the Shiites. The former accept the Sunna as their authority (Chapter Five). They consider themselves orthodox and compose the larger division. The Shiites are the followers of Ali, the prophet's cousin and son-in-law, whom they regard as the vice-regent of God and, with his descendants, as infallible and sinless. The Shiites fostered many sects, among which were the Assassins, the Druses, the Fatimids, the Ismailis and the Karmathians. Some of these became known to and proved their fighting mettle against the Crusaders. The Assassins were so named from being given a foreglimpse of Paradise through the use of hashish and promised permanent residence there if they died fighting for Islam. For a religion as abstemious regarding liquor as is Islam, such means seem excessive. Esthetic and idealistic were the Sufis (men of "wool"), who emerged during the late tenth and early eleventh centuries. Gathering concepts from Neoplatonism, Christianity, and Buddhism, they elaborated on the theme of the union of the personal soul with God. Sufism was strongest in Persia, where its members lived in semi-monastic fashion and contributed some of that country's leading poets, among them Hafiz, Jami, Jalai ad-Din Rumi, and Omar Khayyam. Later dervish (Persian for "mendicant") orders, distinguished for their twirling, ecstatic dances, professed Sufism.

The more particularized and personalized the religious embellishment becomes, the more firmly it is clung to, and the more enthusiastically its members seek verification by drawing in local converts and by reaching out as far as their means will permit to proselytize abroad. The early Christian apostles followed the well-established Buddhist practice of traveling on their own initiative and alone, relying on the charities of those to whom they preached for sustenance; but by the time of the Chicago Columbian Exposition, Christian missions had become a long-established career enterprise. A man was accompanied by his family to the scene of his activities, and he devoted the prescribed number of business hours to the profession; he rose in rank and in salary increase as in any other organized institution. The Rev. George T. Candlin, English Methodist Missionary to China, set the figure for the "Christian army in the greater crusade" as $10,000,000 per annum.

There were those who took a broad view regarding what Christian missions should be. Merwin-Marie Snell, chairman of the Scientific Section at the Parliament, said in his opening address, "Every missionary training-school should be a college of comparative religion. Ignorance and prejudice in the propagandist are as great an obstacle to the spread of a religion as in those whom it seeks. The first requisite of successful mission work is knowledge of the truths and beauties of the religion to be displaced, that they may be used as a *point d'appui* for the special arguments and claims of the religion to be introduced." But lacking such a background, the attitude was more often that expressed by Missionary Candlin: "To us the non-Christian religions are little other than archaic forms, however valid and fresh they may seem to their followers. They are crude attempts at theology which have gathered round the personality of men, who, in their own spheres, to their own times and races, were spiritual kings. Each presents a problem the Gospel is bound to solve." This problem solving was often a matter of creating greater perplexity. The Rev. Robert A. Hume, American Congregationalist missionary to India, in his talk on "Criticism and Discussion of Missionary Methods," noted, "There are phases of Christian truth and doctrine which are put before Orientals as essential to Christianity which I do not believe and which some of us do not believe are essential to Christianity. There are things taught in the name of Christ which are only western theology, which are only western comprehensions of truth as we see it. There have been things put about the nature and person of Christ, about the character of his atoning work, about the doctrine of retribution, about the doctrine of scripture, which have, instead of attracting, repelled the minds of non-Christian people."

There also were aspects about Christianity having nothing to do with its "truth and doctrine" but with flaunting its heedless brutality in the face of more civilized people, to which Asians objected. Reference is made to Christians' hard-hearted eating of animals as though the food before them had never had any more feelings than cabbages. Mr. Hume, in another talk on "The Contact of Christian and Hindu Thought," attempted to waive the accusation: "Seeing the early comers from the West killing the cow, eating beef, drinking wine, sometimes impure, sometimes bullying the mild Indian, the Hindu easily supposed that these men from a country where Christianity was the religion, were Christians. In consequence they despised what they supposed was the Christian religion. They did not know that in truth it was the *lack* of Christianity which they were despising." But a native Indian, Narasima Charya, a Brahman of Madras, in his short contribution to the "Criticism and Discussion of Missionary Methods" series (preceding Mr. Hume) not only implied that the missionaries were themselves guilty of the carnivorous deed but attempted to propagate it:

"So long as Christians, by tacit silence, make people believe that the eating of animal food is a necessary preparatory course to be gone through with before baptism, so long, then, will you find you have a stumbling-block in the way of the evangelization of India." This was a reason that their converts were "all men of low type," as Dharmapala observed in the same session about neighboring Ceylon, where the population generally, being Buddhist, were as offended by flesh eating as were the Indian Brahmans.

Dharmapala named the two most objectionable traits of Westerners on his island as intolerance and selfishness. To these he might have added the related one of imperiousness. European nations had extended their empires into Asia, as in Napoleon's invasions into Russia and the Near East. Foremost — and most infamous — of them was the British hegemony of India, where the English first did such things as encourage the manufacture of textiles, then slit the fingers of the weavers when they found that it competed with home industrialization. In the nineteenth century this was matched by the British buildup of the opium market in China, which kindled retaliation in the Boxer Rebellion. Kinza Hirai mentioned the expulsion of foreigners and the closing of Japan in the seventeenth century, due to the replacement of Portuguese by the militant Spanish Jesuits, who tried to take over the empire. And it must not be overlooked that among the motives of the United States for opening Japan in the mid 1850s was gaining a neutral refueling station for its coal-burning battleships, with empire expansion in the Pacific in mind.

Among admissions of this nature by missionaries at the Parliament was that of the Rev. Henry H. Jessup of Beirut, Syria: "We find ourselves confronted and thwarted at the very gateway of the Asiatic and African, as well as the Polynesian races, by that monster of hideous mien, the *sacra auri fames*, the accursed European greed for gold; gold earned at any price, gold in exchange for opium, gold for poisonous, maddening liquors, degrading and crazing with their flood of foulness and death men, women and children, made in the image of God." Prof. C.R. Henderson, of the University of Chicago, added, "The usefulness of Christian missions in India depends greatly on the discipline of the British army and on the habits of European sailors and merchants. After thirty-one years spent in India, Archbishop Jeffries makes this terrible charge: 'For one really converted Christian, as the proof of missionary labor, the drinking practices of England have made a thousand drunkards.' British rum has not only reduced, but actually obliterated the Hottentot. In East Africa German merchants import liquor in face of Mohammedan protest. It is said the Congo land was bought with alcohol, and even savages protested against the factor of 'Christian' commerce. To endure this crime without protest is not meekness, but stupidity and cowardice." And Dr. W.A.P. Martin, president of the Imperial Tungwen College, Peking, noted with regard to the Chinese people: "When Christianity comes to them from Russia, England or France, all of which have pushed their territories up to the frontiers of China, the Chinese are prone to suspect that evangelization under such auspices is only a cloak for future aggression."

The other side of the coin is that whereas these churchmen could condemn their lay countrymen for their depredations in the East, they, themselves, looked on as silent observers and did nothing to remedy the situation. When the opportunity presented itself, they laid the blame on the native populations. Prof. Isaac T. Headland, of Peking University, in his paper about China said that "The country swarms with people — poor people — people who are so very poor that there are, no doubt, thousands who starve every year. It is said that just outside the (Ch'ien men) gate, which stands immediately in front of the emperor's palace, more than four hundred people froze to death in a single cold night during the past winter. In front of this gate is a bridge, called Beggars' Bridge, where half-naked men and boys may be seen at any time — except when the emperor himself passes — eating food which would not be eaten by a respectable American dog." This sounds like a scene outside the Christian Czar's palace at that time, or outside the iron fence of the Marble Court at Versailles prior to the French Revolution. Headland continued, "But while this is all true it does not alter the fact that there are more temples in Peking than there are churches in Chicago. There are temples of all sorts and of all sizes, from the little altar built outside the door of the watchman's house on the top of the city wall to the great Lama temple, which covers many acres of ground, having an idol of Buddha one hundred feet tall, and one thousand five hundred priests to conduct the worship.

"Similar to this great Buddhist temple is the great Confucian temple, not so large, and without priests, but equally well built and well kept. The large Taoist temple, immediately outside of the west side-gate, is expensive and well supported, and contains many priests, while the large grounds of the Mohammedans, with their twenty-one mosques, are worthy to be ranked with those above mentioned. Besides these, the Temple of the Sun, the Temple of the Moon, the Temple of Earth, the Temple of Heaven, and the Temple of Agriculture, are all immense structures of the most costly type. These are all state temples where the emperor performs worship for all the people, and the annual sacrifices of cattle and sheep are by no means inexpensive." The architectural monuments referred to had stood for generations, and their staffs were no more than attend the Vatican City or chapels of the royal courts of Europe. Typically Christian was the objection to the one archaic rite of annual animal sacrifice left in China, not because it was cruel, but because it was not "inexpensive."

Prof. Headland lauded the Roman Catholics in Peking, who "have shown their wisdom in erecting cathedrals, which, though not so expensive [as the existing native temples], far surpass the others in beauty, design and workmanship. They have three very fine cathedrals — the East, the South, and the North, — the least of which would be an ornament to any

city in the United States." Thus it was wrong for the Chinese
to have built their great temples during times of their prosperity, but now that foreigners had invaded the empire and
reduced it to a den of vice and poverty, it was all right for the
newcomers to lavish money (some of it squeezed out of native
converts) on cathedrals.

The Headland paper was read by William Pipe during the
evening session on the tenth day of the Parliament. After he
finished, Swami Vivekananda got up and made a few im-
promptu remarks. "Christians must always be ready for good
criticism, and I hardly think that you will care if I make a
little criticism. You Christians who are so fond of sending out
missionaries to save the souls of the heathen, why do you not
try to save their bodies from starvation? In India during the terrible famines thousands died from hunger, yet you Christians
did nothing. You erect churches all through India, but the
crying evil in the East is not religion — they have religion
enough — but it is bread that these suffering millions of
burning India cry out for with parched throats. They ask us
for bread, but we give them stones. It is an insult to a starving
people to offer them religion; it is an insult to a starving man
to teach him metaphysics. In India a priest that preached for
money would lose caste, and be spat upon by the people. I
came here to seek aid for my impoverished people, and I
fully realized how difficult it was to get help for heathens
from Christians in a Christian land."

7

FAITH AND REASON

FAITH AND REASON are highly evolved human faculties.
Faith is inductive and resides in the emotions. Reason is discerning and operates in the mind. Faith, looking backward,
is belief, and looking forward it is hope. It has tremendous
powers of accumulation and facile assimilation. It accepts
without due process of logic; logic is a property of reason.
Reason organizes and compares. Faith compartmentalizes
everything to its taste. Reason accepts discriminantly and
synthesizes its selections on rational grounds. Faith and
reason are opposing attitudes, and they relate to those two
historic regions of Asia associated with mythology and philosophy religions: the Faith Zone is the Near and Middle East;
the Reason Zone is South Asia and the Far East, the latter
considered in its characteristic achievement and as having
outgrown the archaic stage of its development, and prior to
the backsliding it has suffered in recent times due to foreign
influence.

Rabbi Alexander Kohut of New York attributed the origin
of faith orthodoxy to the Jews. He said, "Faith is [a] spark
of God's own flame, and nowhere did it burn with more
persistence and vehemence than in Israel's devotion. There
worship and virtue glowed with mellow, unpretentious light.
No exterior influence could effectually diminish the unrivaled
radiance of Israel's ever-luminous belief in him and his all-
guiding Providence, even when encompassed by hideous
forms of idolatry and deteriorating influences, which sought
to undermine the innate monotheistic impulse of its immacu-
late creed.

"Faith, the creed of Israel, was the first and most vital

138

principle of universal ethics, and it was the Jew, now the Pariah-pilgrim of ungrateful humanity, who bequeathed the precious legacy to Semitic and Aryan nations; who sowed the healthy seeds of ineradicable belief in often unfertile ground." Thus Dr. Kohut exalted faith and made two fields beholden to it, a monotheistic assumption (which Dr. Sunderland more accurately termed "henotheistic") and what he called the "Vital principle of universal ethics," but which actually consisted of a narrow tribal code (Chapter Eight).

Prof. D.G. Lyon, in speaking on "Jewish Contributions to Civilization," agreed that these people "stand in a preëminent degree for faith." He said, "At the fountain of their being they place a man whose name is the synonym of faith. Abraham, the first Jew, nurtured in the comforts and refinements of a civilization [Sumerian] whose grandeur is just beginning to find due appreciation, hears an inward, compelling voice, bidding him forsake the land of his fathers and go forth, he knows not whither, to lay in the distant West the foundations of the empire of faith. . . . What was it but faith which in later times enabled an Isaiah to defy the most powerful army in the world, and Jeremiah to be firm to his convictions in the midst of a city full of enemies? What but faith could have held together the exiles in Babylon and could have inspired them once more to exchange this home of ease and luxury for the hardships and uncertainties of their devastated Palestinian hills? It was faith that nerved the arm of the Maccabees for their heroic struggle, and the sublimity of faith when the dauntless daughter of Zion defied the power of Rome. The brute force of Rome won the day, but the Jews, dispersed throughout the world, have still been true to the foundation principle of their history. They believe that God has spoken to the fathers and that he has not forsaken the children, and through that belief they endure."

Abraham did not leave the "comforts and refinements" of Sumer to go to the West; he accompanied his father, Terah, to the outpost of Haran, where Terah died. According to

Genesis (Chapter XII), it was from Haran that he set out after God promised him a home in the land of Canaan. When he arrived there he found famine and thus continued on to Egypt. Here he told his fair wife Sarah to say that she was his sister. As such she reportedly was taken into the house of Pharaoh, who "entreated Abram well for her sake: and he had sheep, and oxen, and he asses, and menservants, and maidservants, and she asses, and camels." Upon discovery of the deception, Pharaoh banished them. Abraham, being "very much in cattle, in silver, and in gold," returned to Canaan. Conditions were better, but not, Abraham thought, sufficient to sustain both himself and his brother, who had thus far accompanied him, so Lot and his retinue passed on to Jordan. In Jordan were the infamous towns of Gomorrah and Sodom; Lot settled in the latter and played a role in its destruction. His daughters got him inebriated and engaged him in incest. Abraham assessed the local women, and sent to Mesopotamia for a wife for his son Isaac.

The defiance of the prophet Isaiah was originally against the Jews themselves. In the fourth verse he addressed them: "Ah sinful nation, a people laded with iniquity, a seed of evildoers, children that are corrupters: they have forsaken the Lord, they have provoked the Holy One of Israel unto anger, they are gone away backward." The prophet Jeremiah was charged with going to Jerusalem, where the people "have walked after vanity, and have become vain," where even the priests said, "Where is the Lord? and they that handle the law know me [the Lord] not." It was inadvisable to cite the two prophets as examples of national faith when the Bible itself makes it clear that they were lone adherents at times when the tribe as a whole was predominantly faithless. Regarding the Babylonian captivity or the "heroic struggle" of the Maccabees, these situations were no different from what other peoples endured in the face of oppression, like the Parsees in Iran and the Gypsies in India uprooted by the invading Moslems, or the Canaanites by the Jews.

Dr. Paul Carus, in his talk "Science a Religious Revelation," remarked that the Hebrew word for faith is *ammunah*, "which means firmness of character." Judging by the Israelites' application of it in the Bible, it might better be defined as "recurring tenacity." There is little in it that can be looked upon as praiseworthy.

Christianity inherited its emphasis on faith from Judaism. The Hon. W.H. Fremantle, canon of Canterbury, in discussing "The Religious Reunion of Christendom," named faith as the primary means toward his subject's goal. "Faith is a supreme religious faculty," he declared, "and in St. Paul's hands it became at once the expression of the most intense and positive and of the most universal religious feeling. Such it was also to Luther and to all the great reformers, and as such it must be to us in the new reformation which looks beyond ecclesiastical systems to the Kingdom of God." Fremantle interpreted faith as "the acceptance of God and his Word. Whatever has been known to us as to his nature, his truth or his will, faith is that which says 'Amen' to it. . . . Each individual must for himself open his heart to accept God's message." He moved on to the crux of his argument. "It is certainly not true that to fix the mind upon the central objects of faith – God, Christ, love, truth – instead of on the Thirty-nine Articles, or the Westminster Confession, or the canons of the Council of Trent, or other denominational standards, makes religion weak and flaccid. The experience of many, if not the most of the greatest [Christian] minds, has been that they have tended, as life goes on, to think more of the former and less of the latter." His mode for reuniting Christendom was dissolving its later differences. As the rabbi linked faith with Israel's "vital principle of universal ethics," the canon called it "always a moral attachment. It is trust in a person, and this implies sympathy and admiration; and then it is an aspiration like that which Saint John experienced in the words, 'We know that we shall be like Him for we shall see Him as he is, and every one that hath this hope in Him purifieth himself even as He is pure.' And faith, again, as we see in the eleventh chapter of Hebrews, is the master principle of life, the source of insight into present and future realities, of obedience, of courage, of endurance; the source of all that is original in thought or action lies within; it is only the issues of faith which can be partially shaped by the ecclesiastical systems."

Chapter XI of the sermons of Paul to the Hebrews begins, "Now faith is the substance of things hoped for, the evidence of things not seen." The text goes on to say that it is through faith we accept the creation myth, by faith Abel offered a "more acceptable sacrifice than Cain" (for which he was killed), by faith Noah "moved with fear, prepared an ark to the saving of his house," and so on down through the Old Testament tales. Some ended happily; some did not, as in the case of Samson, whose confiding of secrets to the various questionable women in his life was his undoing and makes a good object lesson on the visciousness of faith. It is recommended elsewhere in Hebrews that faith be directed to "Jesus, the Son of God," who was made "an high priest for ever after the order of Melchizedec." Melchizedec was the "King of Salem, priest of the most high God," who wined and dined Abraham after he had rescued Lot and "his goods, and the women also, and the people" from being held captive. The king-priest is made out a more remarkable person than the Christ in the matter of his birth. The latter had a human mother and god father, whereas Melchizedec was "Without father, without mother," though how he was born is not revealed. It is easy to see where the New York rabbi and Canterbury canon got their zest for faith, but in the antique incidents there is little evidence of faith, and not much to commend it when found.

The Rev. John J. Keane, rector of the Catholic University of Washington, undertook to show that reason may have its shortcomings. After asking if logic can unite "the creature and the Creator," he observed, "Reason sees that the finite could not thus mount to the Infinite any more than matter of itself could mount to spirit. But could not the Infinite stoop to the finite and lift it to his bosom and unite it with himself, with no confounding of the finite with the Infinite, nor of the Infinite with the finite, yet so that they shall be linked in one? Here reason can discern no contradiction of ideas, nothing beyond the power of the Infinite. . . . Reason sees that to do so would cost the Infinite nothing, since he is ever his unchanging self; . . . it would be most worthy of infinite love thus to perfect the creative act, thus to lift up the creature and bring all things into unity and harmony. Then must reason declare that it is not only possible but it is most fitting that it should be so." The rector made the gross error of confusing the Infinite with a "He" god. His argument has appeal for those whose ego is so colossal as to assume that the Infinite is motivated for their special benefit.

Equally scornful of the efficacy of reason was Col. Thomas Wentworth Higginson, whose views on the subject had been influenced by a statement made by "Professor Tyndall, at the close of his Belfast address" — namely, "that religion belongs not to the *knowing* powers of man, but to his *creative* powers." Higginson took up the theme: "If knowing is to be the only religious standard, there is no middle ground between the spiritual despair of the mere agnostic, and the utter merging of one's individual reason in some great, organized authoritative church," whereas if "man's creative imagination is to be the standard, the humblest individual thinker may retain the essence of religion, and may moreover, have not only one of these vast faiths, but all of them at his side. Each of them alone is partial, limited, unsatisfying; it takes all of them together to represent the *semper, ubique et ab omnibus*." One has dire reservations as to how much could be gained from prying into what of religion is acceptable to the "humblest individual thinker" — less so were the word "believer" substituted for "thinker," which seems to be what Higginson implies — or of what, short of utter confusion, would an aggregate of all of the "vast faiths" make.

The semitic faith religions climaxed in Islam. Dr. George Washburn puzzled over its exact tenets. "It is, in fact, very difficult for an honest inquirer to determine what is really essential to the faith. A distinguished Moslem statesman and scholar once assured me that nothing was essential beyond a belief in the existence and unity of God. And several years ago the *Sheik-ul-islām*, the highest authority in Constantinople, in a letter to a German inquirer, stated that whoever confessed that there was but one God, and that Mohammed is his prophet, is a *true* Moslem, although to be a good one it is necessary to observe the five points of confession, prayer, fasting, almsgiving, and pilgrimage; but the difficulty about this apparently simple definition is that belief in Mohammed as the prophet of God includes a belief in all his teaching, and we come back at once to the question what that teaching was." With the Old and New Testaments taken together as the text of Christianity, each contradicting itself no less than the other, with equal justification one wonders what its exact teaching is.

Faith plays an important role in Parseeism, in its hierarchy (Chapter Two), in the afterlife (Chapter Four), in its scriptures (Chapter Five), and in its teachings and ceremonials (Chapter Six).

Except for the revival of Shinto during the eighth century and the popularization of the Pure Land sect of Buddhism in Japan during the thirteenth century — the latter postulates a paradise for the deceased from which it is an easy step to Nirvāna — faith is incidental in Far East religions. During the dynastic period in the Middle Kingdom, the Chinese believed in and conducted themselves according to the maxims of Confucius, but this relates to social etiquette and government, not religion. There is no place for faith, officially, in Taoism, its guidebook being the *Tao-te*, "Reason-virtue." However, Dr. W.A.P. Martin, president of the Imperial Tungwen College, Peking, pointed out at the Parliament that, by the end of the nineteenth century, Lao-Tzu's "followers have become sadly degenerate; and not to speak of alchemy, which they continue to pursue, their religion has dwindled into a compound of necromancy and exorcism." In other words, Taoism had deteriorated from a system of lofty reason to one of base faith in dubious material phenomena. It had sunk to a level of folk faith, which is and always has prevailed throughout the world.

In India and the sphere of Indian influence, great faith is demonstrated among the common people, faith in their deities and faith in their myths, as in the Judeo-Christian-Islamic and Mazdian region. In India it is also to be found in higher places. D'vivedi, in discussing Hindu scriptures, mentioned that in the Sampradāya period, *jñāna* (knowledge) was replaced by *bhakti* (devotion), and *karma* (deeds) by *prasāda* (salvation). This was during the eleventh and twelfth centuries, when religious refugees from the Near and Middle East had come into India and exerted an influence. The movement was represented at the World's Parliament of Religions by S. Parthasarthy Aiyangar of Madras, who spoke on "The Tenkalai S'ri Vaishnava, or Southern Ramanuja Religion." The five elements it recognized are: the Lord, souls, the goal of endeavor, means to the attainment of the goal (which is by divine grace), and obstacles to be overcome; each of these was divided into five manifestations or parts. On the matter of faith, Aiyangar affirmed what amounts to the Śri Vaishnava creed: "Rāmānujācharya [the founder] is venerated as a saviour, and still more is Krishna, identical with Rāma and an incarnation of God. Faith consists in trusting him; it has no limits. It is the true method of salvation, for which all other means should be abandoned. He who trusts in the Saviour, simply abandoning himself to him without effort of his own, will by God's free grace, without regard to merit, be led through all stages of progress, from the abandonment of hatred to the service of God and the godly. The good deeds of him who does not so trust appear sins to God, while the very sins of him who trusts may appear as virtues." Such intensity of devotion is equal to that of Sufism under Islam, the early Christian martyrs, modern faith

healers of California, and Holy Rollers in the Southern high-
lands.

The other major instance of faithism in India encompasses
the sects originating in the nineteenth century which, unlike
the Śri Vaishnava, combine imported (mostly Christian) elements with traditional Hinduism. At the Parliament, B.B.
Nagarkar of Bombay was sent by the Brahmo Samāja (or
Brahmo-Somaj), founded in 1828 by Ram Mohan Rai. He gave
its articles of faith as "belief in the existence of one true God,
... the unity of truth, ... the harmony of prophets, ...
[and in itself as] a dispensation of this age." Spiritual teachers
accepted included "Vyas and Buddha, Moses and Mohammed,
Jesus and Zoroaster," each of whom "was sent from above
with a distinct message, and it is the duty of us who live in
these advanced times to put these messages together and harmonize and unify the distinctive teachings of the prophets of
the world." Such harmony and unification is not easily imagined inasmuch as at least four out of the six "prophets"
named would not have agreed with the sect's doctrine that
"Self-annihilation and self-effacement are the only means of
realizing the veracities of the spiritual world." Neither they
nor their devout followers would have cared for the reference
to God as the "Universal Mother," although those at the Parliament otherwise generally accorded with Nagarkar's thesis
that "The deeper the realization of the Motherhood of God,
the greater will be the strength and intensity of our ideas of
the brotherhood of man and the sisterhood of woman. Once we
see and feel that God is our Mother, all the intricate problems
of theology, all the puzzling quibbles of church government,
all the quarrels and wranglings of the so-called religious world
will be solved and settled."

Hinduism proper, such as was circumscribed by Manilal M.
D'vivedi during the second day of the Parliament, is a very
complex matter. Various authorities arrive at different conclusions concerning it. It is interesting, in regard to the present
topic, that D'vivedi concluded with two "simple principles"

each of which begins with the word "belief." These are: "1. Belief in the existence of an ultra-material principle in nature and in the unity of the All. 2. Belief in re-incarnation and salvation by action." We are reminded what Kinza Hirai said about religions having an "*a priori* belief in an unknown entity," which means as a starting point. D'vivedi's Hindu intellectualism counters this by putting belief at the end. There is a world of difference between jumping at conclusions through faith, and reaching them by careful observation and clear rationalization.

Faith and mythology are fostered by the same institution, the church or priesthood. To this body they are inseparable, as faith provides the hold that it exercises over its parishioners, and myth is the principal object toward which faith is directed. Its generative power is issuing scriptures under the guise of revelations received from God or the gods, either as inspirations or actual declarations. The propagation of the process is the source of the institution's revenue, which would be seriously curtailed, if not terminated, were the laity to discover that its faith dependency on the organization and its legends is not essential to reaping the benefits proffered, if, indeed, these benefits have any existence other than in the inventiveness of faith. With Zarathustra, Moses, and other early Old Testament prophets, who lived at a time when faith was as far as human thinking had progressed, the insistence upon belief seems natural; but considering Jesus and Mohammed, who postdate the Greek philosophers in the Mediterranean region by a matter of centuries, the emphasis upon faith seems pathetically backward. It is, and by faith their religions have propagated archaisms for most of two millennia.

A special variety of faith was advanced in the Denominational Congresses at the World's Parliament of Religions through a paper written by the Rev. Mary Baker Eddy, founder of Christian Science, and read by Judge S.J. Hanna, editor of the *Christian Science Journal*. Mrs. Eddy claimed that about thirty years earlier she began to formulate her ideas on improving health through modifying traditional Christian beliefs. In the paper she stated, "I learned that all real Being is in the immortal, divine Mind, whereas the five material senses evolve a subjective state of mortal mind, called mortality and matter, thereby shutting out the true sense of immortality and Spirit. Christian Science explains all cause and effect as mental and not physical. It lifts the veil from soul, and silences the false testimony of sense. It shows the scientific relation of man to God, disentangles the interlaced ambiguities of Being, and sets free the imprisoned mind to master the body." The five Christian Science tenets are: (1) accepting "the Scriptures for our guide to eternal Life," (2) acknowledging the Holy Trinity "and man in the Divine image and likeness," (3) acknowledging "God's forgiveness of sin," his punishment of "Whatsoever worketh abomination or maketh a lie," and man's "unity with God," (4) acknowledging "the way of salvation demonstrated by Jesus", and (5) "to strive, watch and pray for that Mind to be in us which was also in Christ Jesus. To love one another, and, up to our highest understanding to be meek, merciful and just." Despite the prominent use of the words "mind," "mental," and "scientific," Mrs. Eddy's code is more concerned with credence than cognition. Mind enters the picture only as will or affirmation employed in the Christian Science healing system.

The principal source of Mrs. Eddy's ideas was Phineas Parkhurst Quimby, son of a blacksmith of Belfast, Maine, himself a craftsman (clockmaker), who applied a smattering knowledge of mesmerism, phrenology, and animal magnetism to the cure of human disorders. Mrs. Eddy (then Mrs. Patterson) was his adoring patient and defender in the press from the fall of 1862 until his death early in 1866. Faith played an important role in Quimby's treatments, but it was faith in himself as the healer. Legendary religious associations were Mary Baker Glover Patterson's contribution to the system, and they proved to be the magnet that attracted iron-clad Victorian Christians to her health-restoring cult by the thousands. The bane of her existence and cause of her death (at least so she charged her intimates to report) was Malicious Animal Magnetism engendered by her enemies.

A decade after the Parliament, Judge Thomas Troward, former resident in the Punjab, covered the salient features of Christian Science in "The Edinburgh Lectures on Mental Science." He discussed spirit and matter; subjective, objective, and subconscious mind; causes and conditions; intuition; healing; the will; and body, soul, and spirit. Though he mentioned indebtedness to the "most illustrious founder of the Most-Christian Fraternity of the Rosecrucians," who preceded Mrs. Eddy by two centuries, Troward's method is free from religious overtones.[1] The beginning of pure mastery of mind over body goes back several millennia to the Indian practical philosophy of Hatha Yoga.[2]

Fabricating beliefs is a wary subject in Buddhism. Dharmapala, in his discourse on "The World's Debt to Buddha," quoted the teacher's views as given in the *Kalama Sutta*: "Do not believe in what ye have heard; do not believe in traditions, because they have been handed down for many generations; do not believe in anything because it is rumored and spoken of by many; do not believe merely because the written statement of some old sage is produced; do not believe in conjectures; do not believe in that as truth to which you have become attached by habit; do not believe merely on the authority of your teachers and elders; after observation and analysis, when it agrees with reason and is conducive to the good and gain of one and all, then accept it and live up to it."

Dharmapala began his talk with a description of the setting that gave birth to such unmitigated rationalism. "Ancient India, twenty-five centuries ago, was the scene of a religious revolution, the greatest the world has ever seen. . . . The air was full of a coming spiritual struggle, hundreds of the most scholarly young men of noble families (Kalaputta) leaving their homes in quest of truth, ascetics undergoing the severest mortifications to discover a panacea for the evils of suffering, young dialecticians wandering from place to place engaged in disputations, some advocating scepticism as the best weapon to fight against the realistic doctrines of the day, some a life of pessimism as the nearest way to get rid of existence, some denying a future life. It was a time of deep and many-sided intellectual movements, which extended from the circles of Brahmanical thinkers far into the people at large." The culmination was "the overthrow of monotheism, priestly selfishness, and the establishment of a synthetic religion, a system of life and thought which was appropriately called *Dhamma* [or *Dharma*] — Philosophical Religion. All that was good was collected from every source and embodied therein, and all that was bad discarded. The grand personality who promulgated the Synthetic Religion is known as BUDDHA. For forty years he lived a life of absolute purity, and taught a system of life and thought, practical, simple, yet philosophical, which makes man — the active, intelligent, compassionate, and unselfish man — to realize the fruits of holiness in this life on this earth." Reason is the ultimate authority in philosophy religions.

The Rt. Rev. Banrui Yatsubuchi, of the Buddhist Church of Japan, characterized the founder of his religion: "Buddha was not a creator, and he had no power to destroy the law of the universe, he had the power of knowledge to know the origin, nature, and end of the universe, and cleared off the cravings and illusions of his mind till he had no higher grace of spiritual and moral faculties attainable." Thus the Buddha *perceived*, he had not *decreed* the Dharma.

The method found by the Buddha was the subject of the first lesson he taught to the bhikshus, or disciples, after his attainment of Enlightenment. Part of it, as rendered by Dharmapala, runs: "There are two extremes, O Bhikshus, which the truth-seeker ought not to follow: the one a life of sensualism, which is low, ignoble, vulgar, unworthy and unprofitable; the other the pessimistic life of extreme asceticism, which is painful, unworthy and unprofitable. There is a

Middle Path . . . which opens the eyes and bestows understanding, which leads to peace of mind, to the higher wisdom, to full enlightenment, to eternal peace. This Middle
Path, which the *Tathāgata* [referring to himself] has discovered, is the noble Eight-fold Path, viz.: Right Knowledge
— the perception of the Law of Cause and Effect, Right
Thinking, Right Speech, Right Action, Right Profession,
Right Exertion, Right Mindfulness, Right Contemplation."
One notes that half of the "steps" in this path have to do
with self-discipline — in one's utterances, doings, means of
livelihood and evasion of sense attachments — whereas the
other four are intellectual achievements. Each has a distinct
function: Right Knowledge Dharmapala defined in the list
itself as "the perception of the Law of Cause and Effect";
Right Thinking is directing one's mind away from frivolous
things and involvement in the mundane toward that which
leads to spiritual attainment; Right Mindfulness is perceiving
deeply into mental and bodily conditions of both oneself and
others, recalling previous lives, and mastering discontent, fear,
and anxiety; and Right Contemplation makes use of the
highest understanding faculty leading to complete deliverance.

Dharmapala commented that "the strongest emphasis has
been put by Buddha on the supreme importance of having an
unprejudiced mind before we start on the road of investigation
of truth. Prejudice, passion, fear of expression of one's own
convictions and ignorance are the four biases that have to be
sacrificed at the threshold."

The Rt. Rev. Zitsuzen Ashitsu, of the Tendai sect of
Japanese Buddhism, spoke on the subject of mind in more
esoteric terms, proper to his persuasion. His English is a bit
quaint in spots, but he puts across the idea that mind (Lao-tzu's
Tao) is inherent in everything. "The fundamental principle of
Buddha is the mind, which may be compared to a boundless
sea, into which the thousand rivers of Buddha's doctrines
flow; so it is Buddhism which comprehends the whole mind.
The mind is absolutely so grand and marvelous that even the

heaven can never be compared in its highness, while the earth is too short for measuring its thickness. It has the shape neither long nor short, neither round nor square. Its existence is neither inside nor outside, nor even in the middle part of the bodily structure. It is purely colorless and formless, and appears freely and actively in every place throughout the universe. But for the convenience of studying its nature we call it True Mind or Absolute Unity. Every form or figure such as heaven, earth, mountains, rivers, trees, grasses, even a man, or what else it might be, is nothing but the grand personality of absolute unity. And as this absolute unity is the only object with which Buddha enlightens all kinds of existing beings, so it is clear that the principle of Buddha is the mind."

The paralytic dependence upon a savior for redemption found in the faith religions has no place in Buddhism. The seeker after enlightenment must rely on his own efforts alone. The term "disciple" here is aptly applied, as the follower must develop rigid discipline in himself. The premise is included in the Buddha's final admonition to members of the order. "Be ye lamps unto yourselves. Be ye a refuge to yourselves. Betake yourself to no external refuge. Hold fast to the truth as a lamp. Hold fast as a refuge to the truth. Look not for refuge to any one besides yourselves. Learn ye then, O Bhikshus, that knowledge have I attained and have declared unto you, and walk ye in it, practice and increase, in order that this path of holiness may last and long endure, for the blessing of many people to the relief of the world, to the welfare, the blessing, the joy of gods and men. O Bhikshus, everything that cometh into being changeth. Strive on unceasingly for the consummation of the highest ideal."

This consummation refers to that which is attained in the final step of the Noble Eightfold Path. It has been called "Right Contemplation" (as by Dharmapala), "Right Concentration" and "Right Meditation," the last term being that most widely used today. Unlike faith, which suppresses the thinking process, meditation is a technique for intensifying it.

The Rt. Rev. Horin Toki, another member of the Buddhist Church in Japan at the Parliament, stated, "meditation in Buddhism is to call out the mysterious and tremendous force from the pure and absolute truth in the universe, and to correspond it with the mental power of ourselves. At this point of correspondence there is again the mysterious function or action which will cause the union of our mental power with that great force of the absolute truth in clear, pure and active manner. This instant of harmony is the instant when our nature of Buddha and that pure truth together become one absolute body; this is called enlightenment, and it is the effect of meditation."

Inasmuch as all of our normal mental processes are colored by the experiences that we have had, some becoming too readily acceptable when our associations with them are pleasant, others being rejected because of bitter connections, the individual thinker suffers from his conditioning. He is misled by the prejudices about which the Buddha warned. Much of this can be eliminated through the disciple's mastering the first seven steps. When he comes to the eighth, the mind ascends to an impersonal level; it leaves behind — as it were — the finite mind and contacts and identifies with the Infinite Mind, where resides all wisdom, all Enlightenment. This Illumination is so refined that it cannot be rendered into words, and even if it could, an unenlightened mind could not grasp its meaning. Thus the endeavor must be accomplished on one's own. "Buddhas merely show the way." He who becomes a Buddha can do no more than indicate the existence of the Dharma; others must encompass it for themselves.

Every man must accept the proposition that the human mind is limited in its scope, but it is folly to accept the hit-or-miss expedient of faith when there is available the heightening method of meditation to enable reason to climb to the absolute pinnacle of understanding.

Confusion arises from the looseness of application of the word "faith." Outside of what Rabbi Kohut called "faith orthodoxy," it may stand for assurance in one's own ability to accomplish something, in the way a friend or intimate will perform, in a perceptiveness of how a certain trend or movement will turn out, and so on, all of which are in a secular sense and based on acquaintance with phenomena. Such confidence is far removed from faith in the unknown quantities of religion, as utilized by the Near Eastern group to propagate their myths and avowed membership compensations. Here it becomes an instrument of brainwashing whereby they maintain their hold upon an unthinking congregation for the support of their own tyranny. Religious faith is a human faculty that is incapable of distinguishing between fact and fiction, or truth and falsehood. That which is believed on faith alone does not stand one chance in thousands of having anything to do with reality. Faith is a circuitous following after many masters, ranging from gods, demi-gods, prophets, priests and preachers to scriptures and legends. Faith is a soothing balm for fear and anxiety, but its curative powers are restricted and provisional. Faith transforms illusions into deeper illusions and makes them appear factual. It appeals to the sentiments, to what the ego wishes had being, submitting improbable assurance that it is so. Faith magnifies the finite and the momentary, making them false apparitions of the infinite and the eternal. Faith jealously guards its identity; it turns a deaf ear to counter faiths. It fabricates its own conditions. It harbors faith in its own faithness. Faith is the fastness of its own credibility. And Faith is the bottomless pit of gullibility. Adherence to a faith religion condemns one to its errors and to an isolation that "divides the human family not seldom into hostile factions."[3]

Reason, by contrast, attains to universality. It originates not in limited and questionable, so-called revelations imposed from outside, evoking emotions, but from that reliable agent, the ultimate arbitrator within the individual — too rarely employed in the field of religion — the mind itself. Reason is subject to no extraneous master. It faces facts squarely and has no cause to seek justification. It adjusts the self and its operation to actual conditions, rather than inflicting a distorted will upon the world beyond. Reason lays its sills upon firm foundations, it builds its walls of solid substances, it frames its roof of impenetrable fabrics, and its structure stands the test of time and clime. As it is not drawn inward, but observes from the inside out, reason seeks ever-broader horizons. Attuned to truth, reason converts easily to greater truths. Pure reason is the divine spark of the cosmos of which all higher beings partake. Reason is a precious endowment that must be guarded against the distractions and distortions of ulterior sources. It must be sublimated by its own unadulterated freedom in functioning. It becomes the fearless pilgrim, insusceptible to appeasement, impervious to vagaries, unaffected by threats and promises, cognizant of and dissatisfied by falsehoods, unfulfilled by approximations, and ever striving toward that utmost attainment which is the goal of true religion — union with the Eternal and the All-Knowing. Meditation, as the ultimate stage of reason, perceives Universal Reason. And it will be found that the counterpart of the essence of Universal Reason is the essence of Universal Compassion, which motivates the highest ethics.

CHAPTER SEVEN — notes

1   Thomas Troward, *The Edinburgh Lectures on Mental Science*, New York, 1909.
2   For a popular account of Hatha Yoga see Swami Vishnudevananda, *The Complete Illustrated Book of Yoga*, New York, 1960; and for a more technical résumé, B.K.S. Iyengar, *Light on Yoga*, New York, 1966, Introduction, pp. [21]-54.
3   To those having an interest in the questionable problem of faith reliance is recommended Dr. Gina Cerminara's *Insights for the Age of Aquarius*, subtitled *A Handbook for Religious Sanity* (Wheaton, Madras, and London, 1973), wherein in fifty "insights" General Semantics is shown to be as applicable to religion as to science for arriving at valid deductions.

8

RIGHTEOUSNESS, MORALITY AND ETHICS

A RELIGION may judge itself by its piety, but other religions judge it by the conduct of its members. Most religions discriminate between good and evil, the desirable and the undesirable, but their standards for them differ. They range from what seems best for the individual at the present time, through what is best for the family, tribe, or nation, to what is best for humanity, all sentient beings, and the universe as a whole throughout all time. They differ also as to whether they are oriented toward material or non-material — meaning spiritual — values. There is a breach between being religious and acting justly. The distinction was broached at the Parliament in the talk of Prof. Crawford Howell Toy of Harvard University. It was entitled "The Relation Between Religion and Conduct," in which he entered the subject by saying, "it may be noted that, in the ancient world, about the same grade of morality, theoretical and practical, was attained by all great nations. From this ethical uniformity we must infer that the moral development was independent of the particular form of religion. Another fact of the ancient world is that the ethical life stands in no direct ratio to the religiousness of a people or circle. Several great moral movements were characterized by an almost complete ignoring of the divine element in human thought. These are Confucianism, Buddhism, Stoicism, and Epicureanism. Turning to modern Europe, it is evident that progress in morality has been in proportion to the growth rather of general culture than of religious fervor. If religion alone could have produced morality, the crusades ought to have converted Europe into an ethically pure community; instead of which they oftener fostered barbarity and vice. The English Puritans of the seventeenth century were among the most religious and the most barbarous and unscrupulous of men. In a word, religion has, as a rule, not been able to maintain a high moral standard against adverse circumstances, and has not exerted its proper influence."

In the foreground of Prof. Toy's prospect of the matter is his own culture of America with its roots in England and Europe, the religious background of which is Christianity and Judaism. In the Semitic religions the norm of proper conduct is righteousness, or doing the will of God. Its formulae lodge in scriptures, which, as has been seen, were fabricated by scribes; they are adhered to through faith, an emotional response that fluctuates from unmitigated enthusiasm to complete indifference, and it largely is applied overtly. Its rules are more-or-less arbitrary, and they but loosely span the moral essentials. Righteousness belongs to the realm of religious envelopments. It is something quite different from morality or ethics. Morality, strictly speaking, is avoiding vices, and ethics is sympathetic behavior toward others; it is acting according to the better instincts of the human heart, and, in its broadest sense, it is the goodness that proceeds out of love and compassion, responsive to the feelings of all beings endowed with such feelings. Righteousness, morality, and ethics may overlap — and when the finer instincts of the religious envelopment are at play they do — but as Toy pointed out in his fourth sentence, several great moral (ethical) movements came into existence without dependence upon the "divine element."

The simplest moral code among the ancient Western Asian religions belongs to Parseeism. Zarathustra looked upon the universe as basically a virtuous structure, with the supreme god Ahura-Mazda standing for the good or the increasing spirit Spenta-mainyush, and evil residing in the decreasing spirit Angro-mainyush. As Jinanji Modi indicated in his paper on "The Religious System of the Parsees," quoting Prof. J. Darmesteter: "The history of the world is the history of their conflict; how

Angro-mainyu invaded the world of Ahura-Mazda and marred it, and how he shall be expelled from it at last. Man is active in the conflict, his duty in it being laid before him in the law revealed by Ahura-Mazda to Zarathustra. When the appointed time will come ... Angro-mainyu and hell will be destroyed, man will rise from the dead, and everlasting happiness will reign over the world." Elsewhere Modi said, "what Zoroastrian moral philosophy teaches is this, that your good thoughts, good words and good deeds alone will be your witnesses. Nothing more will be wanted. They alone will serve you as a safe pilot to the harbor of Heaven, as a safe guide to the gates of Paradise." An admirable factor that most religions overlook is that "Zoroastrianism asks its disciples to keep the earth pure, to keep the air pure, and to keep the water pure. It considers the sun as the greatest purifier. In places where the rays of the sun do not enter, fire over which fragrant wood is burnt is the next purifier. It is a great sin to pollute water by decomposing matter. Not only is the commission of a fault of this kind a sin, but also the omission, when one sees such a pollution, of taking proper means to remove it. A Zoroastrianist, when he happens to see, while passing by his way, a running stream of drinking water polluted by decomposing matter, such as a corpse, is enjoined to wait and try his best to go into the stream and to remove the putrifying matter." Bringing waste land under cultivation is cited as a meritorious deed. And a wholesome family life fits into the overall picture favorable to the increasing spirit. Modi says that the "Parsees do not proselyte others." But Zarathustrianism seems to have made some contact with Christianity, as symbolized by the visitation of the Magi.

Judaism is not considered an evangelical religion either, but its adherents and protagonists at the Parliament were eager to accept credit for its influences. Dr. Alexander Kohut of New York, expounding on "What the Hebrew Scriptures Have Wrought for Mankind," stated that "The most remarkable of the distinctions which divide the Jewish people from the rest of the world, is the immutability of their laws. And, indeed, Israel's legislative system, based upon a manifest recognition of a sole divinity, and embellished by those revealed emblems of ethical precept which have served as a foundation of all moral science, may well arouse the astonishment of poet and statesman, orator or scribe, prince or pauper. *Revelation*, the essence of religious belief, was the guiding star in the labyrinth of national and individual progress. . . . Bible ethics, justice, morality, righteousness and all the mighty elements embodied in virtuous life, are summed up in Judaism's great truths, faithfully portrayed and preserved to mankind in that ponderous volume of poetic inspirations."

Judaism's basic laws are given in the Pentateuch, the first five books of the Bible, ascribed to Moses, beginning with Genesis and concluding with Deuteronomy, the "second law," the law repeated. Before the laws were given, the people were dissolute, beginning with Abraham, the first Jew, as told in Genesis. Practices included lying, as in the case of Abraham himself, passing off his wife, Sarah, as his "sister" in return for Pharaoh's gifts (Chapter XX); opportunism and deception, as practiced by Jacob on his brother and father to gain Isaac's blessing and Esau's legacy (Chapters XXV and XXVIII); sexual promiscuity, as with Judah and his daughter-in-law (Chapter XXXVIII); and selling a member of the family into slavery out of envy and jealousy — the first plan was to kill him — as was done by the sons of Jacob with their brother Joseph (Chapter XXXVII). In each case the offenders benefited, thus the Bible sanctioned their iniquities. However, the alternative of the last, the worse crime of fratricide, would not have gotten the entire tribe of Israel asylum in Egypt while famine was raging in the homeland. Jacob, who had vowed in Canaan that he would be faithful to Yahveh so long as he took care of him, in Egypt has the opportunity of blessing his new benefactor, Pharaoh (XXVIII, 20-21; XLVII, 10).

After living in Egypt four hundred and thirty years, the Jews were organized under Moses to return to Canaan. According to Moses' instructions, as told in Exodus, "they borrowed of the Egyptians jewels of silver and jewels of gold, and raiment: And the Lord gave the people favor in the sight of the Egyptians, so that they lent unto them such things as they required [requested]. And they spoiled the Egyptians. And the children of Israel journeyed from Rameses to Succoth, about six hundred thousand" (XII, 35-37). When pursued by the Egyptians, seeking vengeance for the plagues that had been inflicted upon them, or, more likely, to try to get some of their jewelry back, the Lord saved Israel by drowning their pursuers. "And Israel saw the great work which the Lord did unto the Egyptians; and the people feared the Lord, and believed the Lord, and his servant Moses" (XIV, 31).

Having established his sovereignty over the tribe and given them good cause to fear him, in Chapter XX God dictated the Ten Commandments to Moses on Mount Sinai. The first four have to do with himself, these being: (1) to "have no other gods before me," (2) not to "make unto thee any graven image" or to "bow down thyself to them; for I the Lord thy God am a jealous God," (3) not to "take the name of the Lord thy God in vain" and (4) to "remember the sabbath day, to keep it holy." The last betokens the day of rest following the six days of creation. The first four commandments are righteousness rules or worship dictates and have nothing to do with moral behavior. The other six are: (5) to honor one's father and mother, (6) not to kill, (7) not to commit adultery, (8) not to steal, (9) not to bear false witness against neighbors, and (10) not to covet a neighbor's possessions, including his wife, servants (slaves), and livestock.

Chapter XXI largely has to do with ordinances regarding slaves and children of slaves. Nothing is said about there being anything wrong with the institution of slavery; it is accepted as an economic expedient. If a master strikes out a slave's eye or tooth, that slave is to be freed. If a man "stealeth a man, and selleth him, or if he be found in his hand, he shall surely be put to death." But if a master kills one of his own

slaves, he shall merely be "punished." Death also is meted to
him who "curseth his father or his mother," who practices
witchcraft or "whosoever lieth with a beast." It is noted that
"He that sacrificeth unto any god, save unto the Lord only,
he shall be utterly destroyed." Special dispensations are allowed Jews; if a man "buy a Hebrew servant [slave], six
years he shall serve, and in the seventh he shall go out free for
nothing." The last five commandments — including killing and
stealing — are prohibitions that apply only against other Jews,
as when the Israelites come upon and despoil the Midianites,
Moses orders them to "kill every male among the little ones,
and kill every woman that hath known man by lying with
him. But all the women children, that have not known a man
by lying with him, keep alive for yourselves" (Numbers XXXI,
17-18). The plunder of gold and silver and other precious
materials, which prompted such raids, has to be "purified" by
fire or water, depending on which each could "abide," that
is, come through in usable condition. The Jews proceeded
toward Canaan like a plague of locusts. In Deuteronomy they
boasted, "We took . . . threescore cities, all the region of
Argob, the kingdom of Og in Bashan. All these cities were
fenced with high walls, gates, and bars; beside unwalled towns
a great many. And we utterly destroyed them, as we did unto
Sihon king of Heshbon, utterly destroying the men, women,
and children, of every city. But all the cattle, and the spoil of
the cities, we took for a prey to ourselves" (III, 4-7).

The Ten Commandments are repeated in Chapter V of
Deuteronomy. The following few chapters exalt the Lord as
"a faithful God, which keepeth covenant and mercy with
them that love him and keep his commandments to a thousand generations: And repayeth them that hate him to their
face, to destroy them" (VII, 9-10). Chapter XIV lists the
"clean" and "unclean" animals that Jews may or may not
eat. Also forbidden is the creature "that dieth of itself," which
they should give "unto the stranger that is in thy gates, that
he may eat it;" or they might "sell it unto an alien." Farther

on, the laws become fairly petty, as in the following example: "When men strive together one with another, and the wife of the one draweth near for to deliver her husband out of the hand of him that smiteth him, and putteth forth her hand, and taketh him by the secrets: Then thou shalt cut off her hand, thine eye shall not pity her" (XXV, 11-12).

Hypothetical cases and mob violence may be rounded out by examining the private life of one of the Bible's great figures, Solomon. The priest Nathan and Solomon's mother Bathsheba took advantage of King David's dotage to persuade him to depose his elder son Adonaijah in favor of Solomon. Modern notes to the Bible have exonerated David by claiming that there was no rule of succession at the time, but the laws of Moses state that even though a man hates the mother of his first son and loves another wife, the older son is still "the beginning of his strength; the right of the firstborn is his" (Deuteronomy XXI, 17). Adonaijah submitted to the loss of the kingdom, but he went to Bathsheba and asked her to procure for him Abishag, the maiden brought to the palace to try to restore old David's "heat" and whom Solomon had appropriated for himself. Bathsheba appeared before Solomon and asked for "one small petition." Having obtained for him the kingship, Solomon could hardly refuse her and replied, "Ask on, my mother, for I will not say thee nay." When he heard the request, Solomon was furious at being tricked into giving up one of his women (of which, the Bible records, there were 700 wives and 300 concubines). Not being able to go back on his word to his mother, Solomon solved the problem by eliminating the source of the claim. He instructed Benaiah to assassinate Adonaijah (I Kings II, 17-24). Benaiah was retained to murder a few more notables King Solomon wanted out of the way. They included Joab, his father's trusted Captain of the Host, and Benaiah was rewarded by being given Joab's sanctified quarters, the "room over the host." Solomon prospered and "the Lord his God was with him, and magnified him exceedingly" (II Chronicles I, 1); and he was acclaimed the wisest king Israel ever had. Still, his application of the law that was the "foundation of all moral science" and which aroused "the astonishment of poet and statesman, orator and scribe, prince and pauper" left something to be desired. The moral behavior of the people being worse after its establishment than before, the law itself left a good deal to be desired.

There are, of course, passages of merit in the Old Testament, some of which were adopted by Jesus and will be noted below. None exceeds the picture of the peacable kingdom, wherein "The wolf . . . shall dwell with the lamb, and the leopard shall lie down with the kid; and the calf and the young lion and the fatling together; and a little child shall lead them. And the cow and the bear shall feed; their young ones shall lie down together; and the lion shall eat straw like the ox." (Isaiah XI, 6-7). But this was only a poor prophet's vision, and its chief claim to distinction in the Bible is its singularity.

Dr. H. Pereira Mendes, rabbi of the Spanish and Portuguese Synagogue in New York City, speaking on "Orthodox or Historical Judaism," stated that, "Christianity was born, — originally and as designed and declared by its founder, not to change or alter one tittle of the law of Moses." This strong Jewish foundation to Jesus' teacher was underscored by Prof. William C. Wilkinson of the University of Chicago in his lecture on "The Attitude of Christianity toward Other Religions." He noted first the similarities between the faiths of the Jews and the Samaritans. "The two religions had the same God, Jehovah, the same supreme law-giver, Moses, and, with certain variations of text, the same body of authoritative legislation, the Pentateuch. Yet Jesus, and that in the very act of setting forth what might be called absolute religion (in other words, religion destitute of every adventitious feature), definitely and aggressively asserted the truth of particular Jewish religious claim, in contrast to Samaritan claim, treated on the contrary as inadmissible and false, adding, 'For salvation is of the Jews.' These added words are remarkable words. In the context surrounding and commenting [on] them, they can, I submit, be fairly interpreted in no other way than as meaning that the Jews alone of all peoples had the true religion, the one only religion that could save. No doubt in using these words Jesus had reference to himself as born a Jew, and as being himself the exclusive personal bringer of the salvation spoken of."

In the first gospel of the New Testament, after giving the names of the twelve apostles, the evangelist said that Jesus "commanded them, saying, Go not into the way of the Gentiles, and into any city of the Samaritans enter ye not. But go rather to the lost sheep of the house of Israel" (Matthew X, 5-6). And when asked by an enquirer, "what good thing shall I do, that I may have eternal life?" Jesus replied, "keep the commandments." And when asked which, Jesus declared, "Thou shalt do no murder, Thou shalt not commit adultery, Thou shalt not steal, Thou shalt not bear false witness, Honour thy father and thy mother: and, Thou shalt love thy neighbour as thyself." Thus he cited the fifth to the ninth commandments and added one of his own, to love one's neighbor (XIX, 18-19). Later, in reply to a similar enquiry, Jesus said, "Thou shalt love the Lord thy God with all thy heart, and with all thy soul, and with all thy mind. This is the first and great commandment. And the second is like unto it, Thou shalt love thy neighbor as thyself. On these two commandments hang all the law and the prophets" (XXII, 37-40). One recognizes the two statements as direct quotations from Deuteronomy (VI, 5) and Leviticus (XIX, 18). The first embraces one through four of Moses' Ten Commandments, whereas the latter is not enlarged upon elsewhere in the Old Testament.

If the Jewish scriptures emphasize love for God, having a comparable love for man belongs more properly to Jesus. If the fruit of loving God is righteousness, the fruit of loving man is ethics. This ideal is brought out in the Sermon on the

Mount, of which two versions are included in the gospels, the longer in Matthew, Chapters V-VII, and the shorter in Luke, Chapter VI. According to Matthew, Jesus sermonized: "Ye have heard that it hath been said, Thou shalt love thy neighbor, and hate thine enemy. But I say unto you, Love your enemies, bless them that curse you, do good to them that hate you, and pray for them which despitefully use you, and persecute you." And "ye have heard that it hath been said. An eye for an eye, and a tooth for a tooth: But I say unto you. That ye resist not evil: but whosoever shall smite thee on thy right cheek, turn to him the other also. And if any man will sue thee at the law, and take away thy coat, let him have thy cloke also" (V, 43-44, 38-40). Love for man's fellow beings originated in India, and Buddhist missionaries brought the idea to the Mediterranean region during the third century B.C., as will be related later in this chapter. Jesus adopted it conditionally in his teaching, that is, only insofar as *human* beings are concerned. Also, Jesus threatened those who would not accept him as the son of the tribal god and tribune at the forthcoming Last Judgment with the intimidation: "whosoever shall deny me before men, him will I also deny before my father which is in heaven" (X, 33). Thus he *preached* turning the other cheek to those who would be Christians, whereas he adhered to the old Jewish code of an eye for an eye and a tooth for a tooth himself.

The Sermon on the Mount includes the statement: "Ye have heard that it was said by them of old time, Thou shalt not commit adultery: But I say unto you, That whosoever looketh on a woman to lust after her hath committed adultery with her already in his heart. And if thy right eye offend thee, pluck it out, and cast it from thee: for it is profitable for thee that one of thy members should persish, and not that thy whole body should be cast into hell" (V, 27-29). What he meant, apparently, was that thoughts precede deeds, and evil should be nipped at the thought stage. Emphasis upon moral thinking is Zarathustrian: "good thoughts, good words, good deeds." It constitutes another of Jesus' borrowings from older Aryan religions, again only fragmentarily. Jesus seems to have believed in hell as an actual place and was not speaking of it as a metaphorical state of being, but casting out the eye when adultery was committed in the heart is not getting at the root of the trouble.

The significance of the second commandment hinges on what Jesus meant by the word "neighbor." He defined it by means of the parable related in Luke X, 30-35, in which a victim of highway robbery is passed by a Jewish priest and Levite but is succored by a Samaritan. One assumes the victim to be a Hebrew, and his being ignored by the first and second passersby is characteristic of Jesus' recurring condemnation of sanctimonious religious officials; but the man who acted neighborly had the same god and laws, as noted four paragraphs above (and in Chapter Four), and Samaria is only forty miles from Jerusalem. Jesus' concept of a neighbor extended little beyond the strict Jewish pale.

Both recordings of the Sermon on the Mount in Matthew and Luke contain the verse that has come to be known as the Golden Rule and which Christianity looks upon as its concise guide to ethical behavior. The shorter statement in Luke runs, "And as ye would that men should do to you, do ye also to them likewise." It was referred to six times by as many speakers at the World's Parliament of Religions — by a Congregational minister, a Harvard professor, a New York City rabbi, a London minister, a former missionary to China, and the secretary to the Chinese Delegation to Washington.

Dr. Lyman Abbott of Plymouth Church, Brooklyn, said that "in no other prophet, have we found the moral relations of men better represented than in the Golden Rule." Prof. D.G. Lyon declared, "The adoption of the Golden Rule by all men would banish crime and convert earth into a paradise." Dr. Kaufman Kohler of Beth-El Synagogue noted that "Even though the golden rule has been found in Confucius as well as in Buddha, in Plato as in Isocrates, it never engendered true love of man as brother and fellow-worker among their people beyond their own small circle." Dr. George F. Pentecost of London was the most articulate regarding the equivalents: "It has been said that the Golden Rule was borrowed by Jesus from his religious predecessors. But even a casual comparison of the sayings of Christ with those of other teachers will show a vast difference. Instance that of Hilliel, 'Do not to thy neighbor what is hateful to thyself;' or that of Isocrates, 'What stirs the anger when done to thee by others that do not to others;' or that of Aristotle, when asked how we should bear ourselves toward our friends, 'As we would desire that they should bear themselves toward us;' or that of Confucius, 'What you do not want done to yourself do not do to others;' or a maxim mentioned by Seneca, 'Expect from others what you do to others.' These are all fore-gleams from the sun which shines in its fullness in the perfect law of Christ." Dr. S.L. Baldwin, the retired missionary, gave his own clumsy translation of the Confucius adage, calling it "a negative form of the golden rule." And the Hon. Pung Kwang Yu rendered an interpretation of the Confucian saying that is similar to Dr. Pentecost's.

The "positive" version of Jesus, which the Englishman gave as, "All things whatsoever ye would that men should do unto you, do ye even so to them" (Matthew VII, 12), presents snares unforeseen by the Christian enthusiasts. One is in the person of the maturing busybody, who thrives on hearing the most obscene and malicious gossip; this person would be actively applying the Golden Rule by latching onto every-body encountered and pouring into their ears the choicest and filthiest tales — regardless of whether those persons wanted to hear them or not. Or take the young masochist who virtually lives for the "club" meetings, wherein he and other members of like persuasion strip and spend an hour thrashing each other with their leather belts; exhilarated afterward, he pauses on his way home to beat up the first octogenarian he meets, then bestows similar favors upon two five-year-old children playing in the street. Leaving them bruised and bleeding, he goes on his way feeling pleased and virtuous in having fulfilled the master's bidding to the letter. It will be seen that the Golden Rule does not ideally express the "moral relations of men," that it would not "banish crime and convert earth into a paradise," that it does not engender the "love of man as brother and fellow-worker." Except for the axiom from Aristotle, the remaining four quotations given by Dr. Pentecost avoid the loophole that disfigures the Christian Golden Rule. Jesus would have done well to have "borrowed" a more carefully-worded version from one of "his religious predecessors." But, of course, it was not Jesus who took a single sentence out of context and proclaimed it the Golden Rule — this was the doing of his followers.

The "moral code" of Islam was summed up in Pres. Washburn's paper on "The Points of Contact and Contrast between Christianity and Mohammedanism" in the words of Omer Nessefi: "Honesty in business; modesty or decency in behavior; fraternity between all Moslems; benevolence and kindness toward all creatures. It forbids gambling, music, the making or possessing of images, the drinking of intoxicating liquors, the taking of God's name in vain, and all false oaths. And in general, . . . It is an indispensable obligation for every Moslem to practice virtue and avoid vice, i.e., all that is contrary to religion, law, humanity, good manners, and the duties of society. He ought especially to guard against deception, lying, slander and abuse of his neighbor." The taboo against images motivated the magnificent abstract arabesque designs characteristic of Islamic art, but by the fifteenth century Persian painting had reached its greatest height — albeit still strong in formal elements — and in another hundred years the Mughal emperors of India were fond of having portraits painted of themselves and their favorites in the realistic European style. The theistic imperative in Nessefi's analysis is verified by verses from the Koran: "God commands justice, benevolence and liberality. He forbids crime, injustice and calumny;"

and "righteousness is of him who believeth in God and the last day, and the angels and the prophets; who giveth money, for God's sake, to his kindred and to orphans, and to the needy and the stranger, and to those who ask, and for the redemption of captives; who is constant in prayer and giveth alms; and to those who perform the convenant, and who behave themselves patiently in adversity and hardships and in time of violence. These are they who are true, and these are they who fear God." Like other theistic religions, Islam has its dark side. Washburn notes: "The Koran is full of exhortations to fight for the faith," and "The Prophet led his armies to battle, and founded a temporal kingdom by force of arms." In concluding he admits, "It is true that Christians have had their wars of religion, and have committed as many crimes against humanity in the name of Christ as Moslems have ever committed in the name of the Prophet, but the opposite teaching on the subject in the Koran and the New Testament is unmistakable, and involves different conceptions of morality."

An outsider will discern in both the Bible and Koran good and bad features, and there are plenty of passages of the latter kind that negate the good and give the followers of these faiths sufficient scriptural justification to commit just about any enormity they want. It was these "crimes against humanity in the name of Christ," referred to by Dr. Washburn, of which Kinza Hirai was thinking when he ended his speech on "The Real Position of Japan toward Christianity" with the statement: "We, the forty million souls of Japan, standing firmly and persistently upon the basis of international justice, await still further manifestations as to the morality of Christianity."

To China the concept of *T'ien* (Heaven) may be thought of as the divine protective force of the nation much as Yahveh is to Israel, yet as in all things in Eastern as opposed to Western Asia, the viewpoint is broader, *T'ien* being not anthropomorphic but a metaphysical essence underlying nature. Also, it must be remembered, China was a cultivated and sophisticated nation, producing bronzes and jade carvings still prized among the world's foremost art masterpieces, while Israel was still a tribe of shepherds living in tents. And China was a great empire, its prominent families having gardened villas, dressing in silk and practicing fine calligraphy, while Europe's population was still residing in pit dwellings, went naked in warm weather and wrapped themselves in animal skins when it was cold, and could neither read nor write. The Hon. Pung Kwang Yu's lengthiest paper presented to the Parliament has much to say about morality in regard to his subject, "Confucianism." Our selection begins with his reference to one of China's classics: " 'Nature,' says the Book of Rites, 'in the evolution of living things, can only develop such qualities as are in them. She furnishes proper nourishment to those that stand erect, and tramples on those that lie prostrate.' Wise men and great men are men, and being men they can be touched with the misfortunes and infirmities of men. Wise man and great men, therefore, can supplement nature's work by supplying a compassionate heart, and at the same time impart a new life to the animated creation. Thus, if by disciplining themselves and by teaching others, they so live according to nature, and lay up a store of good deeds as to attain to good fortune and happiness without any seeking on their part, this is what is meant by providing against the operations of nature without fear of prevention on the part of nature, and this is also what is meant by saying that those that stand erect receive proper nourishment for their growth. The reverse is also true. Nature is not provided with a compassionate heart. The bounties of nature are shared by the whole creation alike. Man is only a part of the creation. Nature vivifies the whole creation, but cannot exclude a single individual from the range of her influence. Nature acts upon the whole creation, but cannot act upon a single individual in a different manner. She can only develop the innate qualities which belong to each individual. ... That wise men believe in heaven [*T'ien*] and spirits is attributable to the fact that the doings of men invariably react upon the spiritual influences of nature by bringing good or evil fortune, happiness or calamity according to certain laws. This is what wise men cannot lose sight of." Confucianism accords with Prof. Toy's remark that "Rational religious morality is obedient to the laws of nature as laws of God." Very likely it was from Confucianism that Toy adopted the idea. One notes in it the efficacy of positive thinking.

Whereas the Semite looks upon himself as the darling of the universe, specially excluded from the "range of her influence," who must show only nominal obeisance to Yahveh, God, or Allah and he will get his share of material goods, the Chinese regards his position in the cosmic scheme objectively, morally rather than righteously, and by performing altruistic deeds he will attain to a more respected and felicitous position among men. The Hon. Yu sums up the idea in the sentence: "Happiness and goodness, calamity and wickedness, are as inseparable as the shadow and the body or the echo and the sound." He says that the common people need not be troubled about the philosophy regarding man's place in nature: "As long as one fulfills the duties of life conscientiously, one has, in fact, followed the path of virtue, and avoided the path of wickedness, thus holding in his hands the means of securing happiness and keeping back misfortune."

Later in his essay the Hon. Yu quotes Confucius' "Golden Rule" as "Do not unto others whatsoever ye would not that others should do unto you." And he gives another precept illustrative of the predominantly social character of this philosophy: "A noble-minded man has four rules to regulate his conduct: to serve one's parents in such a manner as is required of a son; to serve one's sovereign in such a manner as is required of a subject; to serve one's elder brother in such a manner as is required of a younger brother; to set an example of dealing with one's friends in such a manner as is required of friends." Kung Hsien Ho, who also submitted an essay on "Confucianism," provided another saying of the sage: "Those who multiply good deeds will have joys to overflowing; those

who multiply evil deeds will have calamities running over."
Kung Hsien Ho enumerates the proper facets of domestic-
social-national citizenry, calling them "paths." "To govern
the country and give peace to all under heaven the nine paths
are most important. The Nine Paths are (1) cultivate a good
character, (2) honor the good, (3) love your parents, (4) respect
great officers, (5) carry out the wishes of the ruler and ministers, (6) regard the common people as your children, (7) invite
all kinds of skillful workmen, (8) be kind to strangers, (9) have
consideration for all the feudal chiefs. These are the great
principles." Thus the foremost virtue is developing a "good
character" in oneself, then honoring the same in others, after
which comes respect for those in judiciary, family and legislative authority, having regard for underlings and foreigners,
with the added advisement of patronizing fine craftsmanship,
a trait that China has maintained.

Indian civilization has been China's venerable companion
in Farther Asia, having a comparable highly stratified society,
but whereas China has reached its greatest achievements in
the secular arts, India has attained its — and the world's —
apogee in religion. Its peak was reached two centuries before
Aristotle and five centuries before Christ, with a purer moral
philosophy than that of Jesus. Concerning the ethical content
of Hinduism, here presented is a paragraph by Manilal M.
D'vivedi in reply to a question posed from the audience at the
Parliament regarding the subject of "Human Brotherhood."

"Says the *Bhagavadgītā*. 'The enlightened look with equal
eye upon a *Brāhmana* full of learning and righteousness, upon
a cow, an elephant, a dog, or a chāndāla (a low caste).' And
well says a popular couplet, 'He alone has eyes who looks
upon the wife of another as upon his own mother, upon
other people's wealth as so much rubbish, and upon all beings
whatever as upon his own self.' Other religions teach 'Love
your neighbor as your brother;' the absolute *Advaita* [the
philosophy of the All] teaches 'Look upon all as upon your
own self.' The philosophy of the absolute does not respect

caste or creed, color or country, sex or society. It is the religion of pure and absolute love to all, from the tiniest ant to the biggest man. Above all, the *Advaita* is expressly tolerant of all shades of religion and beliefs, for it looks upon all the different modes of thought as so many ways of realization of the Absolute, devised to suit the capacity of various recipients." Undoubtedly Christian parliamentarians took offense at D'vivedi's implication that their religion only went so far as to advocate fraternal love for neighbors. According to the Sermon on the Mount, love equal to self-love was restricted to a small group, and love for enemies was of vague degree. *Advaita*'s absolute love embraces not only all men but all creatures.

Having sprung full-blown during that religious awakening that animated India during the sixth century B.C., Buddhist ethics is as unsullied by lingering righteousness as its philosophy is untainted by authoritative gods demanding worship. In this "great moral movement" the "divine element" is directed where it has meaning — in reverence for life. The basic operation of nature is set forth in the Dharma as the law of cause and effect. A paper on this subject by the abbot of Engakuji, a Japanese Zen monastery, Soyen Shaku, read at the Parliament by Chairman Barrows, declares that "The law exists for an eternity, without beginning and without end. Things grow and decay, and this is caused not by an external power but by an internal force which is in things themselves as an innate attitude. . . . Just as the clock moves by itself without any interference by an external force, so is the progress of the universe.

"We are born in the world of variety; some are poor and unfortunate, others are wealthy and happy. The state of variety will be repeated again and again in our future lives. But to whom shall we complain of our misery? To none but ourselves! We reward ourselves; so shall we do in our future life. If you ask me who determined the length of our life, I say, the law of causality. Who made him happy and made me miserable? The law of causality. Bodily health, material wealth, wonderful genius, unnatural suffering are the infallible expressions of the law of causality which governs every particle of the universe, every portion of human conduct. . . . the source of moral authority is the causal law. Be kind, be just, be humane, be honest, if you desire to crown your future! Dishonesty, cruelty, inhumanity, will condemn you to a miserable fall! . . . Buddha is not the creator of this law of nature, but he is the first discoverer of the law who led thus his followers to the height of moral perfection."

We might consider what a lay member of the Southern (Theravādin) School of Buddhism has to say on the subject. The author was H.R.H. Prince Chandradat Chudhadharn, brother of King Rama V of Thailand, whose paper was read by William Pipe. The following excerpt is a reply to the question, "What is good and what is evil? Every act, speech or thought derived from falsehood, or that which is injurious to others, is evil. Every act, speech or thought derived from truth and that which is not injurious to others is good. Buddhism teaches that lust prompts avarice; anger creates animosity; ignorance produces false ideas. These are called evils because they cause pain. On the other hand, contentment prompts charity; love creates kindness; knowledge produces progressive ideas. These are called good because they give pleasure."

Prince Chudhadharn's fourth sentence contains what has been called the three cardinal sins of Buddhism. The first is hankering after existence, desire for corporal pleasures and material possessions, which in its extremes becomes lust, avarice, and gluttony. In the prenatal state it is the will to be born, the source of accepting the limitations of a new incarnation. The second is the emotional upsets linked with maintaining one's identity — resentment, fear, hate, envy, pride, and, as mentioned above, anger. Most of the ramifications of the first two have been recognized in the West, as in the Seven Deadly Sins. The third in Buddhism, ignorance, has been the caution of Mediterranean philosophers but one of the virtues of the faith religions, because of its non-critical acceptance of its outpourings, as detailed in the preceding chapter. Prince Chudhadharn connects the sins with pain. Striving after worldly gains and benefits wears one down, is replete with disappointments and invariably leads to loss. Anger is traumatic to the person in whom it is kindled as well as the one who sparked it and likely will be burnt by it. And although the pretty illusions that unthinking faith has grasped may be satisfying temporarily, the final confrontation with actuality can be shattering. Even more devastating is the faith-motivated ignorance that prompts religious fanatics to massacre people not sympathetic to their own brand of ignorance, as in the Inquisition, the Jihad and the Crusades. Neither such acts of barbarism nor anything comparable to them were ever sponsored by the religion of Enlightenment.

The simplest statement of Buddhism's stand on wrongdoing resides in what the Japanese priest Horin Toki called the "five sitas or moral precepts," in his paper on "Buddhism in Japan" read by Kinza Hirai. They were "taught in the Deer Park at Benares by Bhagavat [Siddhartha Gautama] when he first attained his enlightenment." Toki lists them as "Not to kill, not to steal, not to commit adultery, not to [lie or] talk in immoral language, and not to drink intoxicating liquors." The first three correspond to the sixth, seventh and eighth of the Ten Commandments, except that in Buddhism each one means exactly what it says. Dharmapala noted that the Buddhist "lays aside the club and the weapon, he is modest and full of pity, he is compassionate and kind to all creatures that love life." The fourth Buddhist precept relates to the eighth commandment, only instead of being limited to slander of neighbors it covers every aspect of one's speech. The use of intoxicants was not a Biblical vice, whereas coveting a neighbor's property would have been a major source of tribal dispute.

In addition to the five precepts observed by Buddhists of all walks of life were five others binding only on bhikshus, members of the Sangha or monastic order. They regard discipline, restricting the bhikshu to a single meal a day, eliminating the use of ornaments, luxuries, entertainments, and handling money. Austerities to promote spiritual growth were not limited to Buddhist monks but were common among Indian groups. For instance, Jain ascetics pledged to observe the five *vratas*, to abstain from killing, lying, theft, sexual acts, and coveting or owning possessions, and they adopted certain disciplines. But it was Buddhism that disseminated them throughout Asia, and some were adopted in Christian monasticism in Europe, along with the organizational setup itself, centuries later.

The rules just recited were a safeguard against backsliding and becoming more deeply immersed in the allurements of existence, but the finest and most concrete formula as a positive force for ethical good is the Law of Causality or the Dharma. The differences between this principle and rotes of righteousness are vital. Instead of interpreting words to suit one's convenience, as in the case of the object of verbs in authoritative commandments, they have unlimited connotation. Instead of being imposed by a particular agent — a "He" god — who will punish for failure to obey, thereby tempting transgressions that may go unheeded, the responsibility is absolute upon the doer himself. The universal spirit infused throughout all nature makes no exceptions. Its presence is known intuitively by the conscience that has not been perverted by malpractices, which includes evil performances and habits acquired through righteous rules erring in true virtue. The consciousness of the deed, in both perpetrator and receiver or victim, accrues on the Karmic record as a natural consequence, and it becomes a determining factor toward one's impending status. This person, who becomes aware that he foreordains his future by his present acts and that there is no revoking the Law of Causality, has an entirely different attitude than the person possessed of a hazy code of righteousness, further weakened by a stopgap element of grace administered by a proposed proxy. The Dharma is, by contrast, the key to universal morality, begetting universal justice.

The Dharma as taught by the Tathāgata was established during the third century B.C. by the Indian Emperor Aśoka, who sponsored the world's first great religious council (Chapter One). His grandfather, Chandragupta, had been successful in expelling the last of the Alexandrian garrisons from the northwest of the realm and founded the Mauryan Dynasty. Aśoka brought nearly the entire subcontinent of India under his rule, a nation of about 300,000,000 people. He sent missionaries to neighboring lands and beyond, especially backtracking the route of Alexander's conquest as far as Alexandria in Egypt. Dharmapala reminds us that "His only son and daughter were made apostles of the gentle creed; and, clad in the orange-colored robe, they went to Ceylon, converted the king and established Buddhism there." The watchword of Aśoka's regime was *ahimsa*, harmlessness, which prompted the enactment of civil laws protecting the rights of animals as well as men. Slavery and caste, living sacrifices, and slaughtering in general were abolished. The state built resthouses, dug wells, and erected and stocked hospitals, some of which were for beasts. Stone columns were set up on which were inscribed edicts expressing the ruler's sentiments and ordinances. One mentions that henceforth no animal will be killed to provision the royal table. Another reads, "Thanks to the instruction of the religion spread by the king, there exists today a respect for living creatures, a tenderness towards them, a regard for relations and for teachers, a dutiful obedience to fathers and mothers, and obeisance to venerable men, such as have not existed for centuries. The teaching of religion is the most meritorious of acts, and there is no practice of religion without virtue." One notes the typically Farther Asian equation of religion with goodness. "The practice of virtue is difficult, and those who practice virtue perform what is difficult. Thus in the past there were no ministers of religion; but I have created ministers of religion. They mix with all sects. They bring comfort to him who is in fetters." Being "in fetters" is a characteristic Buddhist expression referring to one's involvement in *samsāra*, the illusory environment. Another begins, "The king honors all sects, he propitiates them by alms. But the beloved of the gods attaches less importance to such gifts and honors than to the endeavor to promote their essential moral virtues." Another edict gives the virtues as "Mercy and charity, truth and purity, kindness and goodness."

Dharmapala commented that Aśoka's "glory was to spread the teachings of the Buddha throughout the world by the force of love, and indeed nobody could say that he had failed. . . . When Buddhism flourished in India, the arts, sciences and civilization reached their zenith, . . . Wherever Buddhism has gone, the nations have imbibed its spirit, and the people have become gentler and milder." For high cultural attainments, prolonged periods of peace and prosperity, and the amenities of a humane society, no civilization elsewhere can compare with those under the aegis of Buddhism in Asia: the Gupta period in India, the T'ang and Sung in China, when the Emperors resided at Nara and Kyoto in Japan, the Sailendra in Java, the great cities of Anuradapura and Polonnaruwa in Ceylon, and Pagan in Burma. Nor should we overlook that most splendid of medieval capitals, Angkor Thom, in Cambodia, whose builder, Jayavarman VII, emulated Aśoka in establishing laws and instituting shelters to promote the well-being of humanity and fauna.

The busy Occidental has no time for such irrelevancies. For quiet recreation he takes the children to the zoo, to be amused by the jungle giants restlessly pacing up and down the concrete floor in their iron-bar cages, the comical antics of elephants begging peanuts, and the wry expressions on the faces of the monkeys, imprisoned for crimes not they but men have committed against them. Or, for more strenuous recreation, he takes his gun and goes hunting, to track and kill the forest denizens, which he calls "sport." He may bring home a trophy of his skill, a deer's head, to mount and hang on his wall to attest to what a brute he is. His women folk patronize the trapper, the mutilators of baby seals, the skinner, the furrier — all of those immoral people who make a living murdering and robbing innocent quadrupeds of their natural apparel to become secondhand garments for pitiless bipeds. His contributions support heartless vivisectors, those who conduct caustic experiments on living animals, wherein — as Mark Twain once described it — the victims are "boiled, baked, scalded, burnt with turpentine, frozen, cauterized; they have been partly drowned and brought back to consciousness to have the process repeated; they have been cut open and mangled in every part of the body, and have been kept alive in a mutilated state for experiments lasting days or weeks." Much of this is student "training." Martyrs include dogs, cats, guinea pigs, apes, and so on; mute rabbits have been heard to shriek from excruciating pain during vivisection practices. Mostly such atrocities are performed behind closed doors and in soundproof laboratories, and the public may be excused for its indolence regarding them. But elsewhere the results of such malevolence are exposed to plain view. In the modern supermarket are long rows of shelves stacked high with dismembered carcasses of lambs, calves, cows, and pigs, packaged in transparent plastic, revealing bones, muscles, fat, oozing blood and lymph, with eager shoppers selecting these products of agony, suffering, and death to feed to equally calloused diners. All of these people would be horrified at the thought of their house pets being so killed, maimed, and processed for dining-room consumption as the remains of the less fortunate beings they have purchased; but a more general view of the matter has not entered their heads. At best they offer the excuse that humans are so far above the other animals that it is quite appropriate for the one to be doomed to become the other's food. By the same reasoning, homonoids from outer space, equally superior to man, would be entirely justified in condemning humans to the slaughterhouse and packing plant for their feasts. If this planet is ever invaded by galaxy foreigners with weapons so efficient that they become absolute masters within a matter of minutes, it will be unlucky for man if their recreational and sporting practices, delight in experimentation, and taste in clothing as well as food have no more regard for universal ethics than have the prevailing Western religions.

9

RELIGION AND WAR

THEISTIC RELIGIONS have done very little to promote peace among the nations of the earth. As Prof. Crawford Howell Toy observed, they have not contributed much to ethical progress, which has depended on "the growth rather of general culture than on religious fervor." Ethics in the Western World is concerned with the relations between men in the same society, without being extended to international relationships. What has been accomplished in this province has come about as a political safeguard, and if it has depended little on cultural development, it has been even less beholden to the prevailing religions. These have clung to a basic ethical code that was improvised for a migrant tribe thirty-three centuries ago, which tribe became more predatory after accepting that code than it had been before. Mythology religions are founded on a rapacious concept of nature, and their tribal deities are lords of strife. They may be appealed to for aid in waging war and taking advantage of other social units, which are considered congenial neighbors only as subjected peoples paying tribute to themselves and homage to their gods; but the mythical gods make no provision for advancing peace between nations. How could they? They are the rivals of the gods of other religions, of other nations. War is as natural to adherents of henotheistic, monotheistic, and polytheistic faiths as peace is foreign to their doctrine.

Jinanji Modi began his paper on Parseeism read before the Parliament by quoting Max Müller: "There were periods in the history of the world when the worship of Ormuzd [Ahura-Mazda] threatened to rise triumphant on the ruins of the temples of all other gods. If the battles of Marathon and

181

Salamis had been lost and Greece had succumbed to Persia, the state religion of the empire of Cyrus, which was the worship of Ormuzd, might have become the religion of the whole civilized world. Persia had absorbed the Assyrian and Babylonian empires; the Jews were either in Persian captivity or under Persian sway at home; the sacred monuments of Egypt had been mutilated by the hands of Persian soldiers. The edicts of the king — the king of kings — were sent to India, to Greece, to Scythia, and to Egypt, and if 'by the grace of Ahura Mazda' Darius had crushed the liberty of Greece, the purer faith of Zoroaster might easily have superseded the Olympian fables."

Modi himself continued: "With the overthrow of the Persian monarchy under its last Sassanian king, Vardagard, at the battle of Nehāvand in A.D. 642, the religion received a check at the hands of the Arabs, who, with sword in one hand and Koran in the other, made the religion of Islām both the state religion and the national religion of the country. But many of those who adhered to the faith of their fathers quitted their ancient fatherland for the hospitable shores of India."

It is exhilarating to contemplate the near subjugation of foreigners to the will and religion of one's ancestors, but depressing to recall their actual defeat and humiliation by others. But that is the way this world of involvement works. Little is known about the life of Zarathustra. He may have been born about 570 B.C., either in the northeast or northwest of Iran. He is said to have had three wives and several sons and daughters. At thirty he met the Archangel Vohu Manah (Good Thought), who took him to Ahura-Mazda, by whom Zarathustra was instructed in the doctrines of pure religion. His first convert, ten years later, was his cousin Medyomah, and two years afterward his second was the Achaemenid King Vishtaspa. Vishtaspa raised the worship of Ahura-Mazda to the state religion.[1] According to the *Shah Namah*, or "Book of Kings," Zarathustra was the hero of the "holy wars" against the invading Turanians; he was killed by them while officiating as the priest in the fire temple of Nush Azar at Balkh.[2]

Vishtaspa's son was Darius I the Great. As has been said (Chapter Two), the Achaemenid Dynasty was terminated by Alexander in 331 B.C.; and it was superseded by another Persian house, the Sassanians, in 229 A.D., which ruled for four hundred years. The first Sassanian king was Ardashir I, who ordered collection of the Zarathustrian writings, copies of which had been distributed in distant lands. Near the ruins of the palace of Ardashir I at Firuzabad is a rocky gorge upon which are carved several scenes of the king's military victories. There is also a relief depicting the investiture of the king, a symmetrical composition of Ardashir I and Ormuzd facing one another on horseback. The god presents the king with a circlet representing power, and prone beneath the horse of Ormuzd lies his evil opponent, Ahriman, whereas under the mount of Ardashir I lies Artabanus V, the Parthian king whom he supplanted. Typical of ancient reasoning, a man is allied with his god against his enemy and his enemy's deity.

The Jewish attitude toward war is parcel of its righteous attitude based upon the law of Moses. Rabbi G. Gottheil of New York City, lauding "The Greatness and Influence of Moses" before the Parliament, declared, "We should worship him, for where has the nation's love and veneration ever produced a picture like it? . . . Every Christian church on earth and every mosque is his monument. Peace is the foundation stone, the historic foundation stone on which they all rest." As related in Exodus, Moses was born in Egypt at the time when the Hebrew increase was of such threat that Pharaoh had passed an ordinance that all newborn male children should be cast into the river; but Moses was saved by being placed in an ark to be found and adopted by Pharaoh's daughter. In the same sentence reporting his reaching maturity, Moses "spied an Egyptian smiting an Hebrew," and in the next sentence he killed and buried the Egyptian (II, 11-12). Wanted for murder, Moses fled to Midian, where he married the daughter of a priest and started a family. At the burning bush he encountered Yahveh, who charged him with delivering the Jews from bondage in Egypt. Pharaoh was indisposed to let them go, but instead of selecting a civilized means of dissuading him, Yahveh inflicted the Egyptians with a series of plagues, ending with killing the firstborns in their families and herds. Then Pharaoh ordered the Jews out of the country. After having "spoiled the Egyptians" of quantities of jewelry, the horde of "about six hundred thousand on foot that were men, besides children . . . and flocks, and herds, even very much cattle" departed. The Egyptians pursued them but were drowned in the sea. Yahveh provided the migrants with food, bread of manna in the morning and the flesh of quails in the evening. At Sinai, Yahveh gave Moses the Ten Commandments and the jurisprudence that became the Hebrew code of righteousness. Then they wandered in the wilderness forty years before reaching God's "Promised Land." Rabbi Gottheil's comment on Moses was, "Think of it! Among a nation escaped from bondage, too degraded even to be led to war, that needed the education, the hammering, as it were, into a people for forty years, to go among them with the sublimest truth that the human mind ever can conceive and say to them: 'Though you are so benighted and enslaved, any truth that I know is not too good for you nor any child of God.' Whence did the man derive that inspiration?"

Moses was inspired to train the Israelites in warfare, and when they got to Canaan and were resisted by King Arad, who took a few of them prisoners, "Israel vowed a vow unto the Lord, and said, If thou wilt indeed deliver this people into my hand, then I will utterly destroy their cities. And the Lord hearkened to the voice of Israel, and delivered up the Canaanites; and they utterly destroyed them and their cities; and he called the name of the place Hormah" — "Wasteland" (Numbers XXI, 2-3). Moses headed an army of "twelve thousand armed for war" (XXXI, 5), only technically it was not war but the most brutal form of massacre and pillaging of towns. Arriving at the Jordan River, the tribesmen hesitated; Moses urged them on: "if ye will go armed before the Lord to war, and will go all of you armed over Jordan before the Lord, until he hath driven out his enemies from before him, And the land he subdued before the Lord; then afterward ye shall return, and be guiltless before the Lord, and before Israel; and this land shall be your possession before the Lord. But if ye will not do so, behold, ye have sinned against the Lord: and be sure your sin will find you out" (XXXII, 20-23). Yahveh's "enemies" were the indigenous inhabitants of a prosperous and peaceable land coveted by his chosen predators, and, if the latter refrained from engaging in the war god's outrageous campaign, amounting to genocide, they became depraved sinners. Exonerating fiendish murder and looting for self-gain on religious grounds is the most degraded sophistry and perversion of decency that was ever devised.

Inasmuch as holy writ itself reveals Moses to be the master warmonger and mentor of marauders, instead of praising him as the peaceful foundation of churches and mosques, he should be condemned for having provided the lawful excuses for every bloody atrocity later committed by Jews, Christians, and Moslems motivated by "I"-god personal interest.

After Moses' death, Joshua was appointed the new leader, and his first command was that all soldiers born after leaving Egypt should be circumcised. After recovering from this ordeal, they continued the martial carnage. Chapter XII of the Book of Joshua lists "the kings of the land which the children of Israel smote, and possessed their land on the other side Jordan toward the rising of the sun, from the river Arnon unto Mount Hermon, and all the plain on the east," which had been under Moses. It is followed by a list of the kings on the west side of Jordan "from Baalgad in the valley of Lebanon even unto the mount Halak, that goeth up to Seir," annihilated by Joshua. The two lists total "all the kings thirty and one." Included among Joshua's victims was the "King of Jerusalem" (which name, incidentally, means the city "founded in peace"), who was beheaded with five other kings, at which event Joshua chided the executioners to "be strong and of good courage: for thus shall the Lord do to all your enemies against whom ye fight" (X, 25).

As the Jews multiplied, they continued to take over adjoining lands and amass plunder, and their combatants increased proportionally. Among the genealogies given in I Chronicles it is noted that one contingent went to the Valley of Gedor "in the days of Hazekiah king of Judah, and smote their tents, and the habitations, that were found there, and destroyed them utterly unto this day, and dwelt in their rooms: because there was pasture there for their flocks" (IV, 41). Again, "The sons of Reuben, and the Gadites, and half the tribe of Manasseh, of valiant men, men able to bear buckler and sword, and to shoot with bow, and skilful in war, were four and forty thousand seven hundred and threescore, that went out to war" (V, 18). The descendants of Issachar formed "bands of soldiers for war, six and thirty thousand men" (VII, 4). The "sons of Jediael [Benjamin's son], by the heads of their fathers, mighty men of valour, were seventeen thousand and two hundred soldiers, fit to go out for war and battle" (VII, 11). And the descendants of Asher "that were apt to the war and to battle was twenty and six thousand men" (VII, 40). Among the victims of the horde of Reubenites, Gadites and half the tribe of Manasseh were the Hagarites, from whom were taken "away their cattle; and their camels fifty thousand, and of sheep two hundred and fifty thousand, and of asses two thousand, and of men an hundred thousand. For there fell down many slain, because the war was of God" (V, 21-22). Without Yahveh, all that manpower might have been put to honest labor.

The European Christian conquest of the New World adopted the Bible strategy. Due to military technical advances, for ruthlessness, cruelty, greed, and destruction, Spanish Catholics in Central and South America surpassed the Israelites in Canaan. However, as in Africa and India, it differed in that surviving humbled "Niggers" were allowed to live, becoming slaves and retainers supporting successive generations of white masters.

However much the Old Testament vaunts the Jews'

inhumane exploits, it yet contains passages that admit of a finer awareness. In Proverbs, for instance, it is noted that: "A soft answer turneth away wrath; but grievous words stir up anger. The tongue of the wise useth knowledge aright; but the mouth of fools poureth out foolishness" (XV, 1-2). A chapter in Ecclesiastes ends thus: "Wisdom is better than strength: nevertheless the poor man's wisdom is despised, and his words are not heard. The words of wise men are heard in quiet more than the cry of him that ruleth among fools. Wisdom is better than weapons of war: but one sinner destroyeth much good" (IX, 16-18).

Dr. H. Pereira Mendes of New York City, speaking on "Orthodox or Historical Judaism," cited universal peace as one of the ideals first introduced by Hebrew prophets. "When Micah and Isaiah announced the ideal of Universal Peace, it was the age of war, of despotism. They may have been regarded as lunatics. Now all true men desire it, all good men pray for it." Micah's concept of "universal peace" was having "many nations" say "Come, and let us go up to the mountain of the Lord, and to the house of the God of Jacob . . . [and] all people will walk every one in the name of his god, and we will walk in the name of the Lord our God . . . and the Lord shall reign over them in mount Zion for henceforth, even for ever" (IV, 2, 5, 7). This god ruler of "many nations" was he who "will execute vengeance in anger and fury upon the heathen, such as they have not heard" (V, 15), which is hardly conducive to a felicitous state of peace.

Isaiah presented the peacable image of the wolf and lamb, leopard and kid, and the calf and young lion dwelling together (Chapter Eight). Later he had the Lord declare: "He that killeth an ox is as if he slew a man; he that sacrificeth a lamb as if he cut off a dog's neck" (LXVI, 3). Unfortunately, this only has to do with sacrifices. Yet unlike other contributors to the Jewish Bible, Isaiah stripped Yahveh of some hitherto vengeful characteristics, as indicated in that oft-quoted verse: "And he [God] shall judge among the nations, and shall rebuke many people; and they shall beat their swords into plowshares and their spears into pruning hooks; nation shall not lift up sword against nation, neither shall they learn war any more" (II, 4). But, as Jeremiah noted, the leopard can not change his spots, and with the worship of an entirely different god it was ill-advised to retain the name of the old war god. In polytheistic Rome the common people knew when they were worshipping the war god Mars and when the peace goddess Pax, whereas in henotheistic Israel even the prophets made no distinction between them. It was Isaiah who proclaimed the coming of the savior: "For every battle of the warrior is with confused noise, and garments rolled in blood; . . . For unto us a child is born, unto us a son is given . . . and his name shall be called Wonderful, Counsellor, The mighty God, The everlasting Father, The Prince of Peace" (IX, 6-7).

The "Prince of Peace" of Christianity refuted the designation by his own declaration, "Think not that I am come to send peace on earth: I came not to send peace, but a sword" (Matthew X, 34). This was meant in a domestic sense, as his following statement was, "For I am come to set a man at variance against his father, and the daughter against her mother, and the daughter in law against her mother in law," which was counter to his injunction to honor parents. Another of his sayings was, "And ye shall hear of wars and rumours of wars; see that ye be not troubled; for all these things must come to pass, but the end is not yet. For nation shall rise against nation, and kingdom against kingdom; and there shall be famines, and pestilences, and earthquakes, in divers places" (XXIV, 6-7). That Jesus considered wars inevitable is indicated by his linking them with famines, pestilences, and earthquakes, and his suggestion during such emergencies was, "Then let them which be in Judaea flee into the mountains" (XXIV, 16). He reportedly fed the multitude that came to listen to him, cast out devils from those possessed, restored a few years more of life to those who were dead, but for matters of catastrophic significance, his solution was that his own people could "flee into the mountains."

Jesus' teaching is fragmentary, disconnected, and inconsistent. In the Sermon on the Mount, he had said, "Love your enemies, bless them that curse you, do good to them that hate you, and pray for them which despitefully use you, and persecute you" (Matthew V, 44), but he did not develop it into a system. He never said that killing or stealing has any further application than not killing or stealing from Jews, as in the Old Testament. At one time he remarked, "Are not two sparrows sold for a farthing? and one of them shall not fall on the ground without your Father [knowing of it]. But ... ye are of more value than the sparrows" (X, 29-31). With his putting a monetary price on the sparrows, recalling that put on human beings in Leviticus, this naturally makes one wonder how many shekels Jesus considered people worth. Having embraced a partial ethics, a step beyond Jewish righteousness, if he had not tormented the priests for not accepting him, thus prompting them to have him eliminated after only a year or two of his ministry, and had he not been encumbered by that same righteousness himself, Jesus might have arrived at a broader doctrine. The other consideration is that his followers were men of low station, such as fishermen, who had no compunction against killing, and the teaching was limited to their capacity.

In Revelation, John beheld heaven open and Christ ride through on a white horse; a sword came out of his mouth to smite the nations, which he would rule with an iron rod (XIX, 11-15). Parallels with the legendary Hindu final judge, Kalki, are unmistakable (Chapter Three). Constantine may have used the passage for inspiration when he set the cipher of Christ on his soldier's shields and took the City of Rome. He marched through the carnage to the forum, where he later erected a statue of himself holding a spear in the shape of a cross. Constantine's conquest was the death rattle of the Classic period and the birth wail of the Dark Ages (Chapter

Three). His dubious sanctity was forerunner to that fearsome group the Warring Saints of Christendom. Legends commemorate many hundreds of saints and martyrs mostly known only by name. Byzantine mosaics depict saints George, Theodore, Demetrius, and Mercurius, dressed in chlamys and breastplate and armed with short sword and lance. Mercurius is said to have conducted irascible acts after his death at the bidding of the Virgin, reentering the tomb with blood-stained weapons to await the Day of Judgment. A Roman legionary named Saint Victor is popular in Lombardy, and another of the same name in the vicinity of Marseilles. Maurice, the patron saint of infantry, was commander of a legion of seven-thousand men, whose scruples against the duties of their profession extended only to Christians.[3]

Saint Jeanne d'Arc had no conscience against killing Christians so long as they were English, just as the invaders had no hesitancy against killing Christians so long as they were French. Theoretically, both nations had worked together during the three preceding centuries sending armies to the far end of the Mediterranean. The Crusades were launched by no less a person than Christ's vicar in Rome, Pope Urban II, toward the close of the eleventh century. He it was who originated the battle cry, *"Deus volt!"* while distributing crosses, from which the movement derived its name; and he promised full penance, no matter how black their sins, to participants. The purpose was to rescue the sepulcher of Christ in Jerusalem from the Moslems, who were making it difficult for Christians to visit it. Early German recruits to the cause began by robbing and murdering Jews in the Rhine Valley. German and French Crusaders marched through Hungary and sacked the Balkans. Frankish, Norman, and Flemish armies collided with Byzantine Greek Christians, fought among themselves, bargained with Italian commercial interests, and conducted an infamous advance along the coast from Constantinople to Jerusalem, which they took in July of 1099. Splashing through the blood of Moslems and Jews running in the streets — estimated at 50,000, fiendishly murdered — the Crusaders proceeded to the Church of the Holy Sepulcher and clasped their gore-stained hands together to pray to him who came to save Israel.

Thus was set up the Latin Kingdom of Jerusalem. Holy Roman emperors, French and English kings joined in later crusades and quarreled over its ownership, which, with disputes between the Knights Hospitalers and Knights Templars, left an opening for Egyptian Moslems and their Turkish allies to recover Jerusalem in 1244. The Children's Crusade was formed on the proposition that the innocence of youth could accomplish what greedy maturity had failed to achieve: the French *enfants* ended up sold into slavery in Egypt, and the German *kinder* perished from disease and hunger marching through the homeland of Catholicism, Italy. Louis IX, the "Crusading Saint" of France, set out against Egypt, where he was captured, released, organized another crusade, then died. The Crusaders substantially weakened Christian power in the Near East through campaigning against the Byzantines, including ravaging Constantinople, and their last stronghold fell to Islam in 1291. After this the term "Crusade" was used to refer to military expeditions sponsored by the popes against wayward Christians in Europe, such as the Albigenses and Hussites. It was accompanied by the Inquisition, in which people were condemned for not having the same contestable faith as their bigoted judges, without knowledge of their accusers, without counsel, without public trial, their property confiscated, and they themselves tortured, maimed, and executed. Christian righteousness had plummeted to the absolute nadir of human depravity.

Aside from their internal conflicts, the butt of the Crusaders' campaigns in the Levant was Islam. As referred to previously, Islam and war are not strangers. In the second chapter of the Koran, Mohammed recommended giving alms to "parents and kinsmen, and the orphan and the poor, and the son of the road;" and in the following verse he stated, "Prescribed for you is fighting, but it is hateful to you. Yet peradventure that ye hate a thing while it is good for you, and peradventure that ye love a thing while it is bad for you; God knows, and ye, — ye do not know!" A little later on he said, "but whosoever of you is turned from his religion and dies while still a misbeliever; these are those whose works are vain in this world and the next; they are the fellows of the Fire, and they shall dwell therein for aye. Verily, those who believe, . . . and those who wage war in God's way; these may hope for God's mercy, for God is forgiving and merciful" (II, 211-212, 214-215). Mohammed made good his sermon by leading his warriors in the taking of Mecca, which submitted without resistance in 630. By the time he died, two years later, most of Arabia had been converted to Islam, and missionaries were at work in the Eastern Empire, Persia, and Ethiopia.

On the morrow of Mohammed's death, his followers embarked upon the Jihad, the "Holy War." Within a couple of years the Arabs had taken the Byzantine provinces of Palestine and Syria, and in another decade they were masters of Egypt and Persia. They pushed across the north shore of Africa, and in 711, the Moors — Moslems of mixed Arab-African descent — crossed the Strait of Gibraltar and defeated the last Visigoth king of Spain. The Arabs established colonies off the coast of Africa, and following raids over a period of two centuries, they took Sicily during the 800s. The Moslems directed their forces against India from the eleventh century onward. First the Turks subdued the Punjab. In the thirteenth century the Afghans took over the basin of the Ganges and founded a sultanate at Delhi. From here the rulers conquered part of the Deccan in the fourteenth century. Meanwhile, the Ottoman Turks had begun to rise in Asia Minor and were acquiring large sections of southeast Europe from the Byzantine Empire. Constantinople fell in 1453, and by the middle of the sixteenth century Transylvania and Hungary had become part of the Ottoman domain. Four-and-a-half centuries after Pope Urban II offered the reward of Heaven to Christian warriors conveying the cross to far-away Jerusalem, the Prophet Mohammed's earlier assurance of Paradise to Moslems for the slaughter of such infidels was to plant the crescent on a solid front, facing Italy, across the Adriatic and Mediterranean seas and on the Danube River. And both factions believed that their god would compensate them handsomely for their murderous piety at the Last Judgment.

Shinto, the indigenous religion of Japan, is referred to as *Kami-no-Michi*, the "Way of the Gods," which incorporates an elaborate mythology giving the descent of the ruling family from the sun goddess, Amaterasu-Omikami. It is the basis for the belief in the "sacred" mission of the Japanese nation, akin to the chosen-people claim of the Jews. Insisting upon unqualified obedience to the Emperor, Shinto has been called the "Religion of Loyalty," and a Japanese, laying down his life in combat for the sovereign, is worshipped as a Kami. Special honors are awarded to the warring Empress Jingo of the fourth century. In the thirteenth century, two large fleets of Kublai Khan's invincible invading armies were destroyed by storms, which the Japanese called *Kamikaze*, "God Winds." They later applied the term to suicide pilots in World War II. Their supposition of divine intervention in the former incident did not prevent invasion by a foreign enemy six-and-a-half centuries later, a direct consequence of their ill-advised offensiveness. Had they not suppressed Buddhism, the Japanese might have seen that its realistic Law of Causality was more reliable than primitive superstitions promoted by warlord imperialists.

Through its rituals, ceremonials and social decorum, Confucianism also has been an instrument favorable to carrying out the royal wishes of an emperor, the representative of Heaven on earth; and when the head of the Chinese state was not a wise one, the populace suffered. He could plunge them into war on a moment's whim. The state temples contained memorabilia of China's great. Among them, of course, was Confucius, and in addition to nature and city deities there were military heroes and martyrs to patriotic causes. One figuring prominently was Kuan Yü or Kuan Ti, who had been a commander during the period of the Three Kingdoms (third-fourth centuries A.D.). He had become the patron lord of army officers, and his temple was the Wu Sheng Miao, the "Military Holy Shrine." Tablets to him and other warriors made this building a devotion hall of martial fame.

The philosophical nature of Taoism excludes endorsement of fighting. The thirtieth and thirty-first paragraphs in the *Tao-te Ching* read: "In time of war men civilized in peace turn from their higher to their lower nature. Arms are instruments of evil and not the tools of the thoughtful man. Only when it is unavoidable he uses them. Peace and quietude he holds high. He rejoices not to conquer. Rejoicing at a conquest means to enjoy the slaughter of men. . . . Conduct your triumph as a funeral."

War is not acclaimed in the numerous Indian religious treatises that were reviewed in Manilal D'vivedi's paper given before the Parliament (Chapter Five). The rigorous social system limited fighting to a specific caste, the Kshatriya, to which belonged temporal rulers and defenders. Warriors were trained according to a high ethical code, which not only forbade them from assaulting members of other castes but other warriors unequally armed. Thus a spear bearer would not attack a swordsman, and an archer would not shoot at either. It would have been unthinkable that they should plunder villages and murder and enslave their inhabitants. Accounts of warfare are given in the Indian epics, the *Mahābhārata*, the Great Bhārata Wars, and the *Rāmayāna*, relating Rama's rescue of Sita, abducted to Lanka by the demon king Ravana. A stanza from the former was quoted in Chapter Three, wherein Krishna extols his divine mission to Arjuna in the *Bhagavadgītā*. The dialogue takes place in the prince's chariot while awaiting the pending battle between the Pandavas and their cousins the Kauravas. The quandary of Arjuna is that of the pacifist foreseeing that "nothing of good can spring from mutual slaughter" because, he says, "If they [the enemy] be guilty, we shall grow guilty by their deaths" (I, 31, 36). He observes that "By overthrow of houses perisheth their sweet continuous household piety, and — rites neglected, piety extinct — enters impiety upon that home; its women grow unwomaned, whence there spring mad passions . . . sending a Hell-ward road that family" (I, 40). Krishna's reply at first tends to minimize the evil of fighting by asserting that the spirit persists beyond the slaying of the body, speaking of the interminable round of existence, "The end of birth is death; the end of death is birth" (II, 27). Then his argument turns to coercion, it being the duty of a Kshatriya to fight: "Nought better can betide a martial soul than lawful war; happy the warrior to whom comes joy of battle;" and "Do thine allotted task; work is more excellent than idleness" (II, 32; III, 8). Krishna, it will be remembered, is the deity speaking, he who has "made the Four Castes, and portioned them in place after their qualities and gifts," and having advised Arjuna of his obligations, he declares, "They who keep my ordinances thus . . . have acquittance from all issue of their acts" (III, 31; IV, 13). We are confronted by the old mythological god's principle of righteousness as opposed to morality, but at least Krishna's bidding includes the honorable requirements of a fair fight, as opposed to Yahveh's spokesman urging his tribesmen to a blackguard raid.

To a Kshatriya family was born Siddhartha Gautama during the sixth century B.C. His father was King of the Sakiyas, in the Himalayan foothills of northeast India. His mother died at his birth, and he was brought up in the martial arts. However, care was taken that he should not know of its consequences — or of any of the other ugly aspects of life. Thus he was grown before encountering disease, old age, and death, and learned that they were inevitable and universal afflictions. His determination to get at the root of the tragedy led to his discovery of the law of cause and effect and the means of escape through suppression of desire and intellectual attainment (Chapters Seven and Eight). As has been shown, the difference between a righteous and ethical religion is that, in the latter, responsibility for one's actions is assumed by the individual; he is his own judge of what is right and wrong without referring to irrelevant religious envelopments — priests, scriptures, gods and emotional involvements. The Buddha declares in the *Dhammapada*, "Evil is done by self alone, by self alone is one stained; by self alone is evil left undone, by self alone one is purified. Purity and impurity depend on one's own self. No one can purify another" (XII, 9). Another runs: "Victory over oneself is indeed better than victory over others. If man subjugates himself and practices restraint . . . [there is no force that] can undo his victory!" (VIII, 5-6). Also, "Let a man conquer anger by absence of anger, wickedness by absence of wickedness, miserliness by liberality, and a liar by the truth" (XVII, 3). A man should stand upright on his own two feet and set the example. He creates the degree and quality of his own Karma, which determines his future; but as he is a member of the social order, the community, state, nation and the world, his Karma is an integral part of each of these aggregate Karmas. Unless he be under a totalitarian system, the individual is able to share in directing the way that these groups proceed. The good citizen is not he who follows blindly any dubious path his society takes but he who makes an effort to steer that society in the right course.

Buddhist teaching is not merely content to declare *ahimsa* a worthy ideal that should be observed if one wishes to improve his own Karma, but, when opportunity offers, one should put it into practice to improve the Karma of many Karmas. The *Sukha Vagga*, in the Pali canon, begins with an account of how the Buddha averted an armed confrontation among neighboring clans, one being his own.

"The story goes that the Sākiyas and the Koliyas caused the waters of the river Rohiṇī to be confined by a single dam between the city of Kapilavatthu and the city of Koliya, and cultivated the fields on both sides of the river. Now in the month jeṭṭhamūla the crops began to droop, whereupon the laborers employed by the residents of both cities assembled. Said the residents of the city of Koliya, 'If this water is diverted to both sides of the river, there will not be enough both for you and for us too. But our crops will ripen with a single watering. Therefore let us have the water.'

"The Sākiyas replied, 'After you have filled your storehouses, we shall not have the heart to take ruddy gold and emeralds and black pennies, and, baskets and sacks in our hands, go from house to house seeking favors at your hands. Our crops also will ripen with a single watering. Therefore let us have this water.' 'We will not give it to you.' 'Neither will we give it to you.' Talk waxed bitter, until finally one arose and struck another a blow. The other returned the blow and a general fight ensued, the combatants making matters worse by aspersions on the origin of the two royal families.

"Said the laborers employed by the Koliyas, 'You who live in the city of Kapilavatthu, take your children and go where you belong. Are we likely to suffer harm from the elephants and horses and shields and weapons of those who, like dogs and jackals, have cohabitated with their own sisters?' The laborers employed by the Sākiyas replied, 'You lepers, take your children and go where you belong. Are we likely to suffer harm from the elephants and horses and shields and weapons of destitute outcasts who have lived in jujube-trees like animals?' Both parties of laborers went and reported the quarrel to the ministers who had charge of the work, and the ministers reported the matter to the royal households. Thereupon the Sākiyas came forth armed for battle and cried out, 'We will show what strength and power belong to those who have cohabitated with their sisters.' Likewise the Koliyas came forth armed for battle and cried out, 'We will show what strength and power belong to those who dwell in jujube-trees.'

"As the Teacher surveyed the world at dawn and beheld his kinsmen, he thought to himself, 'If I refrain from going to them, these men will destroy each other. It is clearly my duty to go to them.' Accordingly he flew through the air quite alone to the spot where his kinsmen were gathered together, and seated himself cross-legged in the air over the middle of the river Rohiṇī. When the Teacher's kinsmen saw the Teacher, they threw away their weapons and did reverence to him. Said the Teacher to his kinsmen, 'What is all this quarrel about, great king?' 'We do not know, Reverend Sir.' 'Who then would be likely to know?' 'The commander-in-chief of the army would be likely to know.' The commander-in-chief of the army said, 'The viceroy would be likely to know.' Thus the Teacher put the question first to one and then to another, asking the laborers last of all. The laborers replied, 'The quarrel is about water, Reverend Sir.'

"Then the Teacher asked the king, 'How much is water worth, great king?' 'Very little, Reverend Sir.' 'How much are Khattiyas [Kshatriyas] worth, great king?' 'Khattiyas are beyond price, Reverend Sir.' 'It is not fitting that because of a little water you should destroy Khattiyas who are beyond price.' They were silent. Then the Teacher addressed them and said, 'Great kings, why do you act in this manner? Were I not here present today, you would set flowing a river of blood. You have acted in a most unbecoming manner. You live in enmity, indulging in the five kinds of hatred.' "⁴ The episode ends with the Buddha pronouncing the following verse, which is one found in the *Dhammapada*: "Oh, happily let us live! free from hatred, among those who hate; Among men who hate, let us live free from hatred."

According to the legend in the *Sukha Vagga*, coupled with a report made at the World's Parliament of Religions, the principle of bipartisan meditation was practised in Asia well over a thousand years before it reached Europe. Prof. Thomas J. Semmes of the law department of Louisiana University, reviewing "International Arbitration" at Chicago, noted that the subject did not apply to Rome because its component states were all under the same rule. But, "At the end of the sixth century, the Goths, the Franks, the Saxons and the

Vandals had divided the western provinces of the Roman Empire into different kingdoms, . . . [which had] become independent sovereigns of their own territory. The church alone, in the midst of this world of dissolution, was completely and powerfully organized. The various states, conscious of their weakness, voluntarily sought pontifical intervention, until the pontifical tribunal became the resort of peoples and princes for the settlement of their controversies on principles of equity and justice. . . . adherence to the Catholic faith . . . [presupposed] general obedience to the decrees of the Pope. But the Protestant Reformation denied the authority of the church. This rendered papal authority no longer possible." Prof. Semmes observed that, in modern society, "there are many patriots of humanity who believe that love of country may be reconciled with the love of humanity, and that the day is not far distant when for happiness of nations and the tranquillity of governments, the policy of life will take a definitive step towards the suppression of the policy of death."

He focused his chronicle on America: "Since the year 1818 the United States has settled by arbitration all of its controversies with foreign nations. The differences with England as to the interpretation of the treaty of Ghent were submitted to arbitration in 1818, and again in 1822, and the third time in 1827." Prof. Thomas O'Gorman, talking on "The Relation of Christianity to America," added that "As early as 1832 the Senate of Massachusetts adopted resolutions expressing 'that some mode should be established for the amicable and final adjustment of all international disputes instead of a resort to war.' Various other legislatures gave expression to the same sentiment, and the sentiment grew apace on the nation." Prof. Semmes took up the sequence: "Arbitration disposed of the controversies with Portugal in 1851, with Great Britain in regard to slaves landed at Napan from the ship 'Creole' in 1853, with Chili in 1858, with Paraguay in 1859, with Peru in 1863 and 1868, with Great Britain as to Puget Sound in 1863, with Mexico in 1868, with

Great Britain as to losses caused by Confederate cruisers during the civil war in 1871, with Columbia in 1874, with France in 1880, with Denmark in 1888, with Venezuela in 1890, and only a few weeks ago [from 23 September 1893] the Behring Sea controversy with England was settled by arbitration in Paris.

"It is interesting to know that during the century from 1793 to 1893 there have been fifty-eight international arbitrations, and the advance of public opinion toward that mode of settling national controversies may be measured by the gradual increase of arbitration during the course of the century. From 1793 to 1848, a period of fifty-five years, there were nine arbitrations; there were fifteen from 1848 to 1870, a period of twenty-two years; there were fourteen from 1870 to 1880, and twenty from 1880 to 1893. The United States and other American States were interested in thirteen of these arbitrations; the United States, other American States and European nations were interested in twenty-three; Asiatic and African States were interested in three; and European nations only were interested in eighteen.

"Peace leagues, the international conferences, and associations for the advancement of social science, have for over thirty years endeavoured to elaborate an international code, with organized arbitration; that is to say, a permanent juridical tribunal, as distinguished from a political congress."

Prof. O'Gorman, who taught at the Catholic University in Washington, completed the story up to the time of the Columbian Exposition: "In 1888 two hundred and thirty-three members of the British Parliament sent a communication to the President and Congress urging a treaty between England and the United States which should stipulate 'that any differences or disputes arising between the two governments, which cannot be adjusted by diplomatic agency, shall be referred to arbitration.' In the same year the government of Switzerland proposed to the United States the conclusion of a convention for thirty years, binding the contracting parties to submit their mutual differences to arbitration. . . . The best known, as it is the latest, arbitration treaty, is the one formulated by the International American Conference under the secretaryship of Mr. Blaine, whereby the republics of North, Central and South America adopt arbitration as a principle of American international law for the settlement of disputes that may arise between two or more of them." Twenty years later this last was to become the Pan American Union, which survived until 1970.

The Hague Conferences, both promoted by Russia, which met in the Netherlands during 1899 and 1907, attempted, unsuccessfully, to reduce armaments and prohibit some of modern warfare's most destructive practices, but out of it grew the Hague Tribunal, which was an agency for settling international disputes by mediation. At the Paris Peace Conference of 1919, concluding World War I, President Woodrow Wilson proposed the League of Nations, its first members being the United States, Great Britain, France, Italy and Japan, joined later (in the 1920s and early 1930s) by Belgium, Austria, Hungary, Germany, Mexico, Turkey and Russia. It was successful in avoiding conflicts between nations during the early years, but the pact was broken in the 1930s by Japan's invasion of Manchuria and later of China, Italy's attack on Ethiopia, Germany's seizure of Austria, and Russia's penetration of Finland. The League collapsed. The Hague Tribunal had been succeeded by the World Court, which began meeting at The Hague in 1921. It virtually ceased functioning with the German occupation of the Netherlands in 1940.

The United Nations came into being in 1942 as a confederation among the opponents of the Axis powers agreeing not to make separate peace treaties. In 1946, after the close of World War II, its headquarters were fixed in New York City. Its principal agency for preserving peace is the Security Council of fifteen members, of which the United States, Great Britain, France, China and the Union of Soviet Socialist Republics are permanently seated, and the other ten are chosen for two-year terms by the General Assembly on their recent contributions to peace and geographic distribution. Hope for accord in the United Nations was impaired by the Cold War between the Western Allies and Communism. A Disarmament Commission organized in 1952 was made ineffectual by the same friction. NATO (North Atlantic Treaty Organization) and other alliances mostly bypassed the United Nations. However, it formed a peace-keeping army in 1950. Not much use was made of it for six years, but from this time onward it has been employed recurrently to allay hostilities between those two factions of war-provoking religions, Israel and Islam. The recent trouble has not been over religion *per se*, though both religious parties and religious feelings have figured in it.

The Zionist movement began striving for a Jewish state independent of the Arabs in the late nineteenth century. Its first glimpse of success occurred in 1922, when Great Britain received Palestine as a mandate from the League of Nations. Arriving at no satisfactory solution to problems there over the next quarter of a century, in August of 1947 the four-months-old United Nations Special Committee on Palestine presented a plan to divide the territory into Jewish and Arab sections, with a small international zone around Jerusalem. Promoted by the United States and Russia, it was adopted by two-thirds vote later in the year, Great Britain abstaining and the Arabian delegation walking out. With the British withdrawal from Palestine, the State of Israel was proclaimed at Tel Aviv on 14 May 1948 and, simultaneously, Arabs from Lebanon, Syria, Jordan, Egypt, and Iraq invaded. The Security Council concluded a cease-fire in July. With an armistice agreed upon in January of 1949, Israel had increased its territory by another half, and it was admitted to the United Nations. In 1950 its government passed the Law of Return, awarding immediate citizenship to all Jewish immigrants. Following Biblical precedent, to accommodate its augmented population, Israel looked covetously at neighboring lands and attacked.

In 1955 it penetrated the Gaza area on the lower Mediterranean coast, and the following year the Sinai Peninsula, which was part of Egypt. Pressure from the United States and the Soviet Union forced a withdrawal, but Israel retained access to the Red Sea. An UN Emergency Force was stationed on the Israel-Egyptian border. In June of 1967 Israel again entered the Gaza and Sinai regions, as well as Golan Heights of Syria and the Arab section of Jerusalem. Five months later the Security Council requested their retreat. Arab guerillas, mostly from Jordan, became bothersome, and Israel proposed peace negotiations, which were to include passage through the Red Sea and Suez Canal. Conditions fermented. Egypt and Syria attacked Israeli positions in Sinai and Golan Heights on 6 October 1973. As this was Yam Kippur, the Day of Atonement, the Jews were not prepared for combat. The Security Council called for a cease-fire on October 22. Two months later an Arab-Israel peace conference opened in Geneva, and it dragged on for nearly two years. In the concluding agreement, signed 4 September 1975, Israel was made to give up part of its recently-acquired gains. But its land grab continued. As this is being written, seven years later, armed peace-keeping forces still are being sent to the scene where Moses established the law and led his commandos.

That the promised land is God's gift only when it is man's taking is in that compendium of texts from which sermons are preached in synagogue, church, and mosque on one or another holy day each weekend. When a person is brought up in a faith in which the sacred scriptures describe God as a "man of war," the savior brings "not peace but a sword" and the prophet was proficient in its use, all of the talk in the world about brotherly love and harmony does not erase the contradictory divine images from his mind. They lie dormant, ready to spring into action at the least provocation. In ancient India, where fighting was limited to a class, and it was conducted according to rules of honor, adherents had more reservations against fighting. It was in such an atmosphere that Mohandas Gandhi was able to conduct his "war without violence," employing the principle of *Satyagraha*, "truth prevails." Better still is a philosophy religion that condemns belligerence altogether, as does Buddhism. It never precipitated a religious war, it never participated in a war of any kind. It would not be true to its own premises if it did. At the Parliament the Japanese Zen abbot, Soyen Shaku, gave a short paper on "Arbitration Instead of War", which is as timely today as it was in 1893. In his somewhat imperfect use of a foreign language, he declared that "International law . . . has done a great deal toward arbitration instead of war. But can we not hope that this system shall be carried out on a more and more enlarged scale, so that the world will be blessed with the everlasting glorious bright sunshine of peace and love instead of the gloomy cloudy weather of bloodshed, battles and war?

"We are not born to fight one against another. We are born to enlighten [*i.e.* to attain] wisdom and cultivate our virtues according to the guidance of truth. And, happily, we see the movement toward the abolition of war and the establishment of a peace-making society. But how will our hope be realized? Simply by the help of the religion of truth. The religion of truth is the fountain of benevolence and mercy."

Other speakers at the World's Parliament of Religions advocated peace, but only a Buddhist could refer to his religion as standing unreservedly for it.[5] How much better the world would have been had the simple advice of the Zen abbot been heeded. Pious Western clerics went out from the Chicago conference, and if they did not actually preach themselves into World War I within a quarter of a century and preach themselves into World War II in another thirty years, they approved and supported those wars; rare was the one who spoke against his nation's involvement. And the same God was invoked to vanquish the enemy on both sides.

CHAPTER NINE – notes

1   Jack Finegan, *The Archaeology of World Religions*, Princeton, 1952, pp. 77-89.

2   Arthur G. and Edmund Warner (translators), *The Shahnama of Firdausi Done into English*, Trauber's Oriental Series, 1905-16, Vol. V., pp. 30-87.

3   A. Jameson, *Sacred and Legendary Art*, London, 1891, pp. 780-801 (Vol. II).

4   Eugene Watson Burlingame (translator), *Buddhist Legends*, Cambridge, 1921, Part III, pp. [70]-72.

5   Aaron M. Powell, editor of the *Philanthropist* and a Friend or Quaker, referred to the "great Krupp gun" on display at the Columbian Exposition as being "appalling in its possibilities for the destruction of humanity." He suggested that if "religious people" would "unite in a general league against war and resolve to arbitrate all difficulties... that that great Krupp gun will, if not preserved for some museum, be literally melted and recast into plow shares and pruning hooks." Nowhere to the records show that the Friends as a society took a pacifist stand at the Parliament.

10

CONCLUSIONS ON THE CONCLUSIONS

THE ENTHUSIASM and the heavy attendance of the opening session at the World's Parliament of Religions were equaled or even surpassed at the final meeting on the evening of September 27. A crowd had begun to gather in front of the Art Institute more than an hour before the doors opened, and it grew to queues extending half a block in either direction. Speculators sold tickets to the secondary Hall of Washington, where speeches were repeated, for three or four dollars. The two great rooms together held over six thousand people. A witness reported next day: "Never since the confusion of tongues at Babel have so many religions, so many creeds, stood side by side, hand in hand, and almost heart to heart, as in the great amphitheatre last night. On the great platform of Columbus Hall sat the representatives of creeds and sects that in bygone days hated one another with a hatred that knew no moderation. The last and closing scene of the great Parliament of Religions is one that will live forever in the memory of those who were so fortunate as to be spectators. The great Hall of Columbus was illuminated by a myriad of lights. Every inch of room was used by the greatest crowd that ever sat within its walls. On the stage, beneath the folds of the flags of all nations, were the representatives of all religions. The dull, black and somber raiment of the West only intensified the radiantly contrasted garbs of the Oriental priests."[1] Thus in seven sentences, using the word "great" four times and "greatest" once, referring irrelevantly to the Tower of Babel with regard to religion, to "hatred that knew no moderation," which is proper to Near Eastern and Western creeds but foreign to those of Farther Asia, and to the obvious

206

color distinctions between the costumes worn by delegates from the two hemispheres while misrepresenting their identity — few of the Orientals were "priests" — we have a characteristically distorted local glimpse of the international religions roundup.

The program for that last session consisted of speeches and farewells from some of the more distinguished of the participants, prayers, hymns, and songs by the five hundred members of the Apollo Club occupying the gallery. Talks were arranged with the visitors from abroad at the beginning, leading up to the home guard putting in their imperious say-so at the end.

The first speaker was Dr. Alfred W. Momerie, who was complimentary about both the World's Fair and the Parliament: "I have seen all the expositions of Europe during the last ten or twelve years, and I am sure I do not exaggerate when I say that your Exposition is greater than all the rest put together. But your Parliament of Religions is far greater than your Exposition. There have been plenty of expositions before. Yours is the best, but it is a comparatively common thing. The Parliament of Religions is a new thing in the world. . . . Here in this Hall of Columbus vast audiences have assembled day after day . . . listening to doctrines which they had been taught to regard with contempt, listening with respect, with sympathy, with an earnest desire to learn something which would improve their own doctrines."

The second speaker was P.C. Mozoomdar of the Brahmo-Somaj, who quoted what his leader, Keshub Chunder Sen, had predicted ten years earlier about Christian sects becoming more liberal and meeting together, as had just happened at the Parliament.

A Russian, Prince Serge Wolkonsky, the Japanese Kinza Hirai, the Chinese Pung Kwang Yu, and a Shinto priest, Reuchi Shibata (the two latter handed prepared statements to Dr. Barrows to read), the English missionary to China George T. Candlin, the Singhalese Buddhist Dharmapala, the Indians Swami Vivekananda and Virchand Gandhi, and then

Prince Momolu Masaquoi of the Vey territory, Africa, appeared in order. Hirai represented four Japanese Buddhists. The Shintoist observed that "our souls have been so pleasantly united here that I hope they may be again united in the life hereafter. Now I pray that the eight million deities protecting the beautiful cherry tree country of Japan may protect you and your Government forever, and with this I bid you goodby." Whatever the establishment thought about a pagan's presumption to a life hereafter was not voiced, but it was greatly offended by Shibata's benediction. Dr. Barrows noted toward the end of his "Review and Summary" that "polytheism had no standing in the Parliament except in a rhetorical blessing at the end of one address." The Jews hailed Yahveh: "Who is like unto thee, O Lord, among the gods?" (Exodus XV, 11). Christians exalt God the Father, God the Son, and God the Holy Ghost, yet they are as horrified by polytheism as of polygamy. With all anthropomorphic gods being mythical — Zeus, Apollo, Osiris, Vishnu, Thor, Mithra and Yahveh equally are fabrications of the human imagination — what real difference is there between worshipping one legendary deity or many?

Vivekananda, who usually leaned toward reconciliation, was in a different mood when he remarked, "Much has been said of the common ground of religious unity. . . . if anyone here hopes that this unity would come by the triumph of any one of these religions and the destruction of the others, to him I say, 'Brother, yours is an impossible hope.' Do I wish that the Christian would become Hindu? God forbid. Do I wish that the Hindu or Buddhist would become Christian? God forbid. . . . But each must assimilate the others and yet preserve its individuality and grow according to its own law of growth." Vivekananda returned to a more characteristic vein in adding, "If the Parliament of Religions has shown anything to the world it is this: It has proved to the world that holiness, purity and charity are not the exclusive possession of any church in the world, and that every system has

produced men and women of the most exalted character."
The chairman-editor's comment was, "Swami Vivekananda
was always heard with interest at the Parliament, but very
little approval was shown to some of the sentiments expressed
in his closing address."

After this group of speakers the Apollo Club sang the
"Hallelujah Chorus" from Handel's "Messiah." "The effect
produced by the Hallelujah Chorus on this occasion is utterly
beyond the power of words to describe. To the Christians
who were present, and all seemed imbued with a Christian
spirit, it appeared as if the Kingdom of God was descending
visibly before their eyes and many thought of the Redeemer's
promise — 'And I, if I be lifted up from the earth, will draw
all men unto me.' Thousands felt that this was the great
moment in their lives, and will never be unmindful of the
heavenly vision granted them in that hour. . . . Three thousand
men and women rose to their feet, waving their handkerchiefs
and cheering, and not until the chorus had sung, 'Judge me,
O God' (Mendelssohn) was quiet restored."

But not for long. Dr. Barrows then introduced Pres.
Charles Bonney "as the man who had done more than any
other to achieve the great success which had come to the
whole series of World Congresses." This "was a great moment, the culmination of a great achievement, and when Mr.
Bonney came forward the vast audience stood up, waved
their hats and handkerchiefs, and poured upon him a flood of
gratitude."

Mr. Bonney announced "that having listened to the representatives from the far-away countries, the audience would
now be addressed by speakers from America in two-minute
addresses." The first to follow was the Rev. George Dana
Boardman, a Baptist minister of Philadelphia, who had spoken
the day before on "Christ the Unifier of Mankind." He simply
stated, "Fathers of the contemplative East; sons of the ex-
ecutive West — Behold how good and how pleasant it is for
brethren to dwell together in unity. The New Jerusalem, the

City of God, is descending, heaven and earth chanting the eternal Hallelujah chorus."

He was succeeded by Dr. Emil G. Hirsch of Chicago, who did not refer to the Messiah music but bid the assembly good-by "in the old Jewish salutation of peace." And after him came representatives of various women's auxiliary groups who had not addressed the Parliament previously. They were followed by Mrs. Julia Ward Howe, who was greeted with a return of cheers and handkerchief fluttering, being the well-known author of the "Battle Hymn of the Republic." Mrs. Howe recited part of a poem that she had composed having to do with a religious dream she had experienced recently.

No doubt invited to participate because they belonged to American minority groups, Bishop B.W. Arnett of the African Methodist Episcopal Church and Bishop John J. Keane of the Catholic University of America made short talks. Then the chairman of the general committee, Dr. Henry Barrows, gave his farewell address, in which he related an incident that occurred at the fair. "While floating one evening over the illuminated waters of the White City, Mr. Dharmapala said, with that smile which has won our hearts, 'All the joys of Heaven are in Chicago;' and Dr. Momerie, with a characteristic mingling of enthusiasm and skepticism, replied, 'I wish I were sure that all the joys of Chicago are to be in Heaven.' " The program was wound up by President Bonney, whose remarks included: "The laws of the Congress forbidding controversy or attack have, on the whole, been wonderfully well observed. The exceptions are so few that they may well be expunged from the record and from the memory. . . . If some Western warrior, forgetting for the moment that this was a friendly conference, and not a battle field, uttered his war-cry, let us rejoice that our Oriental friends, with a kinder spirit, answered, 'Father, forgive them, for they know not what they say.' " The program terminated by all standing and singing the national anthem "America."

Included in Barrow's and Bonney's last remarks and

embellished in the final chapter of the two-volume record of the talks were statements regarding their thoughts on the Parliament, its achievements, and the conclusions that they reached concerning religion after being exposed to many types.[2] The analysis begins:

"The extraordinary success of the Parliament was due to its timeliness, to the amount of work put into it, and to the fact that it was in the hands of men who were fitted to secure the cooperation of the great historic churches and of the representatives of non-Christian faiths. Liberal Christians naturally looked upon it as one of their triumphs, but they could not have gained the cooperation of historic Christendom. Liberal-minded Jews saw in it the fulfillment of the prophecy that the knowledge of Jehovah should cover the earth, but Judaism alone could not have achieved a convention of Christians. The Brahmo-Somaj regarded the Parliament as fulfilling the ideas of the New Dispensation, but the Brahmo-Somaj would have been unable to draw together the representatives of the great faiths. No Christian missionary society could have achieved the Parliament, for the fear of aggressive propagandism would have kept out the non-Christian world. No ecclesiastical body in Christendom, whether Catholic, Greek, Anglican, or Lutheran, could have assembled the Parliament. No kingly or imperial government in which church and state are united could have gathered it, and no republican government where church and state are separated would have deemed it a part of its office to summon it. But, as a part of an international exposition, and controlled by a generous-minded and representative committee, under no ecclesiastical dictation, and appealing in the spirit of fraternity to high-minded individuals, the Parliament was possible, and was actualized. . . . The world needed to wait till English had become an Asiatic as well as an European and American language, before the Parliament could be successfully held. . . .

"It has shown that mankind is drifting toward religion and not away from it; it has widened the bounds of human fraternity; it is giving a strong impetus to the study of comparative religion; it is fortifying timid souls in regard to the right and wisdom of liberty in thought and expression; it is clarifying many minds in regard to the nature of non-Christian faiths; it is deepening the general Christian interest in non-Christian nations; and it will bring before millions in Oriental lands the more truthful and beautiful aspects of Christianity. . . .

"The idea of evolving a cosmic or universal faith out of the Parliament was not present in the minds of its chief promoters. They believe that the elements of such a religion are already contained in the Christian ideal and the Christian Scriptures. They had no thought of attempting to formulate a universal creed. Their objects were more reasonable and important. Dr. Alger conclusively showed that men must be unified in other subjects before they will become one in their intellectual faith. The best religion must come to the front, and the best religion will ultimately survive, because it will contain all that is true in all the faiths. . . .

"One effect of the Parliament will be to bring up more prominently than ever the question of the reunion of Christendom. Dr. A.H. Bradford has said, 'Never again, after the participation of the Roman and Greek Churches in this great gathering, will the union sought be merely a union of Protestant sects.' 'One result of the Parliament,' says *The Churchman*, 'is the demonstration of the fact that the American people appreciate religious courage, which was conspicuously manifested by the Catholics.' Says Bishop Keane: 'Nearly every sentence during these seventeen days tended to show that the positive doctrinal divergences which had held Christians apart during three centuries are fast being obliterated. The Parliament has been a long stride toward the much-desired reunion of Christendom.' . . .

"But to most of the readers of these volumes the supreme question regarding the Parliament is that which concerns the relation of Christianity to other faiths [sic]. It may be safely said that participation in this meeting did not compromise any Christian speaker's position as a believer in the supremacy and universality of the Gospel. There was no suggestion on the part of Christian speakers that Christianity was to be thought of as on the same level with other religions. . . . Dr. Lyman Abbott has well said that 'the difference between Christianity and the other religions is that we have something that they have not. We have the Christ, the revelation of God, the ideal Man, the loving the suffering Saviour.' . . .

"The Christian spirit pervaded the Parliament from first to last. Christ's Prayer was daily used. His name was always spoken with reverence. No word with a shadow of criticism was uttered against him. His doctrine was preached by a hundred Christians and by lips other than Christian. 'The Parliament ended at Calvary.' . . . Jesus Christ is not only the Truth, but he is also the Way and the Life. In him the two ideas which found most universal acceptance in the Parliament — human brotherhood and divine fatherhood — find their proof and explanation. Take away Jesus, the Son of Man, and the silver cord which is binding human hearts into a cosmopolitan fraternity will be loosened. Take away Christ, the Son of God, and the golden bowl on which he has written the name of the Father, and into which he has poured his own life blood, will be forever broken. . . .

"The Parliament has shown that Christianity is still the great quickener of humanity, that it is now educating those who do not accept its doctrines, that there is no teacher to be compared with Christ, and no Saviour excepting Christ, that there is no assured and transforming hope of conscious and blessed immortality outside of the Christian Scriptures, and that all the philosophies do not bring God so near to man as he is brought by the Gospel of Christ. The non-Christian world may give us valuable criticism and confirm scriptural truths and make excellent suggestions as to Christian improvement, but it has nothing to add to the Christian creed. It is with the belief, expressed by many a Christian missionary, that the Parliament marks a new era of Christian triumph that the Editor closes these volumes."

Thus attention was called to the "extraordinary success of the Parliament," promoted by the Chicago group, at the expense of pointing out that neither "historic Christendom," nor any Jewish, Christian missionary society, ecclesiastical, or other religious body could have done it. The enthusiasm of those in attendance, largely drawn from the metropolitan area, signified that *all* "mankind is drifting toward religion and not away from it." The organizers had no idea of "evolving a cosmic or universal faith" because they considered it to be already in existence, in that to which they and the other Christian groups — though not so competent as themselves — adhered; and it was their own victory in having gotten the Roman and Greek churches to participate. They declared their gospel, consisting of a conglomeration of myths, mandates, common precepts, accounts of belligerents, lineages, laments, self-adulation, chieftains and prophets of an aggressive desert tribe worthy of "supremacy and universality." They permitted no implication that "Christianity was to be thought of as on the same level with other religions." Its unique feature was the Jewish messiah, Jesus, who "is not only the Truth, but he is also the Way and the Life." There is no "hope of conscious and blessed immortality outside of the Christian scriptures." And Christendom was due for imminent reunion.

As has been seen, many of the Christian speakers made little attempt to heed the exact wording and meaning of the scriptures, but interpreted (actually falsified) them according to what suited their purpose at the moment. Some admitted that assurance of immortality was a tenuous matter as stated, and that it was limited to Jews in both the Old and New Testaments. Others pointed out how unreliable the book was due to its dubious authorship, questionable translations, haphazard arrangement, erroneous grammar and poor choice of terms. There might have been some justification for acclaiming Jesus the unparalleled prophet if his character as presented in *The Gospel of the Holy Twelve* had been accepted. Here his kindness is consonant, extending to all manner of creatures; he speaks against officials who defile the temple, but he does not resort to savage violence against them as in standard versions of the episode. However, this greater Christ requires the observance of universal ethics, which Christians do not want. They prefer a carnivorous, wine-bibbing Jesus of righteous wrath, so that they can act the same way themselves yet remain among the "elect" without the additional burden of having to practice goodness.

A parallel may be drawn between what Louis Sullivan said about the preponderance of Classic architecture at the Columbian Exposition and the paramount orthodoxy of faith that was meted out at the World's Parliament of Religions. Sullivan's comment was that the retarded style would delay the progress of architecture in this country fifty years. The overwhelming enthusiasm over an archaic religion impeded any advance toward spiritual truths in like measure. Both indicated that the discerning factor in these matters, in late-nineteenth-century America, was taste rather than intellect. But the situation was not as hopeless as it sounds. As the pavilion imported from Japan and set up on Wooded Island at the fair stimulated a new type of building proper to the Chicago School and known as the "Prairie House," so some of the Oriental speakers at the Parliament remained in or returned to America to teach their greater insight and broader viewpoints.[3] Their voices had been heard, and those who were ready for a step forward were provided with guidance. Thus works the evolutionary process. And those who proceed raise the standards of the rest, this being the Law of Causality at its positive best, counterbalancing the retardatory forces contentedly seething in traditionalism.

Typical of the faith religions is the deadly seriousness with which they regard their gods, their scriptures, their institutions, and themselves. A little wit is as good as a soft answer in turning away wrath. To him who feels, life is a tragedy; to him who thinks, life is a comedy. Christians put the emphasis upon believing rather than thinking, whereas Buddhists lay it upon reason. Did anyone ever see a smiling Jesus or a Buddha who is not smiling in traditional art? Typical of Buddhism is the story about the crisis on the Rohini River, with humor in the telling and humor in the settling of the matter. The Bible has none. If King Solomon had not taken himself so seriously and had seen the irony in Adonijah's submitting to losing the kingdom while requesting just one of his thousand women, he would have had a good laugh instead of ordering his brother's murder, and he might have felt virtuous on both scores. Jesus' self-centered intolerance as the savior foreboded catastrophe, and it betokens a heavenly eternity of dismal gloom. As a concept the up heaven is so contrary to galaxy geography and natural law that anybody gullible enough to believe in it becomes a pathetic figure. Even a growing child recognizes the inevitability of change and the absurdity of perpetually-arrested development. Only to the egomaniac, reluctant to give up, personal salvation has great appeal.

Dr. Barrows related that at one of the secondary Parliament meetings, when Dharmapala inquired "how many had read the life of Buddha, five persons responded affirmatively by holding up their hands, whereupon the gentle ascetic exclaimed: 'Five only! Four hundred and seventy-five millions of people accept our religion of love and hope. You call yourselves a nation — a great nation — and yet you do not know the history of this great teacher. How dare you judge us!' The principle of justice here affirmed should be taken to heart, though the application of it was not altogether fair. If Mr. Dharmapala had inquired of the three thousand people at the Parliament: 'How many of you have read, in whole or in part, Arnold's *Light of Asia*, with its account of Buddha?' many hundreds of hands would have been held up. The ignorance is not so dense and wide as was imagined." It would be interesting to learn how many at the Parliament *had* read Edwin Arnold's fine poem, and what they thought it was about if not of the Buddha.

Toward the end of his summary Barrows again referred to Orientals. "The mild and gentle Asiatic may seem a feeble or incomplete type of manhood compared with the Scotsman, the Englishman, the German, the American, with centuries of Christian training behind him, inured to self-government, and strong in the manly virtues, but this same Asiatic, is in some respects superior to his rougher and more vigorous brethren. He is certainly responsive to the touch of love and gentle kindness, but he resents the iconoclasm which rudely smites the idols of his heart. One of the most beloved of the Oriental speakers at the Parliament said: 'I was trained in a Christian school. I took prizes for my knowledge of the New Testament, and if I had respected the ways and words of my teacher, I should undoubtedly have become a Christian.'"

The Christian-trained man of the West was given plenty of opportunity to display his manly virtues in the wars in which his religion involved him, but he was not able to engage in self-government until after he had extricated himself from the yoke of Christian despotism. Though his churches and cathedrals are running over with crosses, pictures, and carved figures in front of which he genuflects and makes petitionary prayers, any religious art other than his own he considers idolatry. In all likelihood the Asian attending the Christian school was Dharmapala, as Ceylon had been a crown colony for a century, and the British overlords suppressed other types of higher education. If he had not been exposed to the free intellectual and spiritual breadth of the religion of Enlightenment, he might have been satisfied with that which had fostered the Dark Ages.

Failure of the principals of the Parliament to grasp the truths of the Farther Asian religions was matched by their ignoring the facts of science given at their conferences. Although, as has been said, the Scientific Section, meeting in Hall III during eight days, dealt with religious "papers of a more scientific and less popular character" rather than with science proper, a conference on evolution was held from

September 27 to 29, yet not one of its talks was recorded. This is unfortunate, inasmuch as if Darwin brought out that the survival of the fittest is one law of nature, he followed it up with the prevalence of mutual assistance within — and sometimes going beyond — animal species as another.[4] Lacking covetousness arousing hostility toward other groups, this natural morality of beasts constitutes a less brutal code than Mosaic righteousness, and it is free of the bigotry that prompted Christian and Islamic aggressiveness (Chapters Eight and Nine). The more technical contributions of D'vivedi, Vivekananda, Gandhi, Hirai, and other Orientals at the Scientific Section also were omitted from the Parliament publications. Barrows included a short Chapter IX on the "Report of the Connection of Religion with the Arts and Sciences." Nothing was mentioned about the arts. He cited Washburn as having noted that "While darkness reigned in Europe," from the eighth to the thirteenth century, "science and philosophy . . . flourished at Bagdad and Cordova, under Moslem rule." Reference was made to Max Müller's paper in favor of an ante-Nicene Christianity, to Bruce's "Man's Place in the Universe," which is theistic, to Dawson's "The Religion of Science," and to Dharmapala's remarks on evolution in his talk on "The World's Debt to Buddha," which latter two will be touched on shortly.

As indicated by the quotation furnished by Dr. Moxom from John Fiske regarding the relation of spirit and body, the investigation of multiple personalities, and psychic regressions conducted by modern psychologists — grown out of the Edgar Cayce recordings — (Chapter Four), contemporary science is more in sympathy with the tenets of Farther Asian religions than with those of the West. They accord because both have derived from the same method of investigating phenomena critically and without previous bias. India's contribution to modern mathematics is threefold — its digits (called "Arabic" from the intermediary), the decimal (replacing the sexagesimal) place-value system, and the current use of zero — and it made possible the many advances that have come about because of this facile vehicle. What few further comments regarding science preserved to us from the Parliament meetings are equally consonant. Sir John William Dawson, author of the book *Story of the Earth and Man*, stated in his Chicago paper that certain deluded scientific thinkers "represent man as engaged in an almost hopeless and endless struggle against an inherited 'cosmic nature,' evil and immoral. This absurd and atheistic exaggeration of the theological idea of original sin, and the pessimism which springs from it, have absolutely no foundation in natural science.

"Natural science does, however, perceive a discord between man, and especially his artificial contrivances, and nature; and a cruel tyranny of man over lower beings and interference with natural harmony and symmetry. In other words, the independent will, free agency, and inventive powers of man have set themselves to subvert the nice and delicate adjustments of natural things in a way to cause much evil and suffering to lower creatures, and ultimately to man himself. Science sees, moreover, a great moral need which it cannot supply, and for which it can appeal only to the religious idea of a divine redemption." Such a moral need was fulfilled millennia ago by Buddhist teaching and national law enacted by the Emperor Aśoka and other Buddhist rulers in Asia.

Following Dr. Dawson was Dr. Thomas Dwight, Parkman Professor of Anatomy at Harvard Medical School, who spoke on "Man in the Light of Revelation and Science." Looking at the matter from the medical standpoint he observed, "It concerns us to know whether the accepted truths of biology science, more particularly those of anatomy, anthropology, and physiology, harmonize with those of revelation. Turning, then, from revelation to science, we have to examine man and to classify him — to determine, in short, according to Huxley's happy phrase, his place in nature. If we subject the tissues of his body to chemical analysis; if, with the highest powers of the microscope, we examine the minutest elements of structure of bone, muscle, blood, brain, and all the rest,

220 THE INCREDIBLE WORLD'S PARLIAMENT OF RELIGIONS

there is nothing implying essential difference between man and animals. We next dissect man's body and examine the various so-called systems, the bones, muscles, vessels, the brain and nerves, and the internal organs. Comparing system by system, we find differences in degree, and in degree only, between the bodies of man and ape. The difference is vast, but it is a difference only in degree after all." Later he added: "Animals rose from the simple to the complex and finally to man, by gradual changes. Instinct is the result of the inheritance of accumulated ancestral experience. There is no essential difference between it and reason." If the race producing scientists had not been so deluded by Near Eastern religion's "revelations," the phenomena revealed to it in the microscope and other highly-developed aids would not have seemed so remarkable. Living at a time before the remains of present man's forerunners had come to light, and still misled by his religious upbringing, Dawson concluded his thesis with: "Revelation teaches that man has fallen; that there is in him a tendency to evil. What is the cause? It is foolish to pretend that it is in the persistence of animal passions. Let the student of Sociology consider the refinement of vice in the luxury, lust and cruelty of the decadence of the Roman Empire, or of Oriental despotism, to look no nearer home, to see that there is a malice in it very different from mere savageness. There is in it a perverseness in evil that suggests a closer resemblance to devils than to beasts. It is not a return to a lower estate, but the corruption of a higher." Here Dr. Dwight misses the fine point that he might have arrived at from what he had said earlier — namely, that if man patterned his behavior more after the natural life styles of his nearest physiological kinsmen on earth, the anthropoid apes, suppressing his desires for excessive possessions and luxuries, his mania for restless travel and infantile amusements, his self-destructive and pointless vices, his penchant toward sectarianism, clannishness and nationalism, accompanied by his arrogance toward outsiders, and especially his pride and self-esteem, which relegates

others to unjustified subjugation, man would avoid the brut-
alities and decadence that he periodically undergoes. As we
have seen, revelation has contributed to the proposition that
man "has fallen" to the level of "devils" by establishing perverted righteousness in place of a decent moral code (Chapters
Eight and Nine).

It was the apostle Paul who brought the Judaic-Christian
bigotry against learning and science to a head, setting the
policy for antagonism and persecution against those who
sought truth in natural philosophy for well over a millennium
and a half. Having been brought up in backward Palestine,
neither Jesus' teaching nor the accounts about him indicates
that he had any contact with the factual knowledge about
the world that the ancient Greeks had accumulated, but
when the apostles began preaching outside of the provincial
Jewish community they ran headlong into a new obstacle.
Thus Paul noted that "the Jews require a sign, and the Greeks
seek after wisdom" (I Corinthians I, 22), which is a frank
admission that the Jews resorted to token superstitions,
whereas the Greeks used their heads. Paul subscribed to the
former, and he lashed imprecations against the Corinthians
for thinking, saying, "the foolishness of [my] God is wiser
than men," and "God hath chosen the foolish things of the
world to confound the wise" (I, 25, 27). To the Colossians he
thundered, "Beware lest any man spoil you through philosophy and vain deceit, after the tradition of men, after the
rudiments of the world, and not after Christ" (II, 8). Such a
twisted attitude bore fruit in 1543, when Copernicus' *Revol-
utions of the Heavenly Bodies*, restating what the Greeks had
known, came from the press. Although dedicated to the pope
and supplied with a groveling preface, the book was put on
the Index of Prohibited Literature; and Copernicus himself
was saved from a martyr's pyre only by conveniently dying a
natural death a few hours after receipt of the book. Galileo
substantiated Copernicus' thesis by observations made through
his telescope, for which he was hauled before the Inquisition

at Rome in 1615 and menaced with torture, his life was spared only because he agreed to relinquish discovered facts and give lip service to the prevalent Christian errors.[5] It seems inconceivable today that less than four hundred years ago the orthodox view of the world still adhered to the primitive Biblical idea that the earth is stationary with the sun moving over it, and that the sky consists of a solid dome with windows to let in the rain and a door for the passage of angels.[6] It seems equally inconceivable that medieval Europeans believed that meteorological phenomena and plagues were inflicted as punishments, and that relief from such calamities required prayer, penance and priestly intervention, even after repeated demonstrations of utter failure. The Christian church fought every worthwhile discovery of science as a threat to its own fallacies and political/religious supremacy, and woe unto those heroic investigators who stood up against that stifling establishment.

Dr. Barrow's last reference in his "Science" chapter states, "The eleventh-day paper of H. Dharmapala remarked especially upon the teachings of Buddha on evolution. They are the generalized idea of Buddha, that the entire knowable universe is one undivided whole, both the phenomena of nature and those of human nature and human life lying under one grand law of the development of all things." This falls short of the essence. To all of the Buddhists at the Parliament, no matter from what country they came, as well as to the representatives of some of the other Farther Asian religions, the key to the cosmos is the Law of Cause and Effect, which stands for the constant operation of the universe on which science bases its principles. And due to its breadth of application to every facet vital to religion, nothing more is essential. As Dr. Paul Carus said in his talk on science as a religious revelation, "The theological questions of past ages have [or ought to have] disappeared, but religion remains a factor in the evolution of mankind. . . . That conception of religion which rejects science is inevitably doomed. It cannot survive and is destined to disappear with the progress of civilization. Nevertheless, religion will not go. Religion will abide. Humanity will never be without religion. For [true] religion is the basis of morals, and men could not exist without morals.

"Religion is as indestructible as science; for science is the method of searching for the truth, and religion is the enthusiasm and good will to live a life of truth." Only someone immersed in the higher Farther Eastern religions, like Dr. Carus, would conceive of a single truth proper to both science and religion.

We also should be reminded of what Col. Thomas Higginson said after recalling the ceremony witnessed in the Portuguese cathedral (Chapter Six), that the "priests and attendants . . . had only removed the darkness they themselves had made." His advice was not only to unveil the darkened windows but to remove the darkening walls, and to replace the stifling incense with pure air, because "the broadest religion is the best."

At that final meeting of the World's Parliament of Religions, when the Apollo Club's "Hallelujah Chorus" reverberated through the Hall of Columbus, the dedicated scientist and the earnest seeker after spiritual attainment and enlightenment must have sat silent in mutual understanding and sympathy, while the emotionally motivated catapulted themselves to their feet, shouting and waving their handkerchiefs in passionate salutation to their Redeemer — who failed to respond.

CHAPTER TEN — notes

1 In the two-volume work, *The World's Parliament of Religions*, Chicago, 1893, Chapter V describes "The Close of the Parliament," pp. 155-187, from which the early quotations in this chapter are taken.

2 *Ibid.*, Part Fifth, "Review and Summary," Chapter II, "Grandeur and Final Influence of the Parliament," pp. 1568-1582.

3 Clay Lancaster, *The Japanese Influence in America*, New York, 1963, reprinted 1983, pp. 76-96; Rick Fields, *How the Swans Came to the Lake*, Boulder, Col., 1981, pp. 128-145.

4 Charles Darwin, *The Descent of Man and Selection in Relation to*

Sex, London, 1871, Chapter IV, "The Moral Sense."

5   Andrew Dickson White, *A History of the Warfare of Science with Theology in Christendom*, two volumes, 1896, reprinted New York 1960, Vol. I, pp. 120-144.

6   As in Psalms XCIII, 1; Psalms CIV, 5; Genesis VII, 11-12; Revelation IV, 1.

APPENDIX: A LISTING OF THE TALKS BY AUTHOR
(numbers to the right refer to page references in the two-volume
The World's Parliament of Religions, Chicago, 1893)

A PORTFOLIO OF THE SETTING AND PARTICIPANTS

THESE PICTURES are reproduced from *The World's Parliament of Religions*, published at Chicago in 1893. Views depict the Hall of Columbus during the morning session of the fifteenth day, 25 September 1893, and the exterior of the Art Institute of Chicago. Portraits occupying a full page in the two-volume work include the Rev. John Henry Barrows, chairman of the General Committee on Religious Congresses of the World's Congress Auxiliary and editor of the publication; Prof. Alfred Williams Momerie, King's College, London; Dr. Isaac M. Wise, rabbi of Cincinnati; Kinza Riuge M. Hirai, Rinzai Zen, Japan; Dharmapala or David Hewivitarne, general secretary of the Maha-Bodhi Society, Colombo; Swami Vivekananda, disciple of Ramakrishna, Bombay; Virchand A. Gandhi, Jain, Bombay; and Jeanne Sorabji, Christian, Bombay. The promoters' attitudes toward the limited knowledge of religions not their own are indicated by captions to photographs of a tattooed New Zealand native, tritely designated "an idol worshipper," and a group of simple Thailand monks and novices labeled "Buddhist high-priests of Siam." The selection of small circular portraits includes: Manilal M. D'vivedi, Hindu scholar from Bombay; Mohammed Russell Alexander Webb, Moslem; Mgr. Robert Seton, Catholic, Jersey City; the Very Rev. Augustine E. Hewitt, Paulist; Col. Thomas Higginson, Unitarian, Boston; Dr. Eliza R. Sunderland, Unitarian, Ann Arbor; Prof. Crawford Howell Toy, Baptist, Harvard University; and Dr. Paul Carus, editor and publisher, Chicago.

241

AN ACTUAL SCENE AT ONE OF THE SESSIONS OF THE PARLIAMENT

(frontispiece, Vol. I)

THE ART INSTITUTE OF CHICAGO, WHERE THE PARLIAMENT OF RELIGIONS WAS HELD. (p.35)

244

Rev. *JOHN HENRY BARROWS, D.D., Chicago.*

"I desire that the last words which I speak to this Parliament, shall be the name of Him to whom I owe life and truth and hope and all things, who reconciles all contradictions, pacifies all antagonisms, and who from the throne of His heavenly kingdom directs the serene and unwearied omnipotence of redeeming love — Jesus Christ, the Saviour of the world."

(p.41)

Rev. ALFRED WILLIAMS MOMERIE, D.D.

"Your Parliament of Religions is far greater than your Exposition. There have been plenty of Expositions before. Yours is the best, but it is a comparatively common thing. The Parliament of Religions is a new thing in the world. It seemed an impossibility, but here in Chicago the impossible has been realized."

(p.273)

246

Rev. Dr. ISAAC WISE, Cincinnati

"Truth unites and appeases; error begets antagonism and fanaticism. It seems therefore the best method to unite the human family in harmony, peace and goodwill is to construct a rational and humane system of theology, as free from error as possible, clearly defined and appealing directly to the reason and conscience of all normal men."

(p.293)

KINZA RIUGE M. HIRAI, Japan

"We cannot but admire the tolerant forbearance and compassion of the people of the civilized West. You are the pioneers in human history. You have achieved an assembly of the world's religions, and we believe your next step will be toward the ideal goal of this Parliament, the realization of international justice."

(p.447)

248

A NATIVE OF NEW ZEALAND, AN IDOL WORSHIPPER
(p.615)

THE BUDDHIST HIGH-PRIESTS OF SIAM

(p.657)

250

H. DHARMAPALA, Ceylon

"*The Parliament of Religions has achieved a stupendous work in bringing before you the representatives of the religions and philosophies of the East. The Committee on Religious Congresses has realized the Utopian idea of the poet and the visionary; a beacon light has been erected on the platform of the Chicago Parliament to guide yearning souls after truth.*"

(p. 861)

Swami VIVEKANANDA, India

"The Parliament of Religions has proved to the world that holiness, purity and charity are not the exclusive possessions of any church in the world, and that every system has produced men and women of the most exalted character. My thanks to those noble souls whose large hearts and love of truth first dreamed this wonderful dream and then realized it."

(p.973)

VIRCHAND A. GANDHI, India

"*Do we not wish that this Parliament would last seventeen times seventeen days? Do we not see that the sublime dream of the organizers of this unique Parliament has been more than realized? I now thank you from the bottom of my heart for the kindness with which you have received us, and for the liberal spirit and patience with which you have heard us.*"

(p.1225)

MANILAL M. D'VIVEDI

(p.259)

Very Rev. AUGUSTINE F. HEWITT

(p.259)

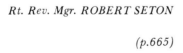

Col. THOMAS W. HIGGINSON

(p.665)

Rt. Rev. Mgr. ROBERT SETON

(p.665)

MOHAMMED RUSSELL
ALEXANDER WEBB

(p.965)

Prof. C.H.TOY

(p.965)

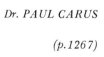

Dr. ELIZA R. SUNDERLAND

(p.475)

Dr. PAUL CARUS

(p.1267)

Miss JEANNE SORABJI, Bombay, India.   *(p.1469)*

INDEX

Abbott, Rev. Lyman: on the
uniqueness of man, 31
on the Golden Rule, 166-7
Abraham: account of in the Bible,
139-40
ahimsa (harmlessness): 177, 196
Ahitsu, Rt. Rev. Zitsuzen: on the
principle of mind in Buddhism,
151
animals: sharers in immortality,
92-3
overlooked in Western ethics,
172-3
science shows close link with
man, 219-21
Aśoka, Emperor: called world's
first known convocation of
religions, 26
reforms in India, 177
avatāra (incarnation): 51, 62-3

Baldwin, Dr. S.L.: on the Golden
Rule, 167
Barrows, Rev. John Henty: appointed chairman of the General
Committee of the Parliament, 10
defines policy of the Parliament,
12-13
dedication of the two volume
publication on the Parliament, 14
disdain of polytheism, 208
conducted final meeting of the
Parliament, 209
remarks about Orientals, 210, 217
discussion on the success of the

Parliament, 211-13
Bhagavadgītā: verses quoted from,
62-3, 172
regarding war, 194-5
Bible: its sanctity, 76
concept of salvation in, 77-8
general remarks on, 104-11
on morality, 159-63
on pacifist remarks in, 187-8
Bodhisattvas: in Mahāyāna, 54
Bonney, Charles Carroll: opening
address as President of the
World's Congress Auxiliary, 29
final address to the Parliament,
209
Blacks: anniversary of the Emancipation Proclamation observed
at the Parliament, 13
progress made by them in America, 13
final appearance of delegates at
the Parliament, 210
Brahmo-Somaj: articles of faith,
146
founder's prediction on Christian unity, 207
Briggs, Prof. Charles A.: talk on
world's scriptures, 17-18
biographic sketch, 23
gives shortcomings of the Bible,
107
Brown, Rev. Olympia: paper given
at the Parliament, 14
Buddha: see Gautama, Siddhartha
Buddhism: essence of, 35

257